T0248012

THE ACCIDENTAL EQUALIZER

THE
ACCIDENTAL
EQUALIZER

HOW LUCK DETERMINES
PAY AFTER COLLEGE

Jessi Streib

The University of Chicago Press   CHICAGO AND LONDON

The University of Chicago Press, Chicago 60637
The University of Chicago Press, Ltd., London
© 2023 by The University of Chicago
All rights reserved. No part of this book may be used or reproduced in any
manner whatsoever without written permission, except in the case of brief
quotations in critical articles and reviews. For more information, contact the
University of Chicago Press, 1427 E. 60th St., Chicago, IL 60637.
Published 2023
Printed in the United States of America

32 31 30 29 28 27 26 25 24 23   1 2 3 4 5

ISBN-13: 978-0-226-82931-9 (cloth)
ISBN-13: 978-0-226-82968-5 (e-book)
DOI: https://doi.org/10.7208/chicago/9780226829685.001.0001

Library of Congress Cataloging-in-Publication Data

Names: Streib, Jessi, author.
Title: The accidental equalizer : how luck determines pay after college /
    Jessi Streib.
Description: Chicago : The University of Chicago Press, 2023. | Includes
    bibliographical references and index.
Identifiers: LCCN 2023008562 | ISBN 9780226829319 (cloth) | ISBN
    9780226829685 (ebook)
Subjects: LCSH: Equal pay for equal work—United States. | College
    graduates—Employment—United States. | Opportunity.
Classification: LCC HD6061.2.U5 S87 2023 | DDC 331.2/973—dc23/
    eng/20230525
LC record available at https://lccn.loc.gov/2023008562

♾ This paper meets the requirements of ANSI/NISO Z39.48-1992
(Permanence of Paper).

Contents

Introducing
the Luckocracy

This book is about America's best equalizing system.

You haven't heard of it until now. No one has, not even the people who created it. They built it by accident, on the way to achieving other goals.

What does it do? It awards the same average earnings to graduates of non-elite universities who come from advantaged and disadvantaged class backgrounds, an outcome I refer to as "earnings equalization." That is, it equalizes one of the resources that most determines life chances, earnings, among people divided by one of the most impenetrable inequalities, class.

And that's no easy feat. Class inequalities almost always persist or expand over the life course; they don't usually suddenly disappear.[1] They exist in childhood, where class-advantaged and class-disadvantaged children grow up unequally, the former receiving more academic support, nutrition, stability, and safety than the latter.[2] They persist through children's schooling, as the academic gaps that begin before kindergarten remain lodged in place through their high school years.[3] They swell after high school as class-advantaged students more often attend college and graduate with a four-year degree.[4]

Inequalities even grow between class-advantaged and class-disadvantaged students who attend the same university. With more resources, free time, and opportunities, class-advantaged students enter college with higher test scores and spend more time studying.[5] They begin college with more ties to professionals and then network more.[6] They start college with more knowledge of the college-educated labor market and then do more to learn about it.[7] They matriculate more familiar with status symbols and then participate in more exclusive and expensive activities.[8] And they enter college with more money and leave with more too, incurring less student debt and receiving more money from their parents.[9] In most moments, inequalities in what you know, who you know, what status symbols you show, and how much money you have translate into later inequalities, maintaining or growing the resource gaps between the class advantaged and the class disadvantaged.[10]

But that's not what happens when graduates of non-elite universities transition from college to work. How do we know? A study of nearly *every* student born in a two-year period who attended college—that is, a study of over *30 million* young adults—showed that college students from different class backgrounds who attend the same university go on to earn the same average amount.[11] That is, kids who grow up poor and attend the University of California San Diego go on to earn the same income, on average, as kids who grow up rich and attend the University of California San Diego, and the same is true of kids who grow up poor and those who grow up rich and attend the University of Georgia, Fayetteville State University, or most other universities.

What's more, though some disagree,[12] many scholars find that students don't even have to attend the *same* college to receive the same average earnings—students from different classes who graduate from *any* four-year college experience earnings equalization too.[13] After analyzing a nationally representative data set of American adults, sociologist Michael Hout concluded: "College graduation cancels the effects of background status."[14] After analyzing *five* nationally representative data sets, sociologist Florencia Torche arrived at the same conclusion: "A college degree fulfills the promise of meritocracy—it offers equal opportunity for economic success regardless of the advantages of origins."[15]

Other researchers emphasize the robustness of these surprising findings. They find that earnings equalization has occurred for decades, and not just in the United States but across many other Western countries too.[16] In the United States, researchers find that earnings equalization happens immediately after graduating from college and extends for at least two decades.[17] It even makes little difference how one measures class background—by parents' income, education, or occupation. In each case, the result is the same: students from different class backgrounds earn the same or similar salaries upon graduating from college.[18]

And yet, without knowing about the hidden equalizing system running behind our backs, no one has yet been able to explain how this happens. Some have pointed to selection and socialization,[19] ignoring the vast body of literature showing that students from different social classes enter and exit the same college with resource profiles that typically lead to the persistence of inequality, not its demise.[20] Some point to sorting, but this isn't the answer either. Students from less-advantaged class backgrounds do sort into higher-paying majors at higher rates than students from more privileged backgrounds, but the difference is too small to account for earnings equality.[21] Some also point to merit, but students from higher class backgrounds tend to have higher GPAs and more knowledge of professional jobs, suggesting that this isn't the right explanation either.[22]

To understand the real way inequality transforms into an important form of equality, we must learn about America's best equalizing system—one I discovered by spending five years interviewing students, analyzing their résumés, talking to employers, reading job ads, and observing career events. But before we learn about it, a note about for whom it works. It equalizes earnings among class-advantaged and class-disadvantaged college graduates from non-elite universities.[23] I focus on how it does so for undergraduate business majors who enter the mid-tier business market, one that hires college graduates from non-elite universities to do mid-level business jobs such as selling services or products, monitoring marketing campaigns, tracking money and supplies, hiring and paying employees, managing projects, supporting upper-level managers, and training and assigning tasks to lower-level workers. This labor market is the largest one for college graduates,[24] and while I focus on it, the equalizing system I describe is not limited to it. Rather, it likely exists in the mid-tier technology, healthcare, science, and engineering labor markets too, thereby equalizing earnings for most college graduates from unequal classes, as most college graduates have attended non-elite universities and work in one of these fields.

One last caveat before introducing the hidden system: it's our best *equalizing* system, but that doesn't mean it's necessarily our best *overall* system. It comes with some unfortunate power imbalances, strips control away from job seekers who go through it, creates market inefficiencies, and, once known, disincentivizes hard work and skill building. It's not a system many people would design on their own, and it's not one everyone will want to go through. Indeed, it's our best equalizing system partly because there's so little competition; most of our opportunity structures create inequality, not equality. Thus, our task is to decide whether we want to keep the nation's best equalizing system—whether the mechanisms that create earnings equality are worth their social price.

Now introducing the hidden, imperfect, and best existing equalizing system.

The Luckocracy

The luckocracy is America's best equalizing system. It's an opportunity structure that allocates rewards based upon luck. It operates in the labor market, but to understand it, let's first consider an analogy to a more familiar setting: a game on the show *Let's Make a Deal*.

On a February day, *Let's Make a Deal* host Wayne Brady called an audience member named Chona to the stage.[25] After she jumped for joy at the possibility of winning money, Brady explained the rules of the game. There was a closed and locked door on one side of the stage and fifteen keys labeled 1 to 15 on the other. Only one key would unlock the door. If Chona chose the right key, she could unlock the door and win a Mazda sedan worth $21,365. However, she had no way of knowing which key was the right one, and with a ticking time clock she could not try them all. Chona raced back and forth across the stage, trying keys 6, 15,

4, 8, and 13. She did not grab the right key, number 9. She lost the game, forfeiting a car worth over $20,000.

The game Chona played had two important features. First, the game gave Chona and contestants from all class backgrounds *the same low levels of information*. She needed to select the right key to unlock the door, but she, like any other contestant, would not be told which key was the right one. There was nothing she could do to learn this information. There was no question she could ask, friend she could call, strategy she could use, or preparation she could have completed to identify the winning key. All she could do was guess.

The game Chona played had a second important feature: the keys she could use were *not based on her class background*. No matter who Wayne Brady selected to play the game—a contestant from a poor family or a rich one, born to parents who completed only elementary school or parents with graduate degrees—they would not know which key would unlock the door. Moreover, any additional resources that a contestant had would be of little use. It would not take an expensive key to unlock the door. Personal connections to *Let's Make a Deal* employees would not lead to privileged information about how to win. Knowledge of ski resorts, expensive restaurants, or international vacation spots were irrelevant. Chona was a realtor and short-order cook, presumably without much money to spend, without inside connections, and without detailed knowledge of the leisure activities of the rich. In this game, that did not matter. She had the same chances of winning as any other contestant.

The game Chona played was a form of a "luckocracy" as guessing determines who loses and wins. Luckocracies are created by dual forces. They offer all players the same amount of information—little—ensuring that all contestants' outcomes are dependent on guessing rather than strategy. They also make the key to winning based on class-neutral processes and criteria, allowing the privileged and disadvantaged to compete as equals. In luckocracies, strategy does not matter and neither do resources correlated with class. Those who win are those who guess well, not those who grew up with the most class privileges.

The Labor Market Luckocracy

There's a luckocracy in the mid-tier business labor market, and it's what equalizes earnings among graduates from unequal classes. In this model, colleges give students from each class background the resources they need to compete for the prize, equalizing these resources but little more. It is only once students prepare to leave college that they enter the primary equalizing system: the luckocracy that exists in the mid-tier business labor market, one founded on the dual pillars of the low but even distribution of information and class-neutral selection criteria.

A key feature of a luckocracy is that so little information is available that individuals from all social classes must guess how to get ahead. The mid-tier business labor market distributed little information, giving students even less information than *Let's Make a Deal* contestants. In the game Chona played, she knew the exact worth of the prize: $21,365. Students from all class backgrounds had heard that jobs in some fields paid more than others, but among jobs in their desired field, pay information was largely hidden. As this book will show, most job ads did not inform applicants of their potential earnings, employers rarely revealed earnings information in job interviews, hiring agents kept salaries secret from students' connections, and students had no way of knowing whether websites that agglomerate salary information were accurate or misleading. Without this information, students from all class backgrounds could not purposefully target the highest-paying jobs. Most would only learn what a particular job paid if and when they received an offer, at which point students would need to guess whether each offer was the highest one they could receive. The centrality of guessing made luck pertinent to their outcomes, and unlucky guesses were costly. In the business world, salaries for similar jobs vary tremendously,[26] so much so that the students I studied who had the same credentials, work histories, responsibilities, and employment locations received salaries up to $25,000 apart.[27]

Students, of course, would not only need to guess which jobs paid the most, but how to receive a job offer. In the game show, Chona had access to fifteen keys and no information about which key would unlock the door. From college students' perspective, the mid-tier labor market provided even less information. As we'll see, most hiring agents did not give students detailed information about their evaluation criteria, and they certainly did not give it years in advance, when students would need to start acquiring the "right" experiences, skills, and styles.[28] Moreover, rather than one door, there were thousands, and many hiring agents used their own criteria, some of which they changed regularly. Within and across firms, these criteria were varied and contradictory, with different agents favoring concise or lengthy answers, answering quickly or slowly, showing bubbly enthusiasm or calm reserve. Given that different hiring agents preferred opposing styles, students could not meet every hiring agent's preferences, and without knowing who held which criteria, they were forced to guess. Wrong guesses were again costly, resulting in being passed over for some jobs even as the same presentation could get them hired for another.

And, like in a game show, students from each class had similar chances of winning. Chona had to guess which key to use, but the key that would unlock the door was available to contestants of all class backgrounds. Similarly, mid-tier business employers forced students to guess what experiences, skills, and styles to present, but most of the "keys" they rewarded were accessible to students of all class backgrounds. As later chapters document, mid-tier employers focused on who could do the job—not on who completed the most internships, where they developed their skills, or whether their leisure activities were expensive or free.[29] Their bar for who was employable was also specific but sufficiently low that it did not require great resources to meet; they looked for skills like teamwork and a basic knowledge of Excel. Of course, there were exceptions to the rule of employers using class-neutral hiring criteria, but the exceptions went both ways, favoring advantaged and disadvantaged students alike.

Employers also maintained class neutrality through the rules they enforced. More advantaged students have longer histories of negotiating with authority figures,[30] but just as Chona could not negotiate to receive a Porsche rather than a Mazda, neither could students negotiate their salary in a meaningful way. Most employers I talked to did not allow students to negotiate for pay. The minority who allowed it would only negotiate over a few thousand dollars, a small amount compared to the $25,000 difference in similar students' salaries.

The mid-tier business labor market was also class neutral in that privileged students were unable to use their greater array of professional connections to their advantage. This book will reveal that hidden information made students' connections comparable to audience members at game shows: they could confidently instruct students how to get ahead, but, in reality, they were just guessing. Students' families, friends, and new connections offered advice about how to meet employers' hiring criteria, but as they did not know individual hiring agents' preferences themselves, their guesses were no more useful than students'. At times, too, students' connections found them a job. However, their connections didn't know how much each job paid, so they just as often ushered students into low-paying positions as high-paying ones.

A year into the mid-tier labor force, young workers remained in a low-information and class-neutral system—a luckocracy that distributed prizes by chance. As later chapters will show, companies typically hid information about how much recent graduates could earn if they received a raise or promotion, job ads still omitted pay information, and salary information was secretive enough that no one could get an accurate read on how pay varied among similar jobs at different companies. Hiring and promotion criteria were again class neutral, based more on low levels of competency than classed signals, strategies, or dispositions. So, again, graduates would need to guess where they could earn the most money and how to enter those positions, and graduates of all classes had the same chances of guessing well. Earnings equalization continued as graduates remained in a luckocracy, with luck replacing class in determining students' outcomes.

The Uniqueness of the Luckocracy

Most opportunity structures are not luckocracies and do not sort students on luck rather than the resources most available to the advantaged.

To understand why the mid-tier business labor market and others like it are particularly poised to generate equality, we need to contrast it with other opportunity structures—other systems for allocating rewards.

Table 1 shows four broad types of opportunity structures, with some variation within them. These structures relate to two factors. The first is whether information about how to get ahead is equally or unequally available to opportunity seekers from each class. The equal distribution of information occurs either because there is so little information available that individuals cannot leverage their time, networks, or money to gain more information or because there is so much information available that leveraging time, networks, and money provides no additional insights. The unequal distribution of information occurs when time, networks, or money can be used to gain an informational edge, allowing those with better information to better strategize about how to get ahead.

The second factor is whether gatekeepers use class-neutral or class-biased criteria and processes to select opportunity seekers. Class-neutral selection criteria mean that gatekeepers typically evaluate individuals using standards and practices that are accessible and fair to individuals of all classes, and when they do not, they use some criteria that favor people from each class. Class-biased selection criteria and processes occur when gatekeepers use standards or practices that reward individuals who have resources associated with higher classes: high-status cultural styles, connections to high-status people, and money.

Opportunity structures that equalize outcomes by class ensure the even spread of information across classes *and* that gatekeepers use class-neutral selection criteria. Removing one of these factors creates systems that weakly reproduce social class inequality. Removing both creates systems that strongly reproduce social class inequality.

A *luckocracy* equalizes outcomes for individuals from different classes. As displayed in table 1, a luckocracy is created when gatekeepers select individuals using class-neutral criteria and when individuals of all classes have the same amount of information about how to get ahead: little. The even suppression of information from individuals of all classes means

TABLE 1: Opportunity Structures

		INFORMATION ABOUT HOW TO GET AHEAD	
		Equally Available by Class	Unequally Available by Class
GATEKEEPERS' SELECTION PROCESSES AND CRITERIA	Class Neutral	No Class Reproduction Low Levels of Information: Luckocracy High Levels of Information: Meritocracy, in theory	Weak Class Reproduction
	Class Biased	Weak Class Reproduction	Strong Class Reproduction

that no one has or can gain the knowledge needed to effectively strategize about how to get ahead. Instead, everyone eligible for rewards must guess how to receive them. And as gatekeepers select individuals using class-neutral criteria and processes, all players' guesses have the same chance of paying off. In short, in this opportunity structure, luck will matter since strategy cannot, and luck will matter equally for opportunity seekers from all class backgrounds.

A *meritocracy* also equalizes outcomes for individuals from different classes, at least in theory. As displayed in table 1, a meritocracy is created when gatekeepers use class-neutral selection criteria and when information about how to get ahead is equally available to individuals from each class. The difference between a luckocracy and a meritocracy is in how information is made equally available: the luckocracy denies it to all while a meritocracy makes it available to all. This shift changes how people get ahead. With little information, individuals must guess; with great information, they can strategize. Advantaged and disadvantaged opportunity seekers' strategies are equally likely to pay off when gatekeepers use processes and criteria that are equally attainable to people of all classes. Thus, the high and even distribution of information coupled with class-neutral selection criteria allow the most strategic and skilled opportunity seekers to rise to the top, regardless of class origin.[31] Unfortunately, while particular *organizations* operate as meritocracies, we have no evidence that any *market* is meritocratic. And, as I'll discuss in the concluding chapter, it's unlikely that this type of meritocracy can form.

More markets operate as *weak class-reproduction systems*. One form of a weak class-reproduction system is created by gatekeepers' use of class-neutral selection criteria coupled with the uneven availability of information by class. This system is often erroneously called a meritocracy due to gatekeepers' class-neutral selection criteria. This label, however, is incorrect both because there are multiple class-neutral systems,[32] not all of which select individuals based on merit, and because even if gatekeepers select opportunity seekers on merit, the uneven spread of information prevents the "best" opportunity seekers from receiving the best outcomes.[33] Instead, the uneven availability of information about how to identify and obtain opportunities tilts the playing field by making opportunities more accessible to one class than another.

An example of this type of weak class-reproduction system occurs in school lotteries. In some school districts, students are not assigned to their neighborhood school. Instead, families rank district schools, and administrators use a lottery to determine who receives their top choice. This system uses class-neutral selection criteria: the lottery ensures that students from each social class have the same odds of being assigned to their favored school. However, information about which schools are best is not evenly available to families of all classes. While some information is available to anyone with internet access, other information is only available from social networks and school visits. With more connections and time to visit schools, class-advantaged families gather more information and rank schools differently than class-disadvantaged families. Despite schools' class-neutral selection processes, the smartest or luckiest students do not necessarily end up at the best schools. Rather, unequal access to information enables class reproduction despite gatekeepers' class-neutral criteria.[34]

As shown in the bottom left quadrant of table 1, there are also reversed forms of weak class-reproduction systems: ones created by class-biased selection criteria coupled with opportunity seekers of all classes having the same information about how to get ahead. In these systems, class-biased criteria give the advantaged a leg up, but the even distribution of information prevents the advantaged from forming more successful strategies about how to get ahead. Class reproduction again works through one channel but not two.

The marriage market provides an example of a weak class-reproduction system formed by class-biased gatekeepers and the even spread of information across classes. In this case, each person who wants a spouse serves as a gatekeeper, deciding whether they will share their resources with a potential partner. When looking for spouses, Americans tend to look for people who attended similar schools, grew up in similar families, and took part in the same activities, as well as partners who can secure or advance their class position. These criteria correlate with individuals' class origins and their predicted earnings.[35] Thus, when choosing partners, most Americans are class biased.

The marriage market also distributes relatively even levels of information to people of all classes, doing so by offering some information to all and suppressing other information. Everyone can see the classed signals that potential partners give off by the way they dress, how they talk, and what they talk about. But in partner searches, like in job searches, the monetary payoff to a match is hidden to people from all classes. In the marriage market, spouses' future earnings are unknown, and people from all classes are unlikely to learn how much money their partners' parents will pass down until the relationship is well underway.[36] Suitors from all classes are also unlikely to know if the partner they selected offers the most resources of any partner they could find. There are millions of potential partners, and who is available to marry changes over time, making it difficult for an individual to identify their most profitable potential match. Moreover, even if a person could identify the most-resourced people, they would not know how to marry them. Even within a class, individuals' preferences for a spouse are somewhat idiosyncratic, vary over time, and are never fully advertised. Thus, who marries whom will be only loosely based upon class because the advantaged prefer to marry high-earning partners from their class but have incomplete information about who is and will continue to be the most advantaged. This market will reproduce social class inequality, but it will not be its main driver.[37]

The final opportunity structure is a *strong class-reproduction system*, one that relies on gatekeepers' bias as well as the unequal availability of information across classes. Class-biased gatekeepers favor advantaged opportunity seekers by selecting individuals using criteria that are easier for individuals with more money, connections, and elite styles to meet. The uneven availability of information allows class-advantaged individuals to use their greater resources to gather more information about how to get ahead.[38] The class advantaged then have dual advantages, ones that, together, forcefully maintain class inequality.

Elite college admissions is the quintessential strong class-reproduction system. College admissions officers at elite colleges select students according to the resources associated with growing up in higher classes. They favor students whose academic profile is enhanced by attending a well-resourced school, whose standardized test scores are boosted by access to the best schools and tutors, and who have time for extracurricular activities rather than paid work.[39] They also tend to favor applicants who can pay full tuition, who took the expensive trip to visit, who are raised by parents who attended the same college, and whose parents are in a position to make a generous donation.[40]

The distribution of information about college admissions is uneven, too. Although colleges are ranked, reviewed, and written about in a variety of media outlets and although university websites post information about their admissions criteria, there is still important information that is not evenly available across classes. College admissions coaches, guidance counselors, and college-educated parents offer information about what types of personal statements are most rewarded, who counts as appropriate letter writers, how to study for standardized tests, and the culture of particular colleges.[41] Students and their families who gain an informational edge cannot use it to ensure that any one person gets into any particular school, but they can use it to help students access at least one selective university.

In this strong class-reproduction system, the effects of students' class origins are not erased but are maintained or amplified. About 54% of students with parents in the highest income quartile graduate from college while only 9% of students with parents in the lowest quartile do,[42] and over 80% of students with two college-educated parents graduate from college compared to just 20% of students whose parents have a high school degree at most.[43] At elite universities—Ivy League universities and those like it—the distribution is even more uneven: students in the top 1% of the income distribution are 77 times more likely to attend than students in the bottom 20%.[44] Combine uneven information and class-biased evaluation criteria, and inequalities endure on a massive scale.

What does this all mean for the creation of equality for students born in unequal classes? First, we can see the power of the luckocracy. It stands out for creating forms of equality.

Second, luckocracies are created by the even availability of information and class-neutral selection criteria. We can see how much each matter. Take either one away, and we're no longer in a system that offers equal outcomes for students from unequal backgrounds. Take both away, and we are about as far from a system that produces equality as we can get.

Third, we can see that a luckocracy only produces equality on narrow outcomes. Jobs dole out money, so that is what they equalize. They cannot equalize most other outcomes—not marital partners, wealth, health, or the chance of attending graduate school, all of which remain unequal.[45] They are also narrow in that they equalize earnings for students from different *class* backgrounds, but if gatekeepers' selection criteria relate to gender, race, sexual orientation, religion, or any other factor, they will not result in equality along these lines. And even along class lines, mid-tier labor market luckocracies are narrow because not everyone can participate. Students must pass through a fierce class-reproduction system—college—before they can enter. Most students from disadvantaged class origins do not do so and are therefore excluded from participating in this game of chance.[46]

Fourth, while colleges are called "the great equalizer," this title should go to the labor market's luckocracy instead. Colleges play a supporting role by preparing students to receive equal outcomes in the luckocracy, but they do not create earnings equalization themselves. It is the labor market's luckocracy that does the most to equalize students' wages.[47] Think of it this way: students from different classes graduate from college with different social ties, savings, styles, strategies, and signals of skills.[48] If the labor market operated as a strong or weak class-reproduction system, college would not be a great equalizer.

Fifth, the fact that the luckocracy is an *opportunity structure* has several implications. It means that it is not the case that equal earnings arise because some students get lucky while other students are selected on skill; in a luckocracy, luck is not an individual-level factor.[49] Rather, in a luckocracy, for those who pass a certain employability bar, *everyone's* outcomes are based on luck. The fact that a luckocracy is an opportunity structure also means that it operates regardless of whether opportunity seekers or gatekeepers know they are in it and regardless of whether they believe individuals' outcomes are due to hard work, skill, smarts, strategy, or luck. And the fact that the luckocracy is an opportunity structure means that luck, in this case, is not a residual—an explanation we use when we *cannot* measure relevant factors.[50] Rather, the role of luck is generated by a structure that we *can* measure. We can know whether class-neutral selection criteria and the even suppression of information combine so that outcomes must be evenly allocated by luck.

Sixth, the luckocracy reminds us that equalization is more dependent upon opportunity structures than individuals' resources and strategies. As we'll see, students from different classes entered the luckocracy with different resources—different connections, cultural styles, and access to money. And they used different strategies to find jobs, too. But despite their efforts, neither group could access information about how to direct their resources or what strategies were most likely to pay off. The opportunity structure dissolved the usual connections between resources, strategies, and outcomes.

Seventh, not all labor markets are luckocracies. To be a luckocracy, labor markets must hide information about earnings and hiring criteria and judge candidates in class-neutral ways. In elite labor markets, companies advertise their wages more often and use class-biased hiring criteria, so they do not act as a luckocracy.[51] Labor markets for artistic jobs tend to hire based upon having "classy" tastes, using class-biased criteria that detract from their operating as a luckocracy.[52] Small labor markets and ones with little wage variation are also not luckocracies as individuals can find out which job pays what. In this way, the labor market for archaeologists is not a luckocracy, and neither is the one for teachers. And when unemployment rises high enough, even markets that normally operate as luckocracies may turn into weak class-reproduction systems. In these times, employment becomes more salient than earnings, and class-advantaged students' networks can give them an edge in finding jobs even if they cannot purposefully route students into high-paying positions.[53]

Despite these exceptions, it's in some employers' interest to create luckocracies, and markets outside the mid-tier business market are likely to operate as such. Employers are likely to create luckocracies when they value skills over the display of classed tastes; when their pay is not so high that advertising it is guaranteed to attract candidates; and when markets are so large, varied, and dynamic that transparency becomes difficult to achieve. Thus, mid-tier labor markets in other large, varied, opaque, dynamic, and class-neutral fields such as healthcare, technology, engineering, and the sciences are likely to operate as luckocracies too.[54] This is not necessarily because they care about class equality, but because valuing skills over applicants' classed resources helps their bottom line and because providing little information is more aligned with their interests than providing more.

Finally, as social scientists know of no market that operates as a meritocracy, a luckocracy is our only known system for creating equality. It is therefore our best equalizing system. But it is a system with pros and cons—one that inspires more ambivalence than the title "best equalizing system" suggests.

The Study

I started this study believing that luck was an answer social scientists gave when they did not have the data to provide the real explanation.

I started this study thinking that earnings equalization doesn't exist. I assumed the dozen studies claiming it did were wrong.

I started this study believing that most gatekeepers were class biased.

It took five years to realize I was wrong, and not just on one count. On all counts.

I came to these conclusions by following Southern State University (SSU) business school students as they searched for jobs and by talking to the people who hire them. Southern State University is a pseudonym for a mid-tier public university: one that is selective but not elite, respected but perhaps not well known outside of the region. It admits mostly in-state students who earn a range of As and Bs in high school. The students I spoke to saw it as a place for smart people but not for the "geniuses" who attend Ivy League universities or even the state's flagship school. An SSU professor told me that professors and administrators saw students in much the same way. They were not geniuses but pragmatic: down-to-earth, career focused, and cost aware.

Within Southern State University there is the College of Business—or CoB for short.[55] The CoB is also mid-tier. Students referred to it as a "top 100 business school," a rank they also saw as respectable but not elite.

I focus on business school students for a few reasons. Most simply, I chose this major for its sheer size. It is the most common major nationally, representing about one in four recent college graduates.[56] It is also the most common major for class-disadvantaged students, though class-advantaged and class-disadvantaged students generally select majors at similar rates.[57] Business school students also stand out in that they experience the widest earnings range of students from any major. Business school graduates at the 75th percentile earn $55,000 more than those at the 25th percentile.[58] This range gives advantaged business students plenty of room to outearn disadvantaged students, making it particularly surprising that they do not. Business students are also appropriate to study because only one in five undergraduate business majors later attends graduate school, making them among the least likely undergraduate majors to seek an advanced degree.[59] For these students, their labor market entry is important since graduate school will not reset their career trajectory.

Among Southern State University business school students, I focus on a particular group. Everyone I talked to was raised in the United States, 21 to 24 years old when the study began, and decided not to go straight to graduate school. In the final telling, this book focuses on the students who stayed in the study until receiving a job: 62 students, 25 of whom were class disadvantaged and 37 who were class advantaged.

I spoke with these students several times. I first talked to many at the beginning of their senior year, then monthly until they accepted a job, and then again a year after they entered the professional workforce. My first conversations with them centered on their work history, career preparation, and future plans. Conversations midyear focused on how they looked for work—how they decided where to look for jobs, which jobs to apply to, what to include on their résumés, how to prepare for interviews, how to act within them, how to decide which job to take, and whether to negotiate over salary. At each stage, I also asked them where they received information and who helped them along the way. My conversations with students a year after they entered the workforce centered on their roles, opportunities, and next steps.

Of course, students could only tell me how they searched for jobs, not how they were hired. So, in addition to talking with students, I spoke with or listened to eighty employers at and after information sessions, career fairs, and professionalization events. I also conducted formal one-hour interviews with over thirty hiring managers and recruiters—usually ones I met at career fairs or whom I could ascertain hired business majors from Southern State University or schools like it. These employers were part of the entry-level "mid-tier" business labor market and hired students for entry-level positions in human resources, marketing, operations, finance, and business technology.[60] The people I spoke to were in a variety of roles: recruiters, talent acquisition managers, and hiring managers for specific teams and positions. Most hired students to work in the South—not on Wall Street—in the technology, healthcare, manufacturing, transportation, or financial sectors.[61] Some of the hiring agents worked at firms that were household names, others at companies with quiet but long histories in their field, and others at start-ups. To preserve their anonymity, I refer to the hiring agents I formally interviewed by number. In parentheses, I list their employment sector and the jobs for which they hired. To preserve students' anonymity, I assigned each a fake name.

Students and employers told me about what they did, but I also wanted to learn about the broader environment in which they operated. Therefore, I hung out in the business school's coffee shop, attended professionalization club meetings, sat in the back of information sessions, and lingered at career fairs and networking events. I also collected students' résumés and analyzed their LinkedIn profiles, allowing me to learn if students from different classes presented themselves to employers differently. I spent a lot of time on websites, too. I analyzed SSU's online job board, UJobs, to learn how job openings were advertised and whether they posted earnings. I looked at companies' websites to learn more about how they advertised positions.

Through these means, I came to conclude that my original assumptions were wrong. After students who wanted to get rich applied to jobs without knowing their possible salaries, I started to wonder why. When students entered low-paying positions in the fields in which their fathers worked, I started to question how that came to be. When a student who had completed eight internships received a particularly low salary, my eyebrows raised. After spending years reading and rereading students' and employers' interview transcripts and thinking about the labor market, I eventually began to rethink my old ideas and come to new conclusions. Suddenly, the mid-tier business labor market seemed like a game show.

Of course, I don't want to go overboard. I studied students at one university, the people who hired them, and the labor market they were part of. It is possible the findings are particular to groups like them. Most Southern State University students I spoke to of each class background were in-state students and entered in-state labor markets. The state they were in contained several cities with low unemployment rates for recent college graduates. At universities in which most out-of-state students are class advantaged and most in-state students are class disadvantaged, students from different class backgrounds may enter different local labor markets and experience different equalizing mechanisms. In addition, it is possible that hiring agents in the American South are less concerned with class signals than hiring agents in the Northeast or other areas. We don't know because these studies have not been done. And it's possible that the findings reflect the labor market at the time: a tight labor market without monopsony power, one in which employers had more power than job seekers, and one in which too many firms hired for too many positions for job seekers to learn about them all.

It's important to remember, then, that the finding that a luckocracy equalizes earnings is constrained to students who graduate from college and to earnings equality rather than broader forms of equality, and that this study is constrained to making claims about students who attend one type of college and enter some types of labor markets. Still, this study is important. It establishes the existence of a luckocracy, an opportunity structure that was operating without our knowledge. It's likely that over half of the college-educated workforce experiences this opportunity structure, making it central to many people's lives. And the luckocracy is remarkable for what it accomplishes. The reproduction or amplification of social class inequality occurs in nearly every other moment of the life course, among nearly every other outcome, and in every geographical area.[62] The transformation of inequality into one form of equality during the transition from college to work is unique and important; the equalization of *earnings* in particular is important as money allows individuals to make more choices about how to live. If we are to understand how to create a more even playing field and the externalities of doing so, we should start by understanding the one that already exists: the luckocracy.

Definitions

To understand this book, readers need to know how I define key terms.

I refer to students as coming from class-advantaged or class-disadvantaged backgrounds. There is no official definition of class and no official cutoff for when someone is advantaged or disadvantaged due to their class position.[63] Moreover, no matter whether class background is studied by parents' income, occupation, or education, students earn the same or similar amounts.[64] In this book, I define class by parents' education. Parents' education has a larger impact on children's later class position than any other measure.[65] It is also the largest predictor of children's socialization, which shapes how students search for jobs.[66] In addition, parents who graduated from college can draw upon their personal experience to guide their children's post-college job search. Parents who did not graduate from college themselves can still be helpful, but they cannot rely on their own experience to guide their college-educated children's job search. On average, of course, parents with a college degree are also likely to work in a professional job and have a relatively high income.[67] Often their children are advantaged in many ways.

Using parents' education as a guide, I included two types of students in the study: students who had two parents who graduated from a four-year college and students who had no parents who graduated from a four-year college. I call students with two college-educated parents "class advantaged" and students with no college-educated parents "class disadvantaged." At times, I drop the "class" label and use the terms "advantaged" and "disadvantaged" for short. Of course, this does not mean that students are advantaged or disadvantaged in every dimension of their lives; these labels only refer to their class origins as defined by their parents' education.

I rely on other studies' claims that students from different class backgrounds earn equal wages upon graduating from the same college.[68] These other studies provide more accurate estimates as they use nationally representative samples and, sometimes, tax records rather than self-reports of earnings.[69] Still, it is worth noting that class-advantaged and class-disadvantaged students earned similar amounts in this study too. Nearly all students in the sample were employed after graduation, and nearly all were employed in jobs for college graduates. The median salary for class-advantaged students was \$45,000 for their first post-college job and \$48,000 for class-disadvantaged participants,[70] and the range for each class was from \$0 to \$72,500 for class-advantaged students and \$20,000 to \$72,500 for class-disadvantaged students.[71]

I also write about undergraduate business students in general rather than students in each business subfield. In this sample, there was little difference in earnings across subfields: the median wages ranged from \$45,000 to \$50,000 for students in each area—human resources, marketing, finance, operations, and business technology. Moreover, the difference *within* subfields was always much larger than the difference *between* them. The gap between the highest and lowest salaries for students in each subfield ranged from \$30,000 to \$58,000 per subfield—far greater than the largest gap between the average salaries of two subfields: just \$5,000.

Finally, it is important to remember the focus of this book: *earnings equalization*—or that advantaged and disadvantaged graduates of the same college receive the same earnings, on average. The outcome under consideration is *not* finding a job, or even finding a job easily. The book includes a discussion of how students find jobs only because earnings are attached to employment. The distinction between jobs and earnings is important because the same factors that can help students find a job cannot help them find a job with high earnings for their field. Class-advantaged students' connections, for example, can help them find jobs, but they cannot help them receive *high-paying* jobs when they cannot know which companies pay in the 10th, 50th, or 90th percentile for particular jobs or what pay corresponds to these percentiles.

Why Believe It?

This book makes an argument so far-fetched that it's hard to believe: there's an opportunity structure that no one knows about, and it's been equalizing earnings behind our backs.

So, why believe it?

Because while I provide additional evidence of the luckocracy's pillars, I'm hardly the first to observe them. I'm only the first to explain how their dual existence allows for earnings equalization.

For instance, it's common knowledge that job seekers have little information about pay. Ads on job boards like Monster.com and Indeed rarely include information about earnings. Instead they contain phrases like "competitive salary and benefits" and "salary commensurate with experience," if they provide any reference to pay at all.[72] Given this, it's not surprising that survey researchers find that job seekers' biggest complaint is the lack of information on pay.[73] Researchers also find that three-quarters of recent college graduates do not know what tasks their jobs will involve before their first day of work;[74] job seekers cannot even use the content of jobs to guess about their pay.

Among researchers who observe the hiring process, it's well known that job seekers have little information about employers' hiring criteria. These researchers find that hiring agents use inconsistent and contradictory selection criteria that are invisible to job seekers. Often hiring managers don't know what type of person they want to hire until just before they post an ad,[75] and they regularly change their minds as they interview candidates.[76] Moreover, many managers tell researchers that their hiring procedures are not systematic,[77] amounting instead to asking random questions and evaluating candidates' answers in erratic ways.[78] Because hiring agents routinely revise their ideas about what type of candidate they want, the questions they ask, and the evaluation criteria they use, even they cannot accurately predict who they will hire.[79] Of course, this means that no one else can know either.[80]

The luckocracy also rests on a second pillar: that gatekeepers use class-neutral selection criteria. Though gatekeepers in elite and artistic labor markets tend to select candidates using class-biased cues,[81] researchers note that this isn't what happens in other markets. Instead, those in mid-tier business markets tend to ignore cultural signals that are classed. As a sociologist who studied the security industry put it: "Some forms of culture correlated with class do not get used in the private sector because they are profitless irrelevancies that the upper classes themselves exclude through their intent focus on doing business."[82] This line of thinking corresponds with what sociologists know about class and culture: culture that *doesn't* relate to class creates more cohesion than culture that does.[83] Talking about blockbuster movies, pop artists, and televised sports bonds people; talking about French films, opera, and niche sports divides them. Businesses want cohesion among colleagues and connections with clients; in mid-tier markets, it's in their interest to be class neutral.

Of course, class can matter in other ways as well, and it often matters because class-advantaged students use their greater money and connections to build more skills. Thus, when evaluators select students on their skills, they also select them on their class origin. But this process is only classed if hiring agents look for the best candidate or candidates who meet a high bar. If they instead look for "good-enough" candidates who meet a low bar, then class is no longer relevant as most people can jump over low bars. Theories of organizational decision-making tell us to expect hiring agents to choose "good-enough" candidates—to satisfice. In what's called the "garbage can model of decision making," management scientists maintain that when problems and processes are not well defined, who is involved in the decision changes, and when the decision makers' time and attention are limited, then they will look for a convenient solution that is good enough for their needs, making their decisions in inconsistent and irrational ways.[84] Translated into hiring practices, the theory holds that when ideas about what type of person to hire are unclear, the résumé review and interviewing process are unstandardized, the people on hiring teams change, and the hiring agents are distracted by their other tasks—that is, in a normal hiring setting—then hiring agents will use unstable criteria to pick a good-enough candidate out of an easy-to-access pool. And good enough is often set at a low bar, since many jobs—including professional ones—do not require high levels of skill.[85]

It's then quite believable that a luckocracy exists. It's well established that job seekers have little information, and some evidence suggests that mid-tier business employers use class-neutral selection criteria. If one accepts previous research, then believing a luckocracy exists only requires recognizing that these two factors work together. If they do, then the lack of information will force all job seekers to guess where and how to get ahead, and class-advantaged and class-disadvantaged job seekers' guesses will be equally likely to pay off.

Of course, it may still be hard to believe that a luckocracy creates earnings equality. Usually, the advantaged can maintain their advantages.[86] So why can't they here?

The answer lies in another well-established fact: structure shapes outcomes more than individual actions, a reality that even the advantaged can't escape.[87] Usually, the class advantaged operate in systems with uneven spreads of information and/or class-biased selection criteria. In these systems, the advantaged can identify which gatekeepers offer the highest rates of return and use their resources to meet their expectations or gain access another way. But in class-neutral systems in which they cannot learn *what* skills to acquire, *how* to display them, *who* can help them, and *where* to exchange them, the value of their resources deflates. They spend time, money, and favors on items of unknown value—on building skills, styles, and access that may have neutral or negative rates of return. And there's no strategy that can remove them from this system. They can try to get around it by entering the elite labor market, but these markets reject most applicants without elite degrees.[88] They can try to "win" the luckocracy by waiting until good luck comes their way, but the system disincentivizes doing so. There's too much to lose if luck doesn't come quickly: if students do not receive a job, they lose face among their peers, lose independence from their parents, and lose the ability to search for a new job as an employed person—a position that leads to higher pay later.[89] And so the structure of the luckocracy renders their individual actions unimportant: the class advantaged cannot know how to invest their resources to net a positive rate of return, and they cannot strategize or buy themselves into a more favorable situation.

Still, some might believe that there are simpler ways to explain earnings equalization than attributing it to a previously unrecognized opportunity structure. But while simpler ideas may seem more believable, the evidence shows they aren't true.

One idea is that earnings equality occurs because class-disadvantaged and class-advantaged students who apply for the same job have equal resources—not unequal ones. With equal resources, they receive jobs that pay equal amounts. According to this logic, the particular class-disadvantaged and class-advantaged students who graduate from the same university are likely to have the same resources; the least-resourced class-disadvantaged students rarely graduate from college, and the most-resourced class-advantaged students select into more elite schools. The class-disadvantaged and class-advantaged students who are left are a lot alike.[90]

But while this idea seems believable, it is untrue. No ethnography of class on campus has found that students from different class backgrounds graduate with the same resources or the same labor market savvy; most find yawning gaps.[91] Studies using sophisticated quantitative methods find that the composition of class-disadvantaged and class-advantaged students at selective colleges cannot account for their later equal earnings.[92] Among the students I followed, the same is true: the class disadvantaged included students whose parents, separately, fostered them, were in jail, and were single struggling moms; the class advantaged included students who, separately, had a grandfather who founded a business school, whose father owned a bank, whose father was the vice president of human resources, and whose parents each worked as doctors. Their resources reflected their parents' jobs; graduating from the same college did not equalize them. Their time in college also did not equalize their resources, as we'll see in chapter 4, nor did it equalize their strategies, as we'll see in chapter 5. Equality did not arise due to which of these students selected into applying for mid-tier business jobs. Almost all would enter the mid-tier business market—the market their degree prepared them to enter and that would hire them without an elite college degree.

Others may believe another false story: the luckocracy exists but only because undergraduate business schools aren't doing their job. If they gave students more information, then class-advantaged students would use it to outearn class-disadvantaged students. But business schools cannot distribute this information. They are not clairvoyant; they cannot tell students each hiring agent's criteria before that hiring agent knows the criteria themselves. They are not omniscient; they cannot tell students the pay of jobs that employers keep hidden. They are also not omnipotent; they can distribute surveys to recent graduates to gather information about their salaries, but they cannot make them complete the survey. Thus, they may not be able to achieve the sample size needed to give meaningful information to current students.

A final objection may be that the findings of this study are misaligned with others. But on closer inspection, it's clear that's not true either. For example, Lauren Rivera's *Pedigree: How Elite Students Get Elite Jobs*[93] and Sam Friedman and Daniel Laurison's *The Class Ceiling: Why It Pays to Be Privileged* find that some hiring agents at elite American and English firms use class-biased hiring criteria. But these findings do not provide evidence that a luckocracy does not exist in the mid-tier labor market; they merely suggest that elite hiring is part of a weak class-reproduction system. Elizabeth Armstrong and Laura Hamilton's *Paying for the Party: How College Maintains Inequality* may also seem to contradict my findings. They follow class-advantaged and class-disadvantaged students through college and into the labor force, and observe class differences in students' post-college trajectories. But they do not measure their different trajectories by earnings alone; they include parental subsidies and marital prospects as well.[94] The luckocracy does not equalize the latter, so it is no surprise they remain unequal.

In this light, the nearly unbelievable becomes believable. Each of the luckocracy's pillars are grounded in decades of research; the opportunity structure really does exist. The advantaged cannot get around it; the luckocracy constrains their ability to use their resources to get ahead. Other explanations for earnings equality are undermined by the evidence: there is little that is equal between college students from unequal class backgrounds, even ones graduating from the same school and applying for the same jobs. Also, the luckocracy is not the result of educators not doing their jobs; they, too, act within informational constraints.

So, the idea that a luckocracy produces earnings equality for students from unequal class backgrounds *is* believable, no matter how fantastical it may initially seem. A luckocracy successfully takes students with unequal resources and gives them an equal outcome.

The Chapters

The book provides new evidence that the mid-tier business labor market for recent college graduates offers little information and uses class-neutral criteria, and that these factors fuse to create a luckocracy that equalizes earnings. The first part of the book shows the structure of the luckocracy: the even but low levels of information that employers give students about jobs and pay (chapter 2), and the little and varied information about class-neutral hiring criteria (chapter 3). The next part of the book examines how students prepare for (chapter 4) and go through the luckocracy (chapter 5), highlighting how class-advantaged and class-disadvantaged students' different resources, strategies, and styles are rendered unimportant in this equalizing system. The last part of the book illustrates the consequences and continuation of the luckocracy one year after graduates began their first professional jobs. It shows that the luckocracy not only equalizes earnings but also opportunities for building skills and for mentorship (chapter 6) and that the luckocracy remains in place a year after students enter the professional workforce (chapter 7). The final chapter reviews the advantages and disadvantages of America's best equalizing system, compares them to those in other opportunity structures, and asks a difficult question: Should we keep or replace the luckocracy? Finally, appendix A is written for academics interested in the theoretical contributions of the book, appendix B gives more details about the study's data and methods, and appendix C lists the interview guides and questionnaires I used when talking to students and employers. Taken together, the book reveals a new opportunity structure, one that turns inequality into equality.

PART I

FORMING
THE LUCKOCRACY

Hidden Information on Jobs and Pay

The *Let's Make a Deal* game show designers put a single locked door onstage and a single prize behind it. Before the game began, the host revealed the prize: a brand-new Mazda sedan worth $21,365. The mid-tier business labor market is not so simple or transparent. There are thousands of employers, most of whom hire for multiple jobs, many of which pay different amounts. And, to a certain extent, employers keep both the job and its worth concealed until they distribute offers. If the *Let's Make a Deal* game is designed to let luck determine winners and losers, the mid-tier business market's luckocracy does so to a far greater degree. Earnings equalization results, in part, because hidden information about where to get ahead forces students from all class backgrounds to guess which doors lead to prizes and which lead to duds.

Hidden Information about Jobs

Each year, hiring agents descend on business schools, transforming them from education to employment centers. They advertise jobs in classrooms, clubs, information sessions, professionalization events, career fairs, networking sessions, hallway meet-and-greets, résumé reviews, and mentoring sessions. They post job ads on company websites, campus recruiting sites, and national job boards. Some even pay universities to name classrooms after them.[1] They know students will soon look for internships and jobs. No matter where they look, employers want students to see their company's name and apply for their positions.

Despite employers' constant presence in business schools, they give students little information about the jobs they hire for and what they pay. Their goal is to increase brand recognition and get students to apply, not to provide students with a lot of information about what they are applying for. In each part of their job ads and in each format in which they interact with students, employers tend to keep hidden the most important parts of prospective jobs: tasks and pay.

JOB ADS

I found that employers repeatedly told students to read their job ads. But they did not tell them the truth about the ads: that the job title, job description, and company description gave students little useful information about the actual job.

Job Titles

Job titles did not consistently inform job seekers about what the job would entail. They were crafted by a variety of people—marketing officials, human resources managers, and hiring agents—not all of whom were familiar with each position. Employers told me that when they were unfamiliar with the position, they turned to market research or competitors' ads to write their own. This meant that they labeled jobs at their company using titles designed for jobs at other companies, ones that might bundle tasks in different ways.[2]

Moreover, some hiring agents saw job titles as marketing devices, used to attract job seekers. Therefore, even when the people titling positions knew what their jobs entailed, they did not necessarily choose a job title that reflected the positions. Hiring agents told me that they chose titles that made the jobs sound more appealing or familiar than they actually were. Some hiring agents called positions "specialists" when they were actually "trainees," added or took away the word "sales" depending on whether they believed it would attract or repel candidates, or used generic job titles for non-generic jobs to make the positions seem famil-iar. Some hiring agents also changed job titles despite not changing the jobs, others rarely changed job titles despite the jobs having changed, and some companies used multiple titles to hire for the same position. In any of these cases, the job title might not reflect the position. At a minimum, it could sow confusion.[3]

Employers admitted that their job titles did not accurately inform can-didates about the jobs. Employer 9 (healthcare, marketing) thought job seekers would be confused by their titles: "A specialist to our company is definitely an entry-level position. At other companies that may be some-one with five years of experience." Employer 7 (transportation, analysts) said her company posted misleading job titles. Their "accounting and finance" position hardly included any finance. Employer 25 (research, sales) shared that her company had a "marketing associate" position designated for an employee who did mostly sales and little marketing. And even when employers thought their job titles were straightforward, they could be anything but to job seekers. Employer 32 (transportation, management) assumed that students would know that one word meant another: "Most people when they see management, they usually know it's gonna be sales." Employer 6 (healthcare, consultants) assumed that stu-dents would know the rank of non-hierarchical words: "[Our job titles] basically mirror the consulting industry, where they're differentiating between an associate consultant and an analyst. Associate consultant is considered a step above the analyst position." Job titles, then, were vague at best and misleading at worst. As such, they could not be counted on to contain useful information.

Job Descriptions

Each job ad contained a job description, but each job description did not provide detailed and accurate information about the job. For employers to accurately describe a job, they would need to know what tasks each new hire would do. Typically, they did not know. Some hired in the fall or spring for jobs that would begin in the summer, before they decided what responsibilities students would take on or what teams they would join.[4] Other hiring managers hired large groups of students and only assigned them to roles after the new cohort was in place; they did not know in advance what each new hire would do. Still other hiring managers thought they knew what students' jobs would entail, but they could not be sure. Business needs change quickly, so they considered it safest not to make promises they could not keep.

The result was ads like the ones below, which used many words to say little about the job tasks. The following ad was posted on UJobs, Southern State University's website for advertising jobs:

> The Supply Chain Operations Analyst will play a vital role as the team's primary representative for the evaluation and implementation of end-to-end supply chain and logistics opportunities. Working closely with the supply chain team's functional leaders, the operations analyst will collaborate with internal stakeholders on cross-functional projects, negotiate effective solutions that both deliver value to our customers and remain feasible and sustainable, and translate requirements back to the team for incorporation into current and future workflows. Additionally, the operations analyst will document and drive end-to-end process improvements across Planning, Procurement, Channel Distribution, and Logistics.

A job ad for a business analyst read equally vaguely:

> The Business Analyst is someone who demonstrates both technical and financial knowledge, enjoys analyzing data, and is a team player. You will be responsible for providing ongoing quality assurance support in a rapidly changing environment driven by technical requirements and business needs. You will be working as part of a cross-functional team of Application Developers, other Business Analysts, and Quality Assurance testers. This role will also involve communication with vendors, managers, and technical staff.

These ads provided little information about what tasks students would do if they were hired. The ad for the supply chain analyst relayed information on who new hires would work with but not what projects they would work on. The ad for the business analyst included what skills students would need and who they would work with but not what the new hire would do.

These two job descriptions were not unique. The employers I spoke to admitted that they, too, wrote uninformative job descriptions. Employer 12 (manufacturing, many business roles) said: "The postings do stay very vague." Employer 15 (finance, many business roles) mentioned: "With campus recruiting, you tend to have more generalized rather than specific job descriptions." Employer 24 (technology, many business roles) agreed: "The job descriptions are generalized." Employer 3 (technology, finance, and sales) said the same: "We did use a generic job description." Job descriptions, then, did little to describe the job.

Company Descriptions

Job ads also included little information about the companies themselves. Companies often described themselves by their number of employees, global reach, growth potential, status in the marketplace, and culture. They did not, however, give job seekers a sense of what it was like to work for them. The following examples show how three companies advertised themselves to marketing students. Despite that they were in different industries, all only offered the same vague language about the same aspects of their companies.

(1) Sinclair Broadcast Group, Inc[.] is one of the largest and most diversified television broadcasting companies in the nation, programming 162 stations located in 79 geographically diverse markets after pending transactions. Our success is the result of extraordinary employees and an exemplary management team who believes in a vision and is dedicated to making Sinclair Broadcast Group, Inc[.] a communications powerhouse.

We are advancing the world of Broadcasting and we want YOU to join our winning team!

(2) Belk, Inc. is the nation's largest privately owned and operated department store company with approximately 300 Belk stores and 23,000 associates located in 16 states with revenues of $4 billion and growing. Recently named in Stores Magazine as one of the Top 50 online retailers, we are also philanthropic and provided over $19.0 million in support to local communities, education initiatives, and breast cancer. In 2013, we proudly celebrated our 125th anniversary with a continued commitment to our mission, "To satisfy the modern Southern lifestyle like no one else, so that our customers get the fashion they desire and the value they deserve." We are investing heavily in our business and are looking for talented people to join our diverse and inclusive Belk team.

(3) David Weekley Homes is the largest privately-held home builder in the U.S., operating in 20 cities in 12 states, and has built more than 70,000 homes since 1976. Our primary business is the design, construction, marketing and sales of new, single-family homes, and our product lines continue to grow with multi-family and Central Living homes. Customers actively seek out David Weekley Homes because of our award-winning reputation and our Brand Promise of delivering the best in Design, Choice and Service. We have earned hundreds of industry awards, including being the first builder to receive the Triple Crown of American Home Building: National Builder of the Year two-time recipient, America's Best Builder, and National Housing Quality Award. But to say that we are in the home building business only tells part of the story. We offer a unique working Culture for our Team Members, which earns us workplace accolades like appearing on FORTUNE magazine's "100 Best Companies to Work For'" list nine times and FORTUNE'S "Top Workplaces for Millennials." Because for us, Our Purpose of Building Dreams, Enhancing Lives of our Team, our Customers and our Community is why we exist as a company.

Readers would be hard-pressed to discern what David Weekley Home's "unique working culture" entailed or why it was named a top workplace for millennials. They could not tell what "vision" Sinclair promoted or what made their management team exemplary. There was no information on how Belk's commitment to philanthropy shaped employees' lives. These ads were not unique. Most provided little information.

INFORMATION SESSIONS AND CAREER FAIRS

Hiring agents also visited campuses to tell students about their jobs. One way they did so was by hosting information sessions—lectures about the job followed by question-and-answer sessions. Yet despite their name— information sessions—these formats provided little information. When hosting them, some hiring agents did not know what roles students would fill. Others knew but were hiring for dozens of positions. In an hour-long session, they did not have time to describe them all.

Not able to tell students about jobs, hiring agents treated information sessions as commercials: they gave a broad overview aimed at instilling a feeling rather than providing detailed knowledge. In fact, it was not unusual for information sessions to literally show commercials.

For example, at an information session for jobs at a luxury car company, two company representatives showed three videos. The first video began with a voice-over: "Within the foothills of the Blue Hills Mountains where earth and sky merge . . . there is a place where dreams fuse with steel. . . . Here thousands of parts in thousands of hands are destined for one purpose: to become the ultimate driving machine." Over lofty background music, the video zoomed in on the company's high-tech robots, announced that care is put into each car, and showcased employees who talked of taking pride in their work. A second video focused exclusively on employees, all of whom described why they love working for the company: market dominance, networking, varied work, a fast pace, and calling colleagues by their first names. A third video featured more employees talking about why they loved the company: "to launch a career at one of the most recognizable companies in the world," to "steer your own path to success," and to be part of an internationally recognized company.[5]

The company representatives spoke after showing the videos. However, they offered little useful information. In this case, the firm representatives outlined the divisions in the company, but offered no more than three sentences on each division. They also said where the jobs were located, how many employees worked at a particular plant, the square footage of the plants, the percentage of products they exported, and the number of countries in which they sold cars. At no point during the presentation did either speaker or any of the videos say what students would do if they were hired.

There was typically a question-and-answer period at the end of information sessions, and the luxury car company included one. However, these question-and-answer sessions also tended to yield little information. At the car company information session, students asked the speakers what they do in a typical day ("Get in at 7:15 or 7:30, check email, then assist my mentor with whatever she needs. It's too varied to say more than that"), what hours they work ("I'm not going to give you a number because it will probably scare you"), if any other company tried to steal them away (no), if the company pays for graduate school ("There's a stipend. I'm not going to lie. It's not a lot."), and the deadline for applying (they named it). The answers to students' questions provided little information—they were again vague. Though not all information sessions literally showed commercials, the amount of information conveyed usually paralleled this one, offering an image more than a detailed description. Usually, the job tasks went unstated.[6]

Students also attended career fairs. Career fairs were events in which employees stood next to tables decorated in their company's regalia and spoke to students who approached them. These events were busy; students tried to talk to several employers, and employers tried to talk to many students. Under these constraints, the expectation was that each conversation last only a few minutes. In these conversations, hiring agents were again vague. Employer 23 (residential services, sales) re-layed what he told students at career fairs: "I just give them the over-view. Very similar to the job postings. Talk about the background of the company, what makes us different." Employer 31 (security, finance, and sales) said she keeps the conversations general: "Basically, it's what is in the job description."

Moreover, the information that hiring agents gave students at infor-mation sessions and career fairs was not always accurate or complete.[7] Employer 3 (technology, finance, and sales) didn't mention the long hours associated with the job or that new hires would spend many weekends away from home. Employer 1 (technology, many business roles) didn't tell students how competitive the job could be. Employer 15 (finance, many business roles) told the students "about the really sexy teams" with-out mentioning that many new hires would be assigned to boring teams. Employer 19 (technology, many business roles) said her colleagues made false promises to get students interested in the position.

What's more, by the end of the interview process, employers may still not give students complete or accurate information about the job. Though some employers used job interviews to explain the job in detail, others did not. Interviewing months before the job began, they still did not know themselves what students would do. Candidates would have to decide whether to take a job without knowing what it entailed.

Thus, despite the fact that employers advertised positions widely and were a regular presence at business schools, they offered students little information about their actual positions. Job titles, job descriptions, company descriptions, information sessions, career fairs, and interviews were all uninformative. Often what students would be doing on the job was hidden from them.

Hidden Information on Pay

Equalization is measured in earnings, not in the jobs students do. Most students from non-elite universities are locked out of elite labor markets, ones that more often advertise their earnings but also reject most applicants from non-elite schools.[8] In the mid-tier business market, employers hid information about earnings from students of all classes.

Job ads typically did not post information about wages. On the popular job board Monster.com, 75% of job ads did not include a wage, and 59% did not include either wage *or* benefit information.[9] On another job board, CareerBuilder.com, 80% omitted earnings information.[10]

Southern State University also hosted its own job board, UJobs.[11] UJobs advertised over 10,000 jobs to SSU students in an academic year. Filtered by jobs for business majors, each cohort of business majors was exposed to over 1,800 ads. Filtered by specialization, students could see well over 100 ads related to most subfields. As table 2 shows, these job ads tended to exclude earnings information. On UJobs, 67% of business administration job ads did not include earnings information. When considering jobs posted in specific subfields, 73% of finance, 71% of marketing, 70% of economics, 66% of human resources, 65% of business technology, and 63% of operations and logistics jobs did not list earnings.[12] Moreover, when jobs did list earnings, some only listed a range— for example, $40,000 to $70,000, a spectrum large enough to be fairly uninformative.[13]

In most cases, students could not receive earnings information by talking to recruiters or hiring managers. Not all of them were aware of what students would earn if they were hired. Talking of the salary for the job he recruited for, Employer 9 (healthcare, marketing) remarked: "A lot of it is kept very controlled by the human resources team, so I don't even have access." Employer 3 (technology, finance, and sales) agreed: "With [company], they really keep everything so secret. It's the nature of the beast."[14]

Other recruiters and hiring managers were privy to how much new hires would be paid but would not share that information with students. Employer 5 (healthcare, consultants) did not present it when students asked: "[Management] trains us on the workarounds for not telling them specifically what it is." Employer 6 (healthcare, consultants) did not offer salary information either: "I personally answer, 'We offer a competitive

TABLE 2: Percentage of Jobs Posted on UJobs That Omit Earnings

	PERCENTAGE OF JOBS NOT LISTING EARNINGS	N
Business Administration	66.7	745
Economics	70.0	183
Entrepreneurship	58.3	103
Finance	72.9	140
HR	66.1	165
Business Internet Technology	65.2	69
Marketing	71.0	259
Operations & Logistics	62.5	168

Notes: Jobs were included if they were posted on UJobs between August 1, 2015, and May 1, 2016. Duplicate job postings were excluded so that each job ad was counted only once.

salary' and just leave it at that." Employer 7 (transportation, analysts) also deflected: "We just let them know that's something we can talk about a little bit further on in the process." Employer 15 (finance, many business roles) summarized the (lack of) salary information available to students: "With campus recruiting, [pay information] is a secret until the end."[15] Indeed, hiring agents also rarely shared salary numbers in information sessions. Of the seventeen sessions I attended, only two offered pay information that was not also in the job ad.

Furthermore, students could not use rules of thumb to guess what each position paid. How employers decided to pay employees was hidden from students. Pay could be based on how managers viewed the importance of that position within the firm, whether managers believed employees were motivated by monetary rewards or other benefits, and if the company had recently merged with another company that paid different wages. Some companies also paid all entry-level hires in the same position the same salary while others varied pay based on the experiences and characteristics of each candidate. Pay could also change when new managers imposed new compensation philosophies, when managers believed they were losing too many employees to other firms, or when there were internal complaints about pay. Indeed, several hiring agents told me that these factors related to their company's pay structure changed frequently. Employer 11 (finance, advisers), for example, said that pay for new hires at his firm changed three times in seven years, and Employer 21 (energy, many business roles) said that they updated their compensation packages each year, though for some positions and not for others. With this much variation and change, students could not rely on rules of thumb to gain accurate information about pay or know if any rumors they heard remained true.

Employers were not the only source of wage information. Websites such as Glassdoor and PayScale claim to offer pay information. However, not only were these websites evenly accessible to students of all social classes, but they provided information of unknown reliability. Websites in which employees post their salaries can be misleading.[16] It is not always clear which position they refer to, in which location, if and how their salary depends on applicants' particular experiences or skills, or if the salary information they revealed last year would apply to this year. A *Wall Street Journal* report also claimed that some firms manipulate information on these sites by selectively asking some employees to report their pay or pressuring them to provide particular information.[17]

In addition, most employers I spoke with said that their company kept pay information secret internally. That is, they did not tell their employees how much their colleagues earned.[18] Because of this, current employees could not tell prospective employees what they would be paid. Current employees could also not draw accurate inferences about others' salaries by using their own. As Employer 16 (transportation, HR, and logistics) told me, some of their positions paid above the market rate and some paid below it, and employees were not told which was which.

In most cases, job seekers could only find out what they would be paid when they received an offer. At this point, employers usually gave students one day to two weeks to decide whether to accept the position.[19] In these periods, students would rarely be able to acquire and compare multiple job offers. Job offers that followed from summer internships were often distributed before the fall hiring season began—preventing students from gaining and weighing other offers—and job offers that came later in the year were not coordinated with other firms. Employers then forced students to decide whether to accept an offer without knowing what other jobs would become available, which would be offered to them, and what they would pay.

Most employers also forced students to consider offers as they stood. That is, most employers I spoke with did not allow students to negotiate over pay. As Employer 21 (energy, many business roles) said: "For my new grad job, the rate is the rate. . . . We wouldn't waver on it." Employer 5 (healthcare, consultants) said: "Everybody gets paid the exact same and there's no negotiation." Employer 6 (healthcare, consultants) concurred: "We don't negotiate salary." Employer 2 (technology, sales) agreed: "The pay is the same for everyone. It's not really a negotiable thing." Employer 29 (healthcare, supply chain) added: "Our entry-level offers are pretty much set. . . . We don't negotiate on those at all." Employers refused to negotiate for several reasons: they wanted all new employees in the same role to have the same pay, they did not want entry-level pay to exceed the pay of experienced employees, they had already determined their annual budget, or they viewed students as having little standing with which to negotiate. Moreover, employers who allowed students to negotiate would only raise their salary by a few thousand dollars, not enough to account for the large earnings gaps between students in the same business specialty.

Thus, employers gave students little information with which to decide where to apply and which jobs to accept. Job ads omitted pay information, job titles were not necessarily reflective of the job, job descriptions were often vague, recruiters refused to answer questions about salary, rules of thumb were of little use, websites posted information with unknown accuracy, connections were kept in the dark, and the short window to accept or turn down a job made it difficult for students to weigh multiple offers at once. None of this would matter if most entry-level positions paid the same amount, at least within a specialty area. But this was not the case. The last few decades have witnessed a rise of earnings inequality among workers within the same occupation, especially in business fields.[20] This rise has been so substantial that nearly half of the variation in Americans' wages is now derived from workers with the same skills finding similar employment at different firms, and the pay differentials for similar positions at different firms is so large that economists argue that the phrase "it's who you know" should be replaced with "it's where you work."[21] Of course, with little information available about earnings, students could not tell where their offers landed in earnings distribution for similar jobs. Both advantaged and disadvantaged students would need to guess if the offer they received was worth taking—making luck, not class, central to receiving a high-paying position.[22]

Conclusion

Employers constructed a labor market using a pillar of the luckocracy: hidden information about where to get ahead. If the mid-tier business labor market is compared to a game show, it would be one with thousands of opaque and locked doors, each hiding the content of the prize and its monetary value from contestants of all classes. It would be a system in which advantaged and disadvantaged students had equal chances of winning because neither group could determine where the best prizes were located or how much the grand prize was worth.

Hidden Information on Class-Neutral Hiring Criteria

To win the game, Chona needed to put the "right" key in the door. However, the *Let's Make a Deal* game denied her the information she needed to strategically choose the "right" key. With so little information, strategies were irrelevant to winning. All she could do was guess. On *Let's Make a Deal*, this was true for contestants from all classes, as they were all denied the information they needed to do anything but guess.

Students found themselves in a similar situation. There were thousands of hiring agents, few of whom gave students complete information about what experiences, skills, and styles they reward. Without this information, students could not know how to present themselves to any particular hiring agent, and there was no strategy they could use to find out. Like contestants in a game show, they would have to guess.

And just as in the game show, students from all class backgrounds had the same chance of guessing well. Though employers' hiring criteria varied considerably, they had one thing in common: the criteria were class neutral. Most employers evaluated students in ways that students of all classes could meet—not in the least, as we'll see in the next chapter, because universities helped students meet mid-tier agents' low bars of employability. And when employers veered away from class neutrality, they balanced their biases. The same hiring agent who looked for traits that class-advantaged students were more likely to display also looked for traits that class-disadvantaged students were more likely to possess.

Thus, employers created a luckocracy, one upheld by the dual pillars of hidden information about how to get ahead and class-neutral hiring criteria. They created a system that operates like a game show, where luck, not class, determines the winners.

Hidden Keys

Employers' hiring criteria were hidden from students. Each hiring agent used specific criteria but told students only their criteria that were common across employers.

Job ads provided little insight about employers' hiring criteria. They were not necessarily complete, accurate, or specific. Employer 13 (government, auditors) explained that they did not list all relevant criteria. Managers, even those hiring for similar positions, did not always agree on the hiring criteria so they left some out of the ad. Employer 14 (university, many business roles) and Employer 15 (finance, many business roles) did not list their full criteria because they initially hired students into a cohort and only later placed them on a specific team. When they wrote their ad, they did not know what teams they would have or which hiring managers would be involved. Employer 28 (technology, procurement) said his company used an outdated job ad that did not account for how the job and its qualifications had changed. What was written in the job ad was then not an accurate representation of the skills that applicants would need.

Information sessions provided no more specific information about employers' evaluation criteria.[1] Some employers said they could not provide it since they hired for many positions and each position required different skill sets that were evaluated in different ways. One employer, for example, explained that she hired for twenty-four teams—far too many to discuss in a one-hour session. Other recruiters did not give detailed information because each hiring manager used different criteria, and they spoke to students before knowing which hiring managers would be involved. Others simply believed that selling an image was more effective than providing detail, or that focusing on a specific job was unwise when students could be hired and then moved into another position. Unable or unwilling to give students detailed information, recruiters used information sessions to offer general advice instead. They dispensed advice that was nearly universal: turn off cell phones, spit out gum, bring a résumé, answer behavioral questions in the STAR format (naming the *s*ituation, *t*ask, *a*ction, and *r*esult), remain positive, ask questions, and demonstrate interest in the company.

Students who wanted to ask recruiters about their hiring criteria would have trouble doing so. Some companies made it difficult for students to identify hiring agents. As Employer 8 (telecommunications, many business roles) said: "We make it very difficult to find our recruiters. . . . We have it on lockdown."[2] Of course, some students did know the recruiters—they met them at career fairs, information sessions, résumé reviews, and classroom visits. But even if students asked them how to be hired, there was a limited amount of information the agent would reveal. Some would inform students about the format of the interview, saying that it included a behavioral portion, group interview, case study, or Excel test. But they would not tell students what specific questions they would ask or how they would be evaluated. As Employer 24 (technology, many business roles) put it: "We would never say, 'These are the questions you're gonna be receiving.' We would say, 'It's gonna be a mix of technical and behavioral-based questions' and leave it at that."

There were also websites such as Glassdoor that listed interview questions for popular jobs. On these sites, previous job candidates post questions they were asked. However, as we'll see, interviewers' questions were not always standardized, so students could not know if the questions someone else was asked would be asked of them. Also, job candidates were not well positioned to know how they were evaluated, and there was no telling if the evaluation criteria others surmised had been applied to them would be used on future candidates as well.

In addition, employers' hiring practices did not cohere around jobs or industry, preventing students from knowing whether rules of thumb would land them a particular position. It wasn't that employers hiring for finance positions all agreed on one set of criteria and those hiring for marketing positions agreed on another, or those hiring in the transportation sector used one set of criteria while those in healthcare used another. Often the people designing the hiring process told me they imported what they learned from working at other firms—including firms in different industries that hired people for different roles. In this way, the hiring process for a marketer at a technology firm could resemble the hiring process for an operations manager at a manufacturing plant. And each could change when a new hiring agent took charge. These changes would occur, of course, without students being informed.

Students' connections were not well positioned to uncover how they would be evaluated either. As we'll see below, not all interviewers were required to follow a script, so no one—not students' connections and not even the hiring agent themselves—necessarily knew what they would ask students before they asked it. On some teams, each member used different evaluation practices and criteria, making it difficult even for team members to know how any hiring decision would unfold. Evaluation criteria also changed over time, making any information a connection had prone to be outdated. As Employer 20 (energy, hourly trader) told me, the same team hiring for the same position may prefer a student skilled at Excel or a student skilled at report writing depending on who had recently left the team and how the team's work had evolved.

Finally, employers made it difficult for students to know if their connections could get them around the evaluation process entirely. Companies varied by whether they allowed the CEO to hire whomever they wanted, had a referral system that all employees could use, relied on referrals from professors they paid, or prohibited any applicant from getting around their formal hiring process. Regardless of their policy, employers rarely advertised it, making it difficult for students to know if the people they approached could help them.

Employers then hid information about how they hired. They did not reveal the specifics of their hiring criteria and practices in job ads, information sessions, or informal conversations, and their hiring practices were too dynamic for students' connections to gather accurate information either. In denying information to students of all class backgrounds, they made sure that getting hired would be like playing the *Let's Make a Deal* game: students would have to guess which key to use.

Varied Keys

If all employers used the same hiring criteria, then students could learn the criteria by applying to many jobs. It wouldn't matter that it's hidden. But hiring agents did not use the same criteria—not when evaluating students' résumés or interviews.

RÉSUMÉS

Hiring agents' differences were apparent from the first stage of the hiring process—from when they evaluated students' résumés. Résumés listed students' GPA, leadership roles, extracurricular activities, and work experience. Outside of wanting a well-formatted résumé with no spelling or grammar mistakes, hiring agents routinely disagreed about which statuses and experiences mattered and how they should be evaluated. However, as we'll see below, their criteria had one commonality: mid-tier business employers largely ignored real differences between class-advantaged and class-disadvantaged students' résumés and evaluated them in class-neutral ways.

Hiring agents held different opinions about students' GPA. For Employer 2 (technology, sales), Employer 13 (government, auditors), and Employer 32 (transportation, management), there was not a GPA requirement. As Employer 32 put it succinctly: "GPA isn't something that we consider." However, for Employer 27 (finance, HR, and finance), there was an unadvertised but consistent requirement: "I think the unspoken cutoff is 3.5." For Employer 20 (energy, hourly trader), a different practice was in place. There were internal inconsistencies about how to evaluate students' GPAs: "With GPA, we have a preference but not a requirement. And to be totally honest, it will vary by the hiring manager what that preference is. As a company we would like to hire 3.0 and above. But I have worked with some hiring managers who have been only interested in somebody with a 3.5 and above." For Employer 21 (energy, many business roles), internal GPA requirements varied too: "I can tell you there are some managers who are GPA snobs."

Similarly, employers differed on how heavily they weighed leadership—a category, that, as we'll see below, they defined so broadly as to be classless. Some saw leadership as essential, some saw it as a plus, and others did not care about it at all. Employer 15 (finance, many business roles) said it was one of the first things she looked for. Employer 5 (healthcare, consultants) said that as she read résumés, she asked herself: "Are they portraying themselves as someone who takes initiative, getting leadership roles?" Employer 20 (energy, hourly trader), on the other hand, noticed leadership roles but did deem them essential: "I see a lot of student résumés where maybe they've been involved in a student organization on campus where they're able to take that leadership position. I think it shows that they go that extra mile. But again, not a make-or-break. Just nice to have." Employer 27 (finance, HR, and finance) also considered leadership a "nice to have" feature on a résumé: "If you're a leader in a club, that's always obviously super great, just shows that you have initiative." Not all hiring agents, however, cared about leadership. About a third of employers I spoke to did not mention it at all.

Internships—an experience that 83% of class-disadvantaged and 92% of class-advantaged respondents reported having—followed the same pattern.[3] They were essential to some hiring agents and unimportant to others. Asked what she looked for in college students' résumés, Employer 12 (manufacturing, many business roles) said: "Definitely previous internship experience." Employer 26 (technology, business roles) agreed: "By the time of graduation, students should have an internship." Employer 3 (technology, finance, and sales) stressed the point: "For new grads, definitely internship experience. . . . I do try to remind them: 'internship, internship, internship.' I cannot speak of that enough."

Other employers, however, did not weigh internships so heavily. Some employers saw internships as one of several experiences they cared about and considered other experiences substitutable for them. Employer 1 (technology, many business roles) explained how she reviewed résumés: "Projects, internships, work experience, study abroad, leadership on campus. There needs to be one of those, but generally, I'm like, 'You need three things to make you at least somewhat competitive.'" Employer 25 (research, sales) also saw internships as one of many possible qualifications: "They must possess at least three of the following. Those are sales and fundraising experience [as an intern], customer service experience, experience working in a team environment, experience in an office setting, or leadership experience."

Other employers did not view internships as relevant at all. Employer 5 (healthcare, consultants) said: "We've definitely taken people who don't have internships." Employer 6 (healthcare, consultants) agreed: "Internship experience—it's not necessary." Employer 32 (transportation, management) responded to a question about if internships were required by saying, "No, not at all."[4]

In addition, employers held varied opinions about students' work experience. Some again considered it essential while others considered it irrelevant. Each of the following employers hired college students for sales positions; none of them viewed work experience in the same way. Employer 31 (security, finance, and sales) wanted to hire someone with sales or customer service experience: "I like to see that they're social, that they've done a little bit of sales before. . . . It can be any type of sales experience. It can be retail, it could be restaurant, it could be customer service." Employer 3 (technology, finance, and sales) did not consider customer service positions equivalent to sales: "Working at Barnes and Noble during the school year, or whatever, doesn't make you qualified for a sales position." Employer 2 (technology, sales) did not care if the applicant had any sales experience at all—or any other experience: "The job that we hire for is a really challenging sales job, and we typically hire people that have no sales experience. We're looking for personality traits more than experience."

Employers regarded extracurricular activities in much the same way. To Employer 32 (transportation, management), they were necessary— one of the first things she looked for on a student's résumé. For Employer 22 (healthcare, many business roles), extracurricular activities were a plus: "I think any involvement in clubs or different organizations is helpful too." To Employer 13 (government, auditors), on the other hand, extracurricular activities were unnecessary: "It's not going to hurt the person's qualifications, but it's not something that they're really looking for."

Of course, this was not a full list of the experiences that employers looked for in students' résumés. Less commonly, employers looked for courses, course projects, service, and study abroad. And, not surprisingly, they did not share a standard approach to evaluating any of these. Study abroad (a classed experience that we'll see is balanced out by criteria that favor the disadvantaged), for example, could be important because it showed students' adaptability, in which case most students who studied abroad would benefit from it, or because it signaled foreign language skills, in which case students who studied abroad in English-speaking nations or who did not learn a foreign language would not receive the same advantage from it.

Thus, a student with a high GPA, who led a team, interned, participated in clubs, and had work experience would pass most mid-tier business employers' initial screen. However, if students had to choose what to focus on in advance or what to emphasize on their one-page résumé, they could not know how to do so. Hiring agents did not always advertise their varied preferences—especially not years in advance, when students would need this information to accumulate the "right" experiences. Students who could not check every box were then forced to guess which ones to check. And, as we'll see below, simply checking these boxes did not mean they would be offered a job. Students still had to guess how to meet employers' expectations in an interview.

INTERVIEWS

Hiring agents had varied ideas about how to evaluate students in job interviews. They used interviews to examine students' skills, but looked for different skills, defined the same skills in different ways, used different methods of assessing skills, and evaluated students' answers using varied and changing standards. Again, each of these variations was hidden from students—forcing them to try to please an audience whose preferences they did not know.

Defining Skills

Many employers looked for an overlapping set of *general* skills, ones that were widely sought across firms. The general skills that employers told me they wanted mirrored the skills reported on national surveys: communication, leadership, teamwork, the ability to learn, and job-related skills such as the ability to use the computer program Excel.[5] However, they defined these general skills in *specific* ways—ways that varied across and within firms.

Communication skills serve as a prime example. Most of the employers I spoke with said that they looked for candidates with strong communication skills. This, then, is a general skill—one that employers generally sought. Employers also shared some general definitions of communication skills. Many defined it in the ways that universities like SSU teach: the ability to hold a conversation, make eye contact, and to be clear, confident, engaged, and professionally dressed—often in a suit. In interviews, they also defined strong communication as answers that followed the STAR format, naming the situation, task, action, and result when responding to a question about past behaviors.

However, employers also had *specific* definitions of communication skills—ones that were not widespread. This variation, though, was not that some employers used class-biased criteria and others did not; most of employers' definitions were class neutral. Employer 5 (healthcare, consultants), for example, explained what she considered strong communication: "What we're looking for is detail. We want to hear specifically what they did." She gave an example of a favorable answer to a question about how to address a team member who did not pull their weight—one that went into great detail:

> So what we're looking for is: "This is a project that we worked on. It was our senior project and our project was this. And this is what everybody's role was. So I was supposed to do this, and then I had two other partners and they were supposed to do this," and that was laid out very clearly. "Then we had figured out what our deadlines were gonna be so that we

knew when our work was supposed to be done. Then we came up to the first deadline, and there was a teammate who didn't do their part. So here's what I did. I decided to reach out to them and talk to them candidly about the situation just to let them know we all are going to get the same grade so we just wanna make sure that we are on the same page and wanted to help you out if you were too busy or just wanted to figure out why you weren't able to meet this deadline when we were supposed as a team."

Then typically they say something like, "Then I realized that this person was just really busy or they didn't know what they were supposed to do but felt too scared to ask. So after we talked it out, we figured out what our plan was going to be. I was going to help train him on how to do Excel since he was responsible for building a spreadsheet in Excel and didn't know how to. Then from there we were able to resolve things and talk through what we were gonna do moving forward to ensure that all of our deadlines were gonna be met and that we were gonna be well-rehearsed before we had to present. So then we did a presentation, everything went well. We all got As on it, and I continued to reach out to that person to let them know that if they needed some more assistance with Excel in future that I could help them with it."

Students, however, could not be sure that employers defined strong communication as giving detailed answers. Employer 13 (government, auditors) wanted short answers instead. She evaluated whether "their answer is concise but provides enough information to where they're answering all of the different proponents of the question."

Employers not only differed on whether strong communication meant providing detail or being concise, but also on whether strong communication showcased preparedness. Employer 1 (technology, many business roles) wanted students to answer questions in ways that showed they had prepared: "If you come into an interview and don't know or haven't gone through those top ten [most commonly asked interview questions], you're not going to do well." However, Employer 9 (healthcare, marketing) did not want students to prepare in advance: "One of the biggest pet peeves for me is if it feels like the interview was rehearsed. Did they have scripted answers?"

Similarly, employers held varied ideas about how strong communication related to response speed. Some, like Employer 9, wanted students to pause and reflect: "I would expect, especially with a curve ball question like that, a minute or two of silence." Others would not hire a candidate who took a minute or two of silence. Employer 17 (transportation, management) ended his interviews asking students why he shouldn't hire them. He did not care about the content of students' answers but believed that quick decision-making was the key to success. So he looked for speedy responses: "All I'm really looking for is can you tell me something within a reasonable amount of time, which is ten to fifteen seconds. . . . It's about can you answer this question quickly and decisively?"

Most employers I spoke to thought that strong communication included asking questions. However, they varied in which questions they considered appropriate. Employer 15 (finance, many business roles) and Employer 8 (telecommunications, many business roles) both hired for internships that could lead into jobs. Employer 15 would not hire a student who asked about money: "If someone is talking to you about salary, then you think, 'Okay, this person's just chasing the dollars. They don't actually care what they're doing. They just want to make the most money.' . . . Because they're a dollar chaser, your thought is that they're probably not going to stay with you very long. This is not the candidate that you're looking for." Other hiring agents wanted students to ask about money. Employer 8 said: "Sometimes I don't talk about it being paid. I want them to ask."

Of course, evaluators' specific definitions of communication skills did not end there. Some defined strong communication as avoiding "*ums*" and "*likes*," sending thank-you notes, and being able to write well. Thus, for students, presenting the same communication skills could result in being hired for one job and rejected from another, and they could not know in advance which presentation styles would result in which outcome.

It was not only communication skills that invoked such varied and specific definitions. Employers also *generally* agreed that leadership and teamwork were important skills, and even agreed on some ways of defining them. Strong leadership, for example, meant more than holding a title—it was shown through actions. Strong teamwork skills meant not criticizing teammates or ignoring them. Beyond that, however, employers held more specific definitions of leadership and teamwork as well as specific ideas about how to balance them. For example, Employer 3 (technology, finance, and sales) did not want candidates to focus on their team: "Most importantly, ownership, and not 'we' statements. A lot of candidates say, 'We did this.' Well, I'm not interviewing your team. I want to know what you did." Employer 21 (energy, many business roles) agreed: "When someone only says 'we,' that's a red flag because we do want someone that can work in team but also thinks about themselves." Yet for Employer 1 (technology, many business roles), the answers Employer 3 and Employer 21 preferred were the answers she critiqued. She disliked when "the I, I, I ruins the we, we, we."

Similarly, employers agreed on another general skill—the ability to learn quickly. However, employers defined evidence of learning quickly in specific ways, ones not shared across hiring agents. Employer 3 (technology, finance, and sales) believed that students who took on new activities must have learned new skills. Employer 19 (technology, many business roles) focused on whether candidates asked her many questions. To her, doing so indicated that they had the tools to learn quickly.

Several employers also wanted to hire students with technical skills. What these included varied by the job. For finance positions, it could include generating profit-and-loss statements; for human resources, it could include understanding benefits and compensation. For many positions, it included using Excel. Employers again had specific definitions of proficiency in Excel. Their definition could include the ability to create pivot tables, design macros, or analyze data stored in the program.

Likewise, companies wanted to hire students with another general trait: interest in the work. Again, they defined evidence of interest in varied and specific ways. Each of the following employers worked in the healthcare industry and each used different indicators of interest. Employer 6 (healthcare, consultants) said: "I look at their major, thinking about what kind of classes they are taking. Meaning are they going to be interested in the work that we do?" Employer 5 (healthcare, consultants), however, said: "I will look at the major—just glance at it—but it doesn't really matter what it is." Instead, she wanted students to tell her: "This is why I'm interested in healthcare." Employer 9 (healthcare, marketing) used different criteria than the former two: "We look to see if they have any previous healthcare experience, but that could be so much as volunteering at a nursing home or volunteering at a hospital—something that expresses their interest in the healthcare field."

Finally, employers also stressed that they hired "cultural fits." Fit was determined both at the company and team levels—so while companies *generally* wanted people who fit, they looked for highly *specific* ways of doing so. Employer 8 (telecommunications, many business roles) stated her main hiring criteria: "A lot of times for college students it is purely would they work well with this manager, and do they have the soft skills necessary to complete the job?" She explained that some managers were people who "cut to the chase" and who think in "black-and-white" terms. Others coddled students. She tried to identify students who would work well with each manager. Employer 21 (energy, many business roles) agreed that cultural fit could be very specific: "I have teams that are very no-nonsense. All they do is data and that's their mindset, so if there's a really bubbly interviewee, they might not mesh well with that team. But another group that's very bubbly, really interactive, then someone who's only data driven, very to the point, might not be the right fit for them." Thus, she said: "We could have different managers who look at the same candidate and one could say they're perfect and the other one could say no."

The same applied to other skills that employers sought as well—skills such as problem solving, flexibility, organization, time management, and the ability to multitask. In each case, what Employer 21 said held more broadly—what would get a student hired by one manager would get them passed over by another. And since no one told students each manager's criteria, all students could do was guess.

Evaluating Skills

Even when agreeing on what skills to assess, employers assessed them in different ways. Most employers used interviews to assess candidates' skills, but they asked different questions and evaluated answers in different ways.[6] Thus, even if students knew what skills evaluators cared about, they would not know what questions they would be asked or how evaluators would assess their answers.

There was considerable variation within and across hiring teams in how candidates were considered. Some teams allowed each member to structure each interview themselves. Even when hiring for the same position, different team members asked different questions, sometimes about different skills, to different candidates.[7] At other firms, hiring agents were meant to ask all candidates about the same skills but did not need to ask the same questions. For example, Employer 5 (healthcare, consultants) explained:

> We have a general interview guide that has different boxes for the types of details we're trying to get. So there may be one on dealing with ambiguity. There would be five or six different questions that they could read off just verbatim. Or a lot of interviewers who are a little bit more senior have made up their own questions about ambiguity. And they'll use those questions instead of the ones that are on the interview guide. And that's okay, just because the interview guide is supposed to be just that—a guide and not an interview bible.

Other firms had precise scripts that interviewers were meant to follow. However, as Employer 15 (finance, many business roles) acknowledged, enforcing this was difficult: "Some of them have interviewed for you a lot, and they're very good about sticking to the script and asking the questions. But sometimes, especially if you get newer managers or managers who want to do things their own way, they go rogue." Thus, a student who knew a recent hire could not be sure they'd be asked the same questions as their contact.

Across and within companies and teams, there was also variation in how employers evaluated students' answers. Some companies had no formal evaluation procedures and little agreement among interviewers about what criteria to use. For example, Employer 13 (government, auditors) explained what happened on her team: "With eye contact, for some people that wasn't as big of a deal as it was to other people. Or even just being able to provide an answer itself—to some people that was just horrible, the worse thing in the world [when they couldn't answer the questions]. And then other people went, 'Well, they're nervous. It's not that big of a deal. Cut them some slack, they're young.'"[8] Other companies trained their interviewers to score each candidate's answer to each question, telling them what type of answer received each number of points. Yet even the use of standardized criteria would not necessarily lead to a predictable outcome. As Employer 12 (manufacturing, many business roles) explained: "Each evaluator has a rubric and will score each response an interviewee gives on a numbered scale. However, they may not use interviewees' scores when deciding who to hire. It's gonna depend on the team. Some will look at the interview more strictly and say, 'This person got the highest interview score. They meet my qualifications. They're a good fit. Okay, we're gonna select them for the role.' Others have more deciding factors outside of the interview. So it's not necessarily the person with the highest interview score is gonna get the job." And, of course, each team's evaluation methods changed over time. Employer 13 (government, auditors) was so dissatisfied with her team's evaluation system that she standardized it; other hiring teams also experimented with how to decide who to hire.

Therefore, students could prepare the *general* skills and styles that they knew employers preferred, but they could not prepare for the *specific* ways that employers would evaluate them. Different employers would evaluate them in different ways at different times. Thus, the mid-tier business labor market was structured like a game show: there were thousands of doors, each which needed its own time-sensitive key to unlock, and information about which key unlocked which door was hidden. In this situation, all students could do was make sure they could talk about the skills that employers generally wanted, then guess how to present them to any particular person.

Class-Neutral Criteria

On its own, hidden information about where and how to get ahead would not create earnings equality. For equality to occur, the second pillar of the luckocracy must also be in place: advantaged and disadvantaged students' guesses need to have the same chance of paying off. And yet, employers could use at least five levers to construct a class-biased system. First, employers could set such a high bar for their desired skills that only students with many resources could meet it. Second, employers could define skills in advantaged students' image: Communication could mean showing class-based polish; fit could mean the ability to talk about international vacations, tennis, or art. Third, employers could focus on the settings where students developed skills. That is, they could prefer students who led the ski team rather than the bowling team or who learned Excel by interning at a prestigious firm rather than an obscure one. Fourth, they could care about the number of activities students completed. As class-advantaged students are less likely to work for pay than class-disadvantaged students,[9] the former have more time to participate in more leadership activities and clubs.[10] Fifth, employers could construct barriers to applying that block students with few resources. Despite having five possible levels to pull to create class *inequality*, most mid-tier business employers I spoke to pulled *none* of them.[11] Moreover, as we'll see, even when they did, their biases balanced out—alternating between favoring advantaged and disadvantaged students.

LOW BARS

Employers had low bars for selecting students, ones that did not take many resources to meet. The bar for receiving an internship was particularly low, even for internships with prominent companies. Employer 16 (transportation, HR, and logistics) revealed: "The internships honestly do not have much qualification." Asked if they needed any qualifications to become an intern, Employer 18 (e-commerce, sales) said: "No. Not necessarily." Employer 19 (technology, many business roles) agreed: "If you're a sophomore, just saying that you've done something is important. I don't really care what it is. If you're waiting tables that's totally fine, or you worked in a club, or you volunteered. I'm just looking that you're not sitting on your fanny."

Employers had a low bar for hiring interns because they considered them low risk. They could work with the student for three months and then not hire them again. However, many employers also hoped to offer the majority of their interns full-time positions, making an internship a relatively easy way for some students to get a full-time job.[12] Because business internships tended to pay and some provided housing, they were available to students from all classes.

For students applying without first having an in-house internship, the bar was still low. Employers told me that their jobs were straightforward enough that most students could hit the ground running or specific enough to their company that they would need to train students regardless of their knowledge and skill. Employers then just looked for general competencies. As mentioned above, they wanted people with leadership, teamwork, and knowledge of Excel, among other skills. The bar for successfully meeting these competencies was specific but not high.[13] Often, if the student could tell a single story about showing the competency, they could show that they met the bar.

Moreover, the employers I spoke to seemed more concerned about whether students met their bar than by how much they exceeded it. They could easily tell me about job seekers who failed to meet their bar: how they rejected the student with ripped clothing or a candidate who lied, swore, demeaned their teammates, or could not answer their questions. They had fewer stories of candidates who dramatically exceeded their bar. Employer 12 (manufacturing, many business roles) even said she had never given a job candidate the highest score on her group's rubric. Instead, hiring agents said they wanted to hire students who answered their questions, met their qualifications, and whose values aligned with their company's. Students might not know what these questions, qualifications, and values were or how they would be tested on them, but they only needed to show that they could answers these questions, meet these qualifications, and had these values—not that they were the best possible person among those who met these standards.[14]

DEFINING SKILLS

The employers I spoke to typically defined skills in class-neutral ways. For example, when employers went into more detail about what they considered communication skills, they included styles that were accessible to all. They wanted to hire students who did not fidget, crack their knuckles, check a cell phone during a meeting, or speak in a timid voice. Some employers mentioned polish as well—usually a sign of a class-inflected style. However, when I asked them to describe polish, they listed characteristics that were widely accessible—not least because, as we'll see, the business school taught them. Employer 18 (e-commerce, sales) explained what she meant: "Polish. Executive presence. So, being neat and clean. You don't have to be in a three-piece suit to have executive presence. A balance of confidence and humility. Eye contact, engaging, being able to get your point across in a way that's not rambling or incoherent." Employer 25 (research, sales) also looked for candidates with polish and did not define polish in classed ways: "Polished communication is good communication skills. As I mentioned earlier, lack of filler words is good, ability to engage in conversation, keep the conversation going. Ask questions if needed. Not casual slang language."[15] Employer 4 (finance, advisers) wanted to hire students with something like polish—"professional communication skills." To her this also did not have a classed component: "I've had kids come up to me and they're chewing gum and yawning. I would consider that unprofessional. But then you see students that come up, shake your hand, make good eye contact. They are the ones with a professional demeanor."

Employers I spoke to also stressed that they preferred candidates who were interested in their company. For them, demonstrating interest did not mean being privy to insider information that students could only obtain through knowing someone at the firm. Though some viewed evidence of interest as stories, volunteer experience, courses, or clubs that aligned with the job or the company, almost all also emphasized that demonstrated interest meant glancing at the company's website. Employer 5 (healthcare, consultants) explained: "We just want them to have looked at our website. And to know what [our company] does. That's essentially it." Employer 17 (transportation, management) also wanted students to show interest by visiting the company's website—but did not demand anything more: "Just the ability to say, 'I looked you guys up. Y'all are based in [state], and you've been in business for fifty years. This is just a little bit of something about what I know about you.' And stuff like that. That's all I'm really looking for—just some basics."

In the mid-tier labor market, business employers also defined fit in class-neutral ways.[16] Employer 11 (finance, advisers) defined fit in ways that all students could display: "Fit. If you don't have the drive to go online, apply, follow up, then you're probably not a good fit. You need to be the kind of person that will follow up with people." Employer 24 (technology, many business roles) also defined fit in ways that did not require resources: "For me, it's somebody who's flexible, somebody who is high energy, who knows a little bit about the company and the position." Employer 18 (e-commerce, sales) defined fit as did many others—as living the company's values, ones that students from all classes could express: "We have six values that are who we are on our best day. They range from the foundational level of accountability and integrity, up to passion and curiosity and persistence, the things that we know, in collaboration, will make them successful in our industry." Not about skills or activities that only those with money or time could acquire, fit was a classless metric to those in the mid-tier market.

WHERE STUDENTS LEARNED SKILLS

Employers kept their criteria classless by ignoring where students developed their skills. Though this book is about students who attend the same college, it is worth pointing out that most of the employers I spoke to did not care where students obtained their bachelor's degree. Employers' stated preferences were backed up by how they recruited. Most employers I spoke to said that they recruited by university location (close to their offices) and by whether the universities offered the majors they wanted. Some also looked at where their own employees had attended college and whether the college was racially diverse.[17] Less often, companies looked at university rank.[18] When they did,[19] they did not necessarily focus on the highest-ranked schools—some who cared about rank recruited from universities that were in the *US News & World Report*'s "Best Colleges Rankings" listing the 150–200 top schools.[20] As class-advantaged students tend to congregate at elite universities and class-disadvantaged students at lower-tiered universities,[21] having little preference for students at elite universities—or any particular rank of universities—enforced class neutrality.[22]

Employers also did not care where students developed their leadership skills. This neutralized class differences since students were not expected to lead expensive or prestigious groups. Employer 1 (technology, many business roles) explained: "Leadership, it can be within a fraternity or sorority, leadership within project work if they can find a way to explain that. Anything. Anything that shows that they've taken on jobs. Camp counselor, anything." An energy firm representative said: "We're looking for people in leadership roles. That could be anything. Church choir leader would count. Manager at McDonald's would count. Anything, we're open to anything." Employer 25 (research, sales) agreed: "Any type of leadership experience is helpful. It just shows that they are willing to go above and beyond, to take that initiative and be able to lead groups of people. Smaller groups, bigger groups, it doesn't really matter." Asked if she cared where they developed leadership skills, Employer 24 (technology, many business roles) simply said: "No. I think leadership is leadership." To the extent that employers had particular preferences, it was that the student led a club related to the job they applied to, such as the marketing club or finance club—clubs open to students of all classes.

Similarly, employers did not evaluate where applicants developed their teamwork skills. Employer 18 (e-commerce, sales) said students could use any context to talk about teamwork: "We ask them to describe times in the past that they have shown or demonstrated certain qualities that match up with our values. They can be school related, they can be church related, they can be team related whatever that is—their extracurricular or education work groups." Employer 20 (energy, hourly trader) said that when talking about teamwork in extracurricular activities, which activity it was did not matter: "I don't think I've ever gotten any feedback from a manager that they're looking for or not looking for a specific club. So, I would say that doesn't matter." Employer 9 (healthcare, marketing) concurred, saying of extracurricular activities: "I think they all have value." Students tend to participate in class-segregated social groups.[23] By rarely paying attention to these, employers again made class not matter.

Likewise, some employers cared that students had interned in the past, but they rarely cared if it was with a prestigious firm. Instead, they cared what the student accomplished. Employer 13 (government, auditors) explained: "They really put a lot more value on what the person was actually able to do and what they were able to gain and learn in the internship versus where it was actually at." Employer 12 (manufacturing, many business roles) agreed: "Where they interned is not as important as the value of the work that they've done." Employer 3 (technology, finance, and sales) added: "It didn't have to be another big company. We had plenty of smaller businesses where interns were given a lot of ownership." Employer 28 (technology, procurement) even was suspicious of internships at prestigious firms: "Sometimes if I see a bigger name, I'll ask more challenging questions to actually dig in the weeds more because it may have just been a big name and they may not have actually done anything."

As mentioned above, some employers saw experience in working-class jobs as being just as valuable as internships. For these employers, jobs taught relevant skills. If the student emphasized these skills, they would consider them. Employer 20 (energy, hourly trader) explained: "Maybe they worked at a clothing store, for example. If they have been in a position there where they can show that 'I had to multitask, I had to communicate, maybe I was responsible for drawing up the books.' That would show us that they were able to do something that might help us out in this position." Employer 5 (healthcare, consultants) agreed: "If they were a server, we'll look at what they put on their résumé. We aren't looking for them to say, 'I bused tables and served five tables at a time.' But maybe they were a lead server and helped to train their peers and helped to build a strategy around how many tables each server could take at one time. Different things like that, we'll be like, 'Oh, okay. That's impressive.'"

NUMBER OF SKILLS

The employers I spoke to also did not care about the number of times students signaled a skill. Students from advantaged backgrounds often have more time, money, and connections to gather more signals of skills,[24] but these were ignored by employers. For instance, many of the employers who wanted to hire students with one internship did not care if they had more. Asked if she cared if students had more than one prior internship, Employer 18 (e-commerce, sales) simply said: "No." Employer 19 (technology, many business roles) weighed in: "Not really. Probably the more the better because you get more experience in line to what we're looking for and get up to speed a bit quicker, but it's not necessary." Employer 20 (energy, hourly trader) added: "No, we don't have any kind of requirements for a number of internships."[25]

Employers also did not care too much about another number: GPA. Even employers who had formal or informal cutoffs did not care by how much a student exceeded it. This could matter since class-advantaged students often attend more rigorous primary and secondary schools, spend more time on homework in college, have greater knowledge of which classes to take to earn high grades, and reach out for help from professors more often.[26] They are then more likely to have higher GPAs.[27] But if students were above the GPA cutoff, this difference would not matter. Employer 12 (manufacturing, many business roles) explained: "If you have a 4.0, we're not gonna weigh you any higher than somebody who meets the 3.0 GPA requirement." Employer 29 (healthcare, supply chain) said of GPAs: "If it's a 3.2 versus a 3.8—we're not as concerned about that." At Employer 3's (technology, finance and sales) company, they only hired people with 3.0 GPAs and above. However, after that, they did not consider GPA: "If we looked at two people with similar résumés and they had different GPAs, it doesn't really matter."

Moreover, some employers were sensitive to the fact that not everyone had the same opportunities to receive a high GPA. Employer 15 (finance, many business roles) suggested that a low GPA was fine if there were classed reasons for it: "If you see someone awesome who was putting themselves through school, who notes they were working a certain amount of hours to pay for their education, managers love that. That's huge. That's showing time management. Okay, you still got a 3.2 but you also worked thirty hours a week. It's really impressive." Employer 19 (technology, many business roles) added: "Some hiring managers think GPA's an end-all, be-all. For me, if you're working your entire college career and you're putting yourself through school, you don't have to have a 4.0. Totally okay."

APPLICATION PRICE

Employers were also class neutral in that applicants did not need to spend money to receive a job. For students who could cover college tuition— either through direct payments, loans, or scholarships—money was a minor factor in accessing a job. Unlike applying for college or graduate school, applying for jobs was free. Employers also paid for transportation and accommodations for non-local interviews, paid students to work as interns, often paid for relocation assistance and housing for internships,[28] and then paid those they hired. Other than paying for clothes to wear to an interview and local transportation, employers covered the costs of applying. It was not in their interest to reward students whose families had more money. They would pay the students; the students would not pay them.

BALANCE

Upon occasion, employers used class-biased criteria or processes. However, taken together, they were class neutral because they alternated between favoring class-advantaged and class-disadvantaged students.

Some employers used evaluative criteria or processes that favored the advantaged. Some, for example, favored students who studied abroad or participated in Greek life. These activities were expensive, and class-advantaged students more often participated in them.[29] Some hiring agents also preferred athletes and Eagle Scouts. Not only were these activities more likely to be taken up by class-advantaged students compared to class-disadvantaged students, but they also were stereotypically male and, for Eagle Scouts, white.[30] As, in recent years, a greater share of college men than college women come from advantaged backgrounds, and a greater share of white than black and Hispanic students come from advantaged than disadvantaged backgrounds, these gender and race preferences may indirectly operate as class preferences as well.[31] In addition to the hiring criteria, some processes favored the class advantaged. Companies that allowed their employees to recommend applicants unintentionally favored class-advantaged students—those more likely to know professionals.[32]

But employers' criteria favored the disadvantaged as well. Some hiring agents favored applicants involved in service activities, which disadvantaged students were more likely to report on their résumés.[33] Other hiring agents preferred applicants who received internships through formal processes rather than, in Employer 1's (technology, many business roles) words, "through their neighbor or something."[34] With fewer professional connections, disadvantaged students were more likely to find their internships through formal means.[35] And, of course, many employers valued work experience. Compared to class-advantaged students, class-disadvantaged students tended to start working at earlier ages and for longer hours, gaining more responsibilities and leadership positions at work.[36]

Even a single hiring agent could alternate between criteria that favored the advantaged and disadvantaged. Employer 2 (technology, sales) preferred candidates who had studied abroad and were in Greek life—two activities that advantaged students were more likely to do.[37] However, he also held criteria that disadvantaged students were more likely to meet: paying for school.[38] As he put it: "A lot of times we'll ask them how they are paying for school. Because somebody who is having everything paid for by their parents might not be as motivated as somebody who's having to pay for it all themselves." Similarly, like many hiring agents, Employer 27 (finance, HR, and finance) preferred students who were able to hold a conversation with professionals—something that students from all class backgrounds learned to do, but that tends to comes easier to students with professional parents.[39] Yet she, like many others, disliked a trait that is also more common among more privileged students: a sense of entitlement.[40] She said: "I've turned down students for internships because they felt like they were entitled to a position and not that they wanted to work for it."[41] Likewise, Employer 22 (healthcare, many business roles) looked for students with clear career goals—something that comes easier to students who grow up around more professionals.[42] However, she also disliked an answer about their goals that only advantaged respondents could give: "Everybody in my family did this so that's what I decided to do."

Balance was created not only because employers had preferences that favored each class, but also because students did not know which hiring agents had which preferences. Because hiring agents' criteria were hidden, class-advantaged students could not count on playing up study-abroad experiences or the internships they received through their neighbors, and class-disadvantaged students couldn't count on service or modesty to lead to a job. Of course, even if students did match their styles with the preferences of particular hiring agents, there was no guarantee that doing so would work in their favor. With hidden wages, a class match could lead to a high-paying position or a low-paying one. Class neutrality was then furthered not only because of balanced preferences, but also because of hidden information.

Conclusion

Employers designed a labor market that operated as a luckocracy, an opportunity structure that paralleled a game show. Like a game show, there were many doors and not all could be unlocked with the same key. And, like a gameshow, they hid information about what key to use to win—what experiences, skills, and styles would lead to a job. And, more so than a game show, they kept secret what prizes (the actual jobs) they were offering and that prize's value (the salary). They also did not allow students of any particular class background to have an advantage as they used class-neutral criteria or balanced their biases. In this system, students were akin to game show contestants whose outcomes would be determined by chance rather than class.

The labor market, however, did not equalize students' earnings on its own. Just like the *Let's Make a Deal* staff made the winning key available to contestants of all classes, the next chapter will show that universities helped students from each social class develop the experiences, skills, and styles that made them eligible for the luckocracy.

PART II

PLAYING
THE GAME

Preparing for
the Luckocracy

College is often called "the great equalizer."[1] According to this view, colleges equalize earnings by selecting disadvantaged and advantaged students who are particularly alike or by turning them into similar people. However, despite this moniker, colleges do not do this—not through how they select or socialize students. Even among students who attend the same college, disadvantaged students enter with less money, fewer professional connections, less familiarity with professionals' cultural styles, and lower test scores; and they leave college with more debt, fewer professional connections, less access to high-status culture, and fewer academic accolades.[2] If disadvantaged and advantaged students entered a weak or strong class-reproduction system after graduating, they would receive *unequal* earnings. And then no one would call college the great equalizer.

Of course, equalizing disadvantaged and advantaged students' resources is not the only way to achieve earnings equality. After all, *Let's Make a Deal* doesn't equalize disadvantaged and advantaged contestants' chances of winning by allowing only those with the same resources to play or by equalizing contestants' savings, social ties, styles, and accolades before the game begins.[3] Its equalizing mechanism is simpler: it puts the keys needed to win onstage, making them available to contestants of all classes, and the rest of the game makes offstage inequalities not matter.

Colleges' role in equalization is simple too, at least when students later enter a luckocracy.[4] Colleges do not equalize students' resources, and that means that they cannot equalize the extent to which disadvantaged and advantaged students *exceed* hiring agents' employability bars. But, as this chapter will show, colleges can make some resources available to all students regardless of social class—resources that allow disadvantaged and advantaged students to *meet* many employers' hiring bars and to enter the luckocracy. By putting these resources on campus, colleges contribute to earnings equality, even if they fall short of being *the* great equalizer.

Shared Access to On-Campus Resources

Southern State University's College of Business put many job-related resources on campus and exposed advantaged and disadvantaged students to them as soon as they arrived. These students came with many levels of preparation and motivations—there was, after all, no special test to enter the CoB, and students chose business for a wide array of reasons: wanting to get rich, desiring job stability, feeling drawn in by a charismatic professor, believing their childhood lemonade stand or teenage lawn-mowing gig revealed a natural propensity for business, becoming inspired by a business-related high school club, hoping to follow in their family's footsteps, needing a backup plan after failing classes in another area, or simply not knowing what else to do. Yet as soon as these different students arrived on campus, they would get the same treatment: one of being overwhelmed with general advice about how to meet hiring agents' employability bars.

After opening the front door to the business school, students from all social classes immediately received the message that job-related resources were available on campus. Upon entering the building, the first office that students passed belonged to the career center. Further down the hall, bulletin boards featured interns' stories of how they found positions. Table-toppers displayed flyers about upcoming networking events. Wall-mounted TV screens played slideshows with examples of professional dress.

The CoB made more detailed information about meeting employers' hiring bars available as well. They placed it in students' required orientation course, where all students would obtain the information. One lecture was devoted to finding and navigating UJobs, the university's online job board. Another day, students learned how to write résumés—to include information about their education, experience, and skills in bullet points rather than paragraphs, to highlight their accomplishments by using action verbs and emphasizing results, to avoid too much or too little white space, and to use a standard font. Another day, students practiced answering interview questions—thinking about the "right" answers to questions about why they wanted the job, how they handled a teammate who didn't pull their weight, and how they've changed someone's mind. In doing so, they learned not to tell the full truth but to put a positive spin on it, to think of their lives in story format, and to use college to gather these stories. In their orientation course, they also were assigned professional mentors who worked at local businesses. The mentors attended their course to advise students about the working world and to model the idea that professionals were normal and approachable people—people like they would become.

In their required orientation course, disadvantaged and advantaged students also received the *Job Search Guide*,[5] a booklet that students would later tell me was "gold." The 64-page guide contained advice about each aspect of the job search, from how to gain leadership experience ("Become an active officer or committee chair for a campus organization"; "facilitate group discussions in class or in a campus organization"; "organize and manage an intramural sports team, camp or recreation group"; "train new campus organization members or employees at your job") to focusing on communicating well during interviews ("Speak clearly and effectively, listen attentively, maintain eye contact, and resist distractions"). It also included pages of sample cover letters, résumés, and thank-you notes; lists of action verbs to use on a résumé; common interview questions; useful questions to ask hiring agents; do's and don'ts when negotiating; and scripts of what to say when accepting and rejecting job offers.

As if this were not enough, the College of Business (CoB) made sure that all students were exposed to this information again—this time, through a second required course. In their required business communications course, students reviewed how to write a résumé. If students hadn't learned it yet, they now learned to include keywords from the job ad in their résumé and to use the language of the industry when applying for a job: to, for example, transform a job in the mailroom into a job managing critical parts of the organization's supply chain or to write of scanning books at the library as showing proficiency using advanced robotic technology. They also reviewed the need to have an up-to-date LinkedIn profile, complete with a picture of themselves, alone, wearing business attire.

If students wanted more information about how to meet hiring agents' employability bars, they could join one of over a dozen of the CoB's professionalization clubs. Since some of these clubs were free and provided students with a pizza dinner, they were accessible to advantaged and disadvantaged students alike. There, they reviewed each other's résumés, and recruiters were brought in to offer résumé advice. Club leaders and faculty mentors led discussions about how to answer common interview questions, such as what to say about your weakness (students should describe how they are working to improve it). Professionalization clubs also allowed students to practice job-related skills, such as marketing, fundraising, "onboarding" new students, managing a budget, and leading a group. Some clubs also hosted competitions to see who could earn the most in pretend investments or sell the most products. Students were also encouraged to use these events to practice their communication skills—look a stranger in the eye, shake their hand, and engage them in conversation. Indeed, I was often taken aback by how many students walked over to me, making eye contact while introducing themselves with their hands extended.

The career center, too, organized events to prepare all CoB students to meet hiring agents' employability bars. They hosted a fashion show where students displayed the difference between "business casual" and "business professional" attire. They encouraged students to model these clothing styles for each other, labeling some events business professional and others business casual so that they could see what was appropriate in each setting. They repeated these messages on a Pinterest page and posters that hung on the walls in the building—ones with specific information such as shoulders should be fully covered, hair should be dry, belts should match shoes, and backpacks should be left at home.

The career center staff was also available to students who wanted another set of eyes on their résumé, to conduct a mock interview, or to talk about how to figure out what career was for them. The career center staff gave detailed feedback, telling students if their résumés had too much or too little white space or too few action verbs, and if in interviews they needed to do more to highlight the results of their actions, lean forward, project more confidence, or use a wider array of examples. The staff also trained a select group of students to do the same for their peers, spreading the reach of career advice to students who were more comfortable talking to students than staff.

Hiring agents also regularly made themselves available to all students to offer general job search advice. They sat behind tables in the business school's hallways, conducting "résumé reviews." There, they offered their opinions about whether objective statements were necessary or passé, whether the education portion of a résumé should come first or last, and advised students to include more about their accomplishments. Employers also promoted their companies while giving lectures that students could attend. These lectures included widely agreed-upon generalities about how to find a job: proofread your résumé for spelling mistakes, arrive at interviews early (but not too early), and avoid email addresses with handles like sexykittysexy.

Of course, advantaged and disadvantaged students' courses prepared them to meet employers' hiring bars too. All SSU business students learned how to use Excel, enabling them to brag about their ability to create pivot tables and run VLOOKUPs. They learned how to assign the right number of workers to each shift, design a marketing campaign, recruit new employees, and name the stages of the project management life cycle. The CoB, like other business schools, put particular emphasis on teamwork, too, by assigning many group projects;[6] they also stressed leadership and communication skills. Professors also encouraged students to join one of the CoB's seven leadership clubs to practice these skills again.

Prepared for the workforce, SSU gave all CoB students the resources to apply for internships and jobs. SSU hosted the website UJobs, which allowed advantaged and disadvantaged students to browse nearly 600 business internships and 1,800 job ads per year. Unconnected to job ads, students also could upload their résumé and hope a hiring agent would reach out to set up an interview. Students could also learn of job openings from recruiters who made announcements in their clubs and courses, at information sessions, and through career fairs. Over 100 companies attended each general career fair, and additional career fairs brought in hiring agents for particular types of jobs.

And, of course, faculty and staff gave CoB students detailed advice about how to talk to employers at the career fair. In courses, clubs, flyers, and information sessions, professors and career center staff told their students what to do. In addition to wearing a suit—one that was a dark color, fitted, and not accompanied by dangly jewelry, eye-catching makeup, or white socks—bring a padfolio: a black padded folder with a notepad and a stack of their résumé. Look at the list of companies attending, research them, then choose five to ten to talk to but approach others first to gain confidence. Shake each hiring agent's hand, look them in the eye, and speak confidently. Prepare an elevator speech: tell the representative your name, major, the type of job you are seeking. Be ready to answer employers' questions about your past behaviors and accomplishments. Use the STAR method when you do: name the situation, task, action, and result. Thank them for their time. Ask for their card so you can follow up by email. Don't forget to smile.

SSU's CoB then played an important role in generating earnings equality. They put many job-related resources on campus, where advantaged and disadvantaged students alike could access them. In doing so, they could not help students meet any particular employer's hiring bar, but they could help all students meet some of the most common aspects of them.

————————————

Christina, an outgoing redhead, was one of the beneficiaries of the CoB's efforts—someone who used on-campus resources to meet many employers' hiring bars. Christina was a class-disadvantaged student who transferred to SSU after leaving another university's nursing program, one she found too competitive and with chemistry courses that were too difficult. She then transferred to a community college, completed two years of coursework, then transferred again to SSU.

Christina entered SSU's CoB with a vague idea that she wanted to go into human resources, but few concrete ideas beyond that. She was immediately surrounded by the CoB's resources, which encouraged her to focus. She recalled, "When I got here, I think that the CoB really starts to get you thinking about your next opportunities, so I joined SHRM, the Society for Human Resources Management chapter at the CoB. In their meetings they work a lot with developing you for after college, and that's when I started realizing, 'Oh, this is something I need to start thinking about now.'"

Christina used the university's resources to hit the ground running. She had a résumé from when she had applied for waitressing jobs, one that she called "very rudimentary." With the help of the human resources professionalization group and her orientation courses, Christina revamped it to meet standard formatting and style guidelines: "You learn what's important, what's not important. Formatting is a really big deal. Like, you've got your one-page résumé—how do you fit all of your experience onto it? I took out the objectives portion. They tell you talk about projects that you worked on, so I put in something like that. And one really important tip is when you're talking about your job descriptions, tailor your experiences to that of a job that you want. So if I want to be working in the business field and I worked at Starbucks, I would say I managed the café supply chain daily or I implemented a new product line. You talk about it in a way that will be applicable even though all you did was make coffee."

Christina also listened to the advice she received on campus that told her to gain leadership and extracurricular experience—or at least to frame her existing experiences in these ways. She used opportunities the university provided to label herself as a leader: "In the business school we have a lot of group projects, and a lot of times somebody does need to take a leadership position. That's not always the most fun because you're working with your peers and you have to keep them on track. I'm willing to take that role." Christina also gained extracurricular experience and spun it to sound like job-related experience. She joined a group that monitored the CoB's student-body elections: "Part of HR is you've got employment laws, and sometimes you get people violating some of the laws. So there was definitely a connection between the two."

The university also helped Christina meet and learn to interact with professionals. She heard the university's push to do so, telling me: "The College of Business is all about networking." Christina used the CoB's resources to get more comfortable doing so. She set modest goals: "My goals are to talk to people like colleagues. For other people it might be to get future opportunities if they haven't found a job yet, but I use them as gaining experience, talking to professionals as colleagues when I'm still a student." She struggled at first: "My first meetings I was completely lost. I was shy. I didn't want to talk to anybody." But, she said, the university's approach works: "They teach you just by repetition, having all of these events."

Christina was not exaggerating when she said networking was a struggle at first or when she said that it got better. She relayed a specific incident, one of meeting professionals at a résumé review: "Everybody's in their black business professional suits, and I'm wearing a dress that I wore to a wedding and some beat-up shoes, because it was the best I could do. I left that meeting and I called my mom crying like, 'I don't have anything to wear. I don't fit in here.' So after that I went out and I bought my suit. That was it. And now when I go to events and I see people maybe coming the first time and they're not wearing business professional clothes, I go up and talk to them and help them. I've been there. It gets better." And it did get better for Christina. She not only learned to dress the part, but to research the company before she approached a hiring agent. She started saying to the employers she met, "I really am impressed with your work on this new project that you're doing." Able to start a conversation, she felt more confident talking to people who could hire her.

Having used many of the university's resources, Christina, a class-disadvantaged student, was ready to become an intern. She did so by relying on campus resources. An internship ad was sent to the human resources club, and Christina applied. She went through two interviews, one that asked her about her experiences and one that asked her about behaviors she had exhibited in the past. She believed the business school prepared her for both interviews. She said of the experience-related interview: "I think that through being in SHRM and in the business classes, I knew I had to talk about my experiences in a way that they were looking for, that would show that I could do the job that they wanted me to do." She reiterated the same point in regard to answering behavioral questions: "It was tell me about a time that you had a difficult customer. How did you resolve the issue? Tell me about a time that you worked in a group and you experienced pushback from a team member. Tell me about a time you took a leadership position, things like that. And again, being in SHRM, being in the business school, they teach you to come up with answers. So I was prepared for answering questions and coming up with examples." Christina received the internship.

Christina then relied upon the university's resources to obtain a second internship. Her courses required her to make a LinkedIn profile and taught her how to do so; a recruiter contacted her after seeing her site. Christina attended that internship interview and again drew upon the university's teachings—here, to be prepared to ask specific questions about the job: "Again, through SHRM, they talked about interviewing skills, and you should always have questions that you want answered by them, whether it's what computer systems do you use, how do you track employees, or what training programs do you have." She received that internship, too.

In just two years, Christina had learned to meet many hiring agents' employability bars. She learned to write a résumé, answer standard interview questions, talk to professionals, and dress as employers expected, while also acquiring leadership and internship experience. She did this by relying upon the university's on-campus resources—ones available to students from all social classes.

Indeed, the CoB's approach worked to prepare most students in the same way. When I asked students what made a good résumé, similar percentages of disadvantaged and advantaged students said that a résumé should be one page, include keywords and action words, and demonstrate concrete accomplishments. When I asked students what they tried to do in interviews, a similar percentage of disadvantaged and advantaged students said they tried to form a connection with the interviewer, keep the interview conversational, use the STAR format when appropriate, appear confident, make eye contact, avoid rambling, and show that they researched the company. Most students from each class, too, participated in at least one internship and extracurricular activity, and about the same percentage of students from each social class included at least one leadership experience on their résumé. Students tended to give the university at least partial credit for teaching them to present these experiences, skills, and styles—naming their orientation course, the *Job Search Guide*, a professionalization club, or their professors as communicating these lessons.

By the time students needed to apply for jobs, students of all classes were ready to meet many hiring agents' employability bars. They were ready due to the resources the university put on campus—ones that students from all social classes could access.

Disparities in On- and Off-Campus Resources

Universities can ensure that *some* resources are available to students from all social classes. They cannot ensure that all students have equal access to *all* on-campus resources or to off-campus ones.

Universities cannot create equality because while they can make resources available to all, they cannot equalize students' use of them.

While disadvantaged students work for pay, advantaged students attend more extracurricular events, take on more leadership roles, visit the career center more often, and seek out their professors' help more.[7] While disadvantaged students congregate in the activities that the university makes accessible to everyone, advantaged students more often participate in the activities that the university provides for an extra fee: study abroad, fraternities and sororities, and the club golf and tennis teams.[8] And while disadvantaged students like Christina work their way up to feeling comfortable around the employers the university invites to campus, advantaged students typically enter college more comfortable with professionals.[9] Because their parents, parents' friends, friends' parents, and neighbors tend to be professionals, advantaged students usually don't find them so intimidating.

Universities also cannot create equality because they cannot equalize students' access to off-campus resources. For every piece of professional advice universities give, advantaged students can talk to their professional parents about it. The messages they receive may then be reinforced, added to, or altered to fit their circumstances. For every professional that universities bring to campus, advantaged students can meet them while also reaching out to the professionals they already know in their families and social circles. They, too, can rely on the comfort they developed by growing up around professionals to reach out to professionals they do not know but hope to meet. The disadvantaged student tends to rely solely on the university. The advantaged student does too— *and* on the opportunities their money buys and their networks bring.

Universities, then, cannot act as *the* great equalizer since they cannot equalize disadvantaged and advantaged students' resources. And because they cannot do this, they can only equalize the extent to which students of different classes *meet* particular hiring bars, not the extent to which students *exceed* each aspect of them.

———————

Take Grace, a short, blond, quiet student—a student who used the university's resources to meet many hiring agents' employability bars and used her personal resources to exceed them. Grace was prepared to enter SSU's CoB and feel comfortable there. Her parents, sister, aunts, and uncles had all attended SSU, and Grace grew up assuming she would attend too. Business was also part of her family's life. Her father founded his own bank, her mother fundraised for a nonprofit, her older sister worked as an accountant, and her aunt and uncle owned a company. She grew up talking about business with her family and learning about professional conduct.

Feeling that SSU was a second home, Grace took advantage of the resources the university made available to all students, and she sought out resources that were available to all who asked. She regularly visited the career center for one-on-one advice: "It's very easy to meet them. I know I can go here and ask all my questions." She also regularly asked her professors for personalized advice, asking them about "everything and anything." She asked for their help deciding whether she should go into marketing or sales, whether particular companies were reputable, and how the marketing campaign she prepared to show employers could be improved.

Grace, like other students, also took advantage of SSU's clubs and leadership opportunities. Like students of all social classes, she joined a professionalization club. But without the need to work for pay, she had time to become particularly involved and became the club's leader. She soon was inviting recruiters to club events—tailoring the invitations, in part, toward her own interests and using her position to have one-on-one conversations with hiring agents. As president of the club, she was also invited to a national conference for people aspiring to enter the same field. She flew halfway across the country to attend. There, she met many more professionals and heard their stories of failure and success. She applied some of these lessons while leading another club that her parents' income allowed her to afford: a social sorority.

Grace, too, took advantage of the networking events that SSU made available to all CoB students but that advantaged students typically felt more comfortable attending: a business and baseball networking event, information sessions that also served as networking events, and, of course, career fairs. She followed the university's advice: "I do a little bit of research beforehand so I don't go in blind and am not, like, what's IBM again?" Once at these events, she followed the university's standard advice: "I introduce myself, tell them my elevator speech, and then usually end with a question pertaining to if they have opportunities for things that I'm interested in. Then I guide the conversation based off that." She spoke with representatives of many companies, feeling fairly confident talking to people whose jobs were less prestigious than her parents'.

But Grace did not rely on the university's resources alone, even personalized ones and ones officially available to everyone but used more often by class-advantaged students. She also took advantage of off-campus resources that many disadvantaged students could not access. By the time she searched for a job, she had received five internships through her networks and completed eight internships in total, far exceeding most employers' hiring bars concerning internships. She knew the owners of her hometown pharmacy and interned for them, just to check if pharmacy was a better fit for her than business. She decided it was not; it left her stuck behind the counter with just one or two people when she wanted to be part of a larger team. Her high school best friend's sister worked at SSU's student media business office. Grace got in touch with her and obtained an internship there. She worked in three different positions there, ones she counts as separate internships: as an office assistant, graphic designer, and account executive. She found her next internship by talking to a local business owner who worked with the club she led, then found her next one in a way that relied on her personal resources again. She was on vacation in Paris when she went to a bar to watch the Super Bowl. There, she met a CEO of a marketing agency who offered her an internship in another American city. Grace found her final three internships through the university. Some were arranged through her classes, ones that placed her with companies and gave her course credit.

Grace also used her ease in talking to professionals to learn more about companies—something advantaged students did more often than disadvantaged ones. When she could not tell what one company did from its website, she set up an informational interview to find out. She also reached out to alumni at another company to set up an informational interview. She knew they did sales and marketing but wanted to find out more. And when she wanted advice about finding a job, she turned to the people she met through her internships. Though she had her résumé reviewed in her orientation and business communications courses, she thought the best advice she received came from one of her internship supervisors.

Grace did not take direct advantage of her parents' resources as much as other advantaged students did, especially advantaged students whose parents worked in business fields. Many of these students considered their parents to be experts in the field and turned to them to review their résumés, conduct mock interviews, and ask for help locating internships. Many advantaged students also drew upon their parents' contacts to try to land a job or gain advice about the field. Clearly, this resource was not available to everybody.

These off-campus resources meant that advantaged and disadvantaged students would not look the same when applying for jobs. Grace used her off-campus resources to exceed hiring agents' bars regarding internships, leadership, and extracurricular activities, and she also used her off-campus resources to get additional extra advice about her résumé and which jobs to apply to, as well as to meet people who could hire her. Grace was not alone. On average, advantaged students climbed higher over aspects of employers' hiring bars. Compared to disadvantaged respondents, advantaged participants reported having slightly more internships—having relied more on their connections to get them—and slightly higher GPAs. They also reported telling interviewers more about their internships, extracurricular activities, and travel. And they reported reaching out to more people who could hire them or give them advice—people who might recognize how much they exceeded particular hiring bars. Of course, disadvantaged students further exceeded other aspects of some hiring bars: they reported more community service and work experience.

The university, then, did not equalize students' resources, experiences, or self-presentation styles. Indeed, the university could not make Christina's resources equal to Grace's. They could not offer Christina parents who talked about business around the dinner table. They could not easily give Christina the money to take vacations to Paris, connect her to business owners in her hometown, or give her the time away from work to participate in as many leadership activities as a class-advantaged student. They could not equalize Christina's access to personalized help at SSU, either. Since the time they learn to talk, advantaged children are often encouraged by their parents to seek help while disadvantaged parents more often teach their young children to be self-reliant—meaning SSU would have to counter years of socialization experiences to equalize students' help-seeking behaviors.[10] And it went the other way, too. Without the same amount of family money, students like Christina would gain more work experience than advantaged students like Grace—an inequality that started before they even began college. With so many inequalities in their lives, all universities could do was make some resources available to students from all social classes. In doing so, they played an important role in generating earnings equality. They helped students from each class background meet many hiring agents' employability bars, even if they could not equalize the extent to which students exceeded them.

Conclusion

If advantaged and disadvantaged students left college and entered a weak or strong class-reproduction system, they would receive unequal earnings. Colleges cannot equalize students' resources and, as such, cannot equalize their ability to exceed employers' hiring bars. But students entering the mid-tier labor market were not entering a class-reproduction system. They were entering a luckocracy—a system in which gatekeepers did not weigh the extent that students exceeded their hiring bars as much as whether they could meet them. The university helped students of all classes meet these bars, playing an important part in earnings equalization.

Of course, not all business schools or other academic units provide so many on-campus resources related to finding a job. However, they all provide graduates from all social classes with a critical resource: a credential. Many colleges, too, now have the equivalent of UJobs, hosting an online job board that connects disadvantaged and advantaged students to employers.[11] As for the detailed advice that SSU's CoB provided, it is available to any student through a Google search. Thus, even colleges that do far less to prepare their students for the workforce still give students from all social classes the ability to meet employability bars in the mid-tier market. And as we'll see in the next chapter, getting students of all classes over some of these bars and into the luckocracy was enough to equalize their earnings.

Searching for Jobs

Armed with the experiences, skills, and styles the university provided them, students searched for jobs. When doing so, they quickly realized they were entering a low-information system. Students from disadvantaged backgrounds accepted what they could not change: that they had no way to get the information they needed to successfully strategize. Students from advantaged backgrounds tried to change what they could not accept. Not wanting to be in a low-information system, they reached out to their connections to gather more information and gain more opportunities, all while flashing their high-status signals. Their strategy did not work. Their connections' help was like that of game show audience members—confidently given but uninformed—and their high-status signals were as irrelevant to getting a high-paying job as they were to winning the *Let's Make a Deal* game. Among students who met hiring agents' employability bar, earnings equalization would result with disadvantaged and advantaged students ending up in the same position: in a luckocracy in which they were forced to guess where to apply, how to be hired, and which job to take.

Entering a Low-Information System

Both class-disadvantaged and class-advantaged students came to realize that they were in a low-information system. Their challenge began with job titles. On UJobs, about 80% of job titles related to each business specialization were unique, meaning that they were used by only one company.[1] On Careerbuilder.com, about a third of all jobs were listed with unique titles.[2] Students of each class background could not make sense of the diversity of job titles. Asked what the difference was between "marketing coordinator" and "marketing assistant"—two jobs that she applied to—Natalie (class advantaged) said she did not know. Asked what a "strategic sourcing associate" does, Cody (class advantaged), who applied for the position, replied: "You're asking me. I don't know." Other students found themselves misled by job titles. Mason (class advantaged) applied to a "patient account representative" position only to later find out that it meant collections. William (class advantaged) explained how he ended up interviewing for an insurance sales position: "I guess in retrospect they were purposefully vague in regard to what you would be doing, because they were like, 'You will be a financial services representative,' and I was like, 'Oh, wow that sounds cool.' It doesn't sound like an insurance salesman." Amelia (class disadvantaged) made the same mistake: "They call it 'financial advising,' which sounds legit and interesting, but they don't say anything about the cold-calling. They don't say anything about networking with people you know to bring them into the company."[3]

Students of all class backgrounds could not make sense of job descriptions either. Shawna (class disadvantaged) said that job descriptions did not help her know where to apply, claiming: "They all pretty much say the same thing." Nathan (class advantaged) said that he could rarely tell from a job description if the job included the type of work he wanted to do: "I was always very interested in analytics, which is hard to get from a job description. You never really know. No one says this is an analytic job. They might say it takes analytical skills, but when I think analytics, I'm thinking statistics and data. You never really know until you get there." Likewise, Chloe (class advantaged) said: "Job descriptions are typically pretty vague, so I don't really get too much info out of them."

Class-advantaged and class-disadvantaged students alike also struggled to find useful information on companies from job ads or company websites. For example, Amy (class disadvantaged) said that despite reading job ads, "You don't know much about the corporation." Peter (class disadvantaged) said of a company he considered applying to: "I didn't know what [company] was." John (class advantaged) claimed: "There's only so much you can learn about a start-up online, just because it's pretty new. So I really didn't learn a lot." Andrew (class advantaged) searched for information about an established company. He was frustrated by how little he could uncover: "I tried to look on the website. I tried to research more about the company, but it was a privately held company so I couldn't really do as much research digging into it. They're so large that I didn't really even know what to research. So I looked at some background info about them and tried as much as I could, but gave up."

Since employers provided little information about their positions or companies, students hoped that other websites would tell them more. They regularly turned to Glassdoor for information, a website that included employees' reviews of the company. However, several students said that the information on the website was not overly useful. Framing the information about the company and job as irrelevant or as untrustworthy, students often dismissed what they learned. For instance, Natalie (class advantaged) said that bad reviews often stemmed from issues she did not care about—issues with bad middle managers or complaints that qualified workers were overlooked for promotions. She dismissed these reviews, saying: "Bad people is not the same as a bad company." Keri (class disadvantaged) also looked on Glassdoor but did not take it seriously: "I look at the reviews that people write, the good and bad, take it with a grain of salt." She also did not change where she applied based on what she read on Glassdoor.[4]

With wage information typically absent from job ads, students from each class background used Glassdoor to search for earnings information as well. Again, they tended to find it of limited use. Chloe (class advantaged) found the information incomplete: "Some of the smaller companies I couldn't research like on Glassdoor what were their average salaries." Mary (class disadvantaged) not only found the information incomplete, but questioned its accuracy: "Honestly, I don't think there's any other way [to know what positions pay]. It gives you just a glance, a photo of what could be. Sometimes they're a little higher on Glassdoor, because I think they're just averaging everyone who goes from entry level to senior, so sometimes it helps, sometimes it doesn't."

Students of each social class then realized they were in a low-information system—one in which employers gave them little information about jobs or what they paid. They did not all realize they were entering a class-neutral system—there was no way for them to preemptively discover it. In this situation, they took different strategies. Class-disadvantaged students typically *accepted what they could not change*. Class-advantaged students typically tried to *change what they could not accept*. But neither strategy gave students the information they needed to purposefully target and receive a high-paying position. Neither strategy enabled students to get around the luckocracy.

Class-Disadvantaged Students' Strategies

Class-disadvantaged students tended to accept what they could not change: they were in a low-information environment and without high-status cultural signals to display.

Their acceptance began with decisions about where to apply for jobs.[5] Class-disadvantaged students had little information about each company, its jobs, and their pay, and so they used what information was in job ads to decide where to apply: the company's location and size as well as the position's business area. Typically, they targeted jobs near their university, hometown, or a nearby city, with work in their specialty area, and with a large company—one they assumed would provide job stability. Within these criteria, they had no way to discern one job from another, so they applied to any job within it. Connor (class disadvantaged), for instance, said of the employers he talked to at the career fair: "If they had anything to do with [business] IT, then I talked to them." Andrea (class disadvantaged) took the same approach: "I just applied to [business] IT in [city.]" Asked if she had any preferences beyond working for a bank in the state where she attended college, Ebony (class disadvantaged) said: "No, not really." Karen (class disadvantaged) was not particular either:

"Right now I just want to get my feet in the door and just get a position. I would like to work in those industries, but I'm not picky." Amy (class disadvantaged) shared her strategy: "I feel like the more you apply to, the more opportunities there are." Anna (class disadvantaged) reiterated: "I applied to everything."

Class-disadvantaged students then sent out résumés. They again accepted what they could not change. Most did not know people who could help them tailor their résumé to meet a particular hiring agent's criteria—or even professionals who could give them expert advice.[6] So they prepared their résumés in their courses and clubs and left it at that.[7] The majority also could not change that they had no high-status signals to display, so they made the most of their lower-status symbols. They used the language of the position they were applying to when writing of their working-class jobs. They described a job as a cashier, for instance, as providing experience handling funds for a multimillion-dollar company.[8]

Class-disadvantaged students accepted what they could not change in interviews too. They could not find common ground with interviewers through high-status displays, so they found commonalities in ways that they could: by talking of sports, their university (one their interviewer often shared or who went to the rival university), or their home state. They also asked the interviewers questions about themselves. If they did not have something obviously in common with their interviewers, they could at least show interest in them.

Class-disadvantaged students rarely had connections who could inform them about the hiring team's interview questions or evaluation criteria. They accepted what they could not change by embracing the unpredictability of the interview. Though the CoB had prepared them for typical interview questions and they reviewed common questions listed online, they did less to prepare for interviews than they knew they could. Instead, they said they preferred to spontaneously respond to interview questions. Amelia (class disadvantaged) favored entering interviews unprepared: "I always wing 'em. . . . They tell you to be yourself but also to practice, study all these answers to these questions you might have or might not have. But if you're going to be yourself, then you'll just answer the question with what your self comes up with." Andrea (class disadvantaged) also embraced knowing little about what she would be asked: "I don't like preparing because that way I'm thinking too hard and I'm trying to remember what I prepared to say. I like winging it because it comes off as more genuine." Ben (class disadvantaged) also preferred to enter interviews without knowing what was coming: "I've never been a fan of preparing for interviews. If you're actually a good candidate for the company, it'll come through." Jack (class disadvantaged) explained he did not need to prepare in advance: "I don't have to consciously think of if they ask this question, do I use this example? I don't have to consciously think about that. I look down [at my résumé] and that's how I do it." Sean (class disadvantaged) said of the interview that led to his job: "I just winged it." Being spontaneous fit class-disadvantaged students' predilections. Growing up with few resources and in families with little authority, they often had to quickly read gatekeepers' reactions and respond to please them.[9]

Class-disadvantaged students' ability to obtain particular jobs was then largely based on luck. They applied to jobs that fit broad criteria but could not discern a high-paying position from a low-paying one. They then hoped that employers would approve of their résumés and ask them interview questions they could answer. In other words, like Chona on *Let's Make a Deal*, they hoped they held the right key to fit into the lock.

Taking this approach, some students were unlucky at first. They were asked questions that they were unprepared for and for which they could not spontaneously produce the right key. Ben (class disadvantaged) struggled when interviewers asked him a surprisingly difficult question, one for which he could not prepare:

On their website they recommended going over the two case studies that were online. They posted the questions, good answers, whatnot. So I looked over those, and I thought that was about the level that they were going to do. On a scale of one to ten for difficulty, their practice ones online were probably about a two or a three—they weren't that bad. In the interview it was like an eleven. So it was still a case study, but it was both more difficult and just very involved. Mine was on optimizing costs in a hospital. I know basically nothing about hospital cost structures. So I went into that pretty much blind. I thought I did okay, but not super well. That was where I ended.

Jack (class disadvantaged) also did not receive a job after he thought he badly failed a case interview—one that asked him about information he hadn't predicted and could not produce on the spot. Similarly, Bethany (class disadvantaged) was asked to make a cold call to sell a product. Despite looking online for a company-specific cold-calling script before the interview, she had not found one. She did not know enough about the products or the company's strategy to make a sale. Sean (class disadvantaged) did not pass a personality test and had no idea what personality the employer sought.

These students were not rejected from jobs because they were objectively bad candidates. Using the same approach, they applied to similar jobs and became lucky—they were asked different questions or evaluated in different ways. After failing a case interview with one company, Jack (class disadvantaged) received a very similar job at a firm of comparable prestige. For this employer, the interview was easier: "I thought for sure there was going to be a case-study question. I thought it was going to blow me away. I just was expecting to not do well at that. And it never came." Ben (class disadvantaged), who, as described above, was rejected after interviewing poorly, later received a job after a résumé review, with no interview at all. Bethany (class disadvantaged) received another sales job, one for which she did not have to make an unscripted cold call. Sean (class disadvantaged) was subjected to a personality test by another employer and still did not know what personality the employer preferred. This time, though, the employer thought he fit and offered him a job.

Other students were lucky, too, in that they unknowingly applied to a job that asked them only typical interview questions—ones for which they had learned to prepare for through their courses and clubs. Amy (class disadvantaged) reported being offered a job after only being asked why she was interested in business and human resources specifically.

For the job she accepted, Mary (class disadvantaged) remembered being asked only questions the university had taught her to answer: "What do you think you could bring to this company? What kind of expertise do you have right now? How proficient are you with Excel?" Anna (class disadvantaged) was also offered a position after being asked questions the university had prepared her for: "They asked are you good at multitasking, how do you handle multiple projects being thrown at you at different times, are you good at time management? They definitely asked an ethics question. There was no curve ball that they threw at me."

Class-disadvantaged students could also be lucky in that, without intent, they happened to answer questions in a way that a hiring agent rewarded. Peter (class disadvantaged), for example, told a hiring agent that he did not know the answer to the math question she posed. He asked her to explain the answer. She responded that she was looking for candidates who would admit what they did not know and ask for help. This was not a strategy on his part; Peter was sure he lost the job after missing the math question. Instead, he was lucky. Without intention, he displayed the key that got him through the door.

In a labor market with many jobs for recent college graduates, nearly all class-disadvantaged students from Southern State University would eventually find a professional job. They simply had to keep applying until they happened to have a key that fit into a lock. For class-disadvantaged students, they could usually do so by relying on the information and experiences that the university or the internet provided.

Of course, the role of luck did not end there. Class-disadvantaged students applied to jobs knowing only that the job fit their broad criteria, not necessarily knowing what they would do. Typically, they also applied without knowing what they would be paid and only found out once they received a job offer. Some students happened to apply for and receive jobs that paid more than the average amount for their specialty, while others happened to apply for and receive jobs that paid less. This was not due to strategy on their part. They could not strategize to receive high-paying positions because they did not know which jobs these were.

Using this approach, some students were unlucky while others were lucky. Amy (class disadvantaged), a student with three internships and who was a leader of a professionalization club, was asked to interview for the job she received after the employer saw her résumé on UJobs. It was a human resources generalist job, one in which she and her supervisor would run the human resources department for the entire plant. She would be paid $38,000 a year. Christina (class disadvantaged, discussed in chapter 4), a student with two internships but no official leadership roles, listened to a recruiter talk about a job in one of her human resources courses. She happened to have printed out résumés that morning for an upcoming career fair, so Christina handed a résumé to the recruiter as she left the class. She was later offered the job, one that paid $50,000 a year to run a human resources department with her supervisor—the exact same job as Amy. Karen (class disadvantaged), a student with no internships and one leadership position, received $50,000 a year to do a similar job—to help companies with their human resources needs. She applied to that human resources generalist position because the company's name started with the letter A and appeared at the top of her search results. In these cases, Amy was unlucky, and Christina and Karen were lucky; the latter two happened to apply to jobs that paid more for similar work.

Three class-disadvantaged students who specialized in business technology also received salaries based on luck, not strategy. Connor (class disadvantaged), a student with no internships or leadership roles, happened to run into his friend's sister's husband's friend in a coffeehouse. This person told Connor that the company he worked for was hiring. Connor then looked for positions online. He did not find any in his subfield so he applied to a different position. The recruiter called him and asked if he would like to apply for a business technology position instead. Connor agreed. He would go through an interview the university had prepared him for—one in which he was only asked about teamwork, course projects, diversity, and widely used software. He was offered one of the highest salaries in the sample: $64,000 a year. Joe (class disadvantaged), a student with two internships and a leadership position in a professionalization club, applied to a high-paying job accidentally.

He was at the career fair and saw a sign for a company that he had not heard of but whose free water bottles he liked. He tried to grab one without the recruiter noticing him. He failed. The recruiter stopped him, told him about the company and the business technology position, and convinced Joe to apply. Joe did and was also asked only questions that the university had prepared him for: how he prioritized work, what he did when a project wasn't going well, what he did in his internships, and about job-related skills he learned in his courses. He received the job and was offered $60,000 a year. Andrea (class disadvantaged), a student with one internship and two formal leadership roles, applied to a business technology job after a recruiter announced it in a club. She received it but was offered $17,000 less a year than Connor, or $47,000 a year. The difference was not attributable to the jobs' locations or to the students' experience or skills—none of the students reported that their interviewers asked detailed questions about their technical abilities. Connor and Joe just happened to apply to positions that paid more than Andrea's.

Class-disadvantaged students then made their last decision to accept what they could not change: they rarely negotiated. Some class-disadvantaged students didn't think they were allowed to negotiate, others didn't think to do it, and still others didn't see the need. Moreover, they almost always took the first job in their field that they were offered. That is, only 13% of class-disadvantaged participants turned down an offer for a professional business job when they did not have another offer in hand. They tended to take their first offer for a variety of reasons. Those with low offers did not always know that their offers were low; with hidden pay information, they did not have a comparison. They also tended not to know how much they needed to earn to pay off their student debt and assumed whatever salary they were offered would be enough.[10] In addition, not all class-disadvantaged students were in a position for their parents to financially support them if they received no job at all. A sure bet—even a low-paying one—seemed far better than not having a job at all. This, too, is what researchers tell us people generally do. Most people prefer certain over uncertain outcomes, even if the latter might be better.[11]

On average, class-disadvantaged students' approach of accepting what they could not change and accepting their first offers led them to median salaries of $48,000. This was about the same amount as class-advantaged students—students who held different resources and used different strategies.

Class-Advantaged Students' Strategies

Class-advantaged students took the opposite strategy as class-disadvantaged students. Like class-disadvantaged students, they wanted professional jobs—not gap years, only "fun" positions, or temporary employment. So, instead of accepting what they could not change, they tried to change what they could not accept. They would not settle for a low-information system but tried to turn it into a high-information system, though only for themselves. They would not act as if they were in a class-neutral system but displayed their high-status cultural signals.

Class-advantaged students' strategy to change what they could not accept began with acquiring more information about jobs. Many gathered information to target particular jobs—not knowing, as we'll see below, that this information would not be as beneficial as they imagined. Ryan (class advantaged) said his father helped him figure out which companies to focus on: "I've talked to my dad a lot about good companies to apply for." Lucy (class advantaged) reviewed the list of companies attending the career fair with her father. He recommended she focus on five companies. Jenny (class advantaged) maintained: "Usually you can find someone that you know who has worked there or who knows someone who worked there. . . . You can find people that have a little bit of insight." Tyler (class advantaged) took the same approach: "My dad has a lot of friends in banking. I've talked to them a good bit about their different banks and their roles and what they enjoy, what they don't like." William (class advantaged) tried to find more information too: "If it's a company I'm seriously considering, I check out my LinkedIn, see if anyone works there, and if someone does I ask them: 'How do you like the company you work for? Is there anything you'd like to tell me about it or something that sticks out?'"[12]

Their connections did not know about every company and position, so class-advantaged students also sought information by reaching out to people they did not know. Some set up informational interviews to learn about companies and jobs. James (class advantaged) called the owner-operator of a store, asked about the company, and set up an informational interview for himself. Alice (class advantaged) reached out to a stranger, too: "I asked somebody if I could do an informational interview. I just asked them questions about their job and how they got into the field." During her internship, Katelyn (class advantaged) reached out to many strangers at her company to learn about their roles: "My goal was to do at least one one-to-one informational interview with a person each week. I ended up exceeding that by a ton. I totaled fifty or sixty people that I talked to."

Some class-advantaged students also did not accept the fact that employers offered little information on pay. Chloe (class advantaged) asked her contacts for salary information: "I never ask for a specific number. I just say, could you give me a range, or is it above or below fifty?" Jenny (class advantaged) asked about a salary for a particular job: "I had talked to other people that applied for the job." Ryan's (class advantaged) internship mentor tracked salaries for various positions. Ryan asked for his help targeting industries and companies that paid well. With more information on companies, jobs, and pay, they hoped to target particular jobs and then develop the keys that would unlock them.

As part of this approach, class-advantaged students also sought more information about how to craft their résumés. They were not content with what they learned from their courses and clubs, so they also turned to the career center and their family for help.[13] They were especially pleased with the assistance they received from the career center. They spoke of the advice they received about reformatting, reordering, and rewording, and the way they thought the career center staff made their résumé stand out.

Class-advantaged students would also not accept that they had little information about each interview either. More often than class-disadvantaged students, they went to the career center to receive lists of questions they might be asked and to have their answers evaluated. They asked their parents—especially their fathers—for advice on what questions they were likely to be asked and what answers to prepare.[14] And they reached out to their contacts for inside information, asking them, too, what questions they were likely to be asked and how they would be evaluated. Some even signed up for online services. Lucy (class advantaged), for instance, signed up for a newsletter that sent her the most common interview questions and the ones that tend to catch candidates off guard.

Class-advantaged students also did not accept that they did not know who could open doors for them or that some companies had policies against hiring through referrals at all. They reached out to people who they hoped would open doors on their behalf. Ryan (class advantaged) shared his strategy: "I'll usually try to find someone that I'm closely connected to, preferably a second connection [on LinkedIn]. I look for where they're located. So if they're in [my city] and they're a sales manager, they're probably going to be the ones doing the hiring. I reach out to those people because they'll have the most influence." Owen (class advantaged) also reached out to many people to gain a leg up: "Honestly, ninety percent of it is reaching out. Not necessarily cold-calling, but cold-emailing, and having a quick story about yourself and why you want to get on the phone, and why you think you'd be a good banker. And just sending it out, trying to get as many people as possible on the phone." Carter (class advantaged) also tried to get a job through a social tie: "My dad likes this man a lot. They've actually fished together. So he's a really good guy. My dad said if he were to work for [company], this would be the agency manager that he would want to work with. So just because of the relationship the agency manager and my dad have, I was able to meet him and build a relationship with him also."

Class-advantaged students also did not accept—or know—that they were entering a class-neutral system. They displayed signals of their class background, filling their résumés with international travel, high-status sports such as golf and tennis, and what they considered to be high-status internships. In interviews, they talked more of their fraternities and sororities, golf, and study abroad—all expensive activities that students with less money found difficult to access. They then stood out from class-disadvantaged students, who more often reported telling interviewers about their working-class jobs and community service.

Yet at every step, class-advantaged students' strategies failed. Though they tried to change what they could not accept, most would have to accept what they could not change. Most of the people class-advantaged students reached out to did not provide information or access that helped them find a high-paying position or even a position at all. Most class-advantaged students also did not see their class signals pay off.

This began with preparing their résumés. Compared to class-disadvantaged students, class-advantaged students turned to more people for help with their résumés. These sources recommended different ways of formatting, ordering, and wording their résumés, but they did not have the critical information students needed: specific hiring agents' preferences. Cody (class advantaged) realized this after asking his girlfriend's father for résumé advice: "If I'm working for [my girlfriend's father], his opinion is good to have, but some people might want to see something else than what he recommended. There's no universally accepted way to do it." Indeed, class-advantaged students said they sent out more résumés than did class-disadvantaged students, but they received about the same number of interviews.[15]

Class-advantaged students' attempts to turn the interview process from a low-information system into a high-information system also failed. To avoid needing to guess which key unlocked a particular door, they tried to gather information about what particular hiring agents rewarded. They first asked their parents for advice. However, their parents' information rarely helped since their parents also had little information about what a specific hiring agent would ask in an interview. William (class advantaged), whose father worked as a human resources executive, said that his father's attempts to help him left him locked out: "My dad helped. He was like, 'They may ask you these type of questions, so go ahead and plan.' And I did prepare for those questions. And then when I got to the interview, the questions were not anything like those. It wasn't that bad, but I was definitely scrambling, and I knew I didn't get it." Ethan (class advantaged) had the same experience.

ETHAN: [My dad] was talking about the difference between mutual funds, structured products, bonds, and stocks. I learned some of this from my finance classes, too, but he helped me have a really good base knowledge in case they asked me technical questions [in a job interview].
JESSI: Did they ask you those?
ETHAN: No.

Claire (class advantaged) also said that her father, a hiring manager for financial positions, tried but failed to prepare her for an interview. Claire explained: "He helped me with a lot of the ETFs [exchange-traded funds] and the S&P 500 and mutual funds, just more specific knowledge of each, and what [company I'm interviewing with] really offers and what their website didn't have listed." Claire reported that her interviewers never asked her about the information her father provided. Without information about a particular hiring team, class-advantaged students' parents were forced to guess what their children would be asked. They usually guessed incorrectly.

Class-advantaged students were also more likely than class-disadvantaged students to seek information about interviews from their contacts at companies where they applied. However, even these company insiders were too removed from the hiring team to offer students specific and accurate information about how to be hired. Chloe (class advantaged), for example, reached out to a family friend who worked at a company where she would interview. Her family friend sent Chloe the company's list of official interview questions, then spent hours helping her craft answers. Chloe continued to practice answering the questions on her own and entered the interview confidently. But the information Chloe received did not help her and even threw her off. The team did not stick to the questions on the company's official list. And when they did draw from a theme on the interview guide, they asked about it in multiple ways. Chloe, however, had reviewed a variety of topics and so prepared only one example of how her skills pertained to each theme. Taken aback by the questions and flustered by the gulf between her expectations and the interview itself, she fumbled through several answers and did not answer some at all. She left the interview knowing she would not be offered the job.

Sally (class advantaged) also sought information that would help her unlock a particular door. Sally knew a student who had graduated from Southern State University the year before and who now worked at the consulting company where Sally applied. Sally reached out to her, and she agreed to prepare Sally for the interview. Sally's connection reviewed case studies with her, gave her tips, and reminded her to show confidence. Sally's older sister also worked as a consultant at another company and helped Sally prepare for the case-study portion of the interview. Sally, too, went to the interview confident in her preparation. However, she had focused on preparing for the case interview. There turned out to be a behavioral interview as well. The interview was with a man she found to be awkward and quiet. Sally did not know how to effectively engage with him. She knew the interview went badly and was not surprised when she did not receive the job.

Elena (class advantaged) also believed that the key to receiving a job was to acquire information about the hiring process from people within the firm. She wanted to work as a national consultant for her sorority so she reached out to five women who held the job before her. She talked to each of them about the application process, what she should include in her application essay, and how they would evaluate candidates. They warned her that the hiring process had changed since they applied, but Elena still thought their advice would help. Elena believed that she followed their instructions, but she was not offered the position.

Class-advantaged students' attempts to get others to open doors for them were also blocked by the luckocracy's low-information system. They did not know who was authorized or willing to open doors on their behalf and then reached out to people who could not or would not help them. They first tried to get people they already knew to open doors for them. While this sometimes worked, it also routinely left students locked out. For example, Lucy's (class advantaged) father secured her an interview with a firm with whom he worked. Lucy's father's connection to the hiring manager was weak. When Lucy attended the interview, she realized that the other candidates were older, more experienced, and had stronger ties to the hiring manager. She did not receive the job. Jim (class advantaged) also asked his connections to open doors for him. He said: "I know the president of the company. I don't want to call her and say, 'Hey, I put in an application,' but I might have to." Jim did end up calling the company president. She never returned his calls. James (class advantaged) invited an international student to his family's Thanksgiving. The student previously interned at a company where James wanted to work, and James hoped his invitation would help him in the hiring process. It did not. James also met with his classmate's father, who worked in the division of a company where James wanted a job. James was not offered a position. Carter (class advantaged) went fishing with his father and his father's friend, a hiring manager. Carter still did not receive the job. Chloe (class advantaged) was confident—and wrong—that her connection would help her receive a job offer: "I'm almost a hundred percent positive I will get that [job] because my aunt is the VP of sales there." Chloe did not receive the position. She was told that the hiring committee selected a more experienced candidate.

Class-advantaged students—especially men—not only asked people they knew to open doors for them but asked others they just met to help them as well.[16] Of course, they did so with little information about who was authorized or amenable to helping them. They found that few people were willing to open doors for strangers, leading them to put in great effort for little return. Ryan (class advantaged)—a straight-A student with internship experience, a father in the field, and a grandfather who was a well-established business professional—reached out to hiring managers and vice presidents to build relationships that would help him receive a job offer. Many of the people he contacted responded and complimented him on his drive, but he rarely received an interview. Similarly, Owen (class advantaged) thought that the best way to get a job was to convince an insider to advocate on his behalf. Acting on this belief, he spent as much time networking as studying for his courses. He sent hundreds of emails and talked to dozens of people. None of them led to a job. Dylan (class advantaged) was not any more successful. He attended as many of the university's networking sessions, information sessions, and career fairs as he could with the hope that meeting recruiters would help him. Yet, he said, it "never actually works, as far as I can tell."[17]

Class-advantaged students' classed signals also had little payoff in a class-neutral system. They learned this only after displaying them. Owen (class advantaged) listed golf under the interest section of his résumé but found that his interviewers "really didn't talk about that much." About one interview, he said: "I figured out that he played golf too, but he was very adamant on asking me technical questions. . . . He didn't spend time on my interests." Similarly, Ethan (class advantaged) told an interviewer about his high-status leadership experience. As social chair of his fraternity, Ethan had organized a charity golf tournament. His interviewer did not respond by talking of his shared interest in golf or by sharing memories of fraternity life. Instead, the interviewer asked Ethan if his responsibilities as his fraternity's social chair included buying alcohol for underage students. Chloe (class advantaged) thought that she wowed interviewers with the manners she perfected in cotillion—etiquette classes for the privileged—but she did not wow them enough. She did not get any of the jobs for which she showed off these skills. Jim (class advantaged) applied to a global company and thus highlighted his study-abroad experience. Jim thought he impressed the interviewer, but he did not receive a job offer.

Despite their refusal to accept what they could not change, class-advantaged students ended up in the same position as class-disadvantaged students: forced to accept the system as it was. They could not get around the low-information system: their contacts did not have accurate information about the hiring process, and they had little information about who could open doors on their behalf. Also, they could not get around the class-neutral system, with employers ignoring their high-status displays. Like class-disadvantaged students, they would need to guess where to apply and rely on the advice the university provided.

Without the information they needed to obtain particular jobs, class-advantaged students chose where to apply in the same way as class-disadvantaged students: with the only information they could. They, too, used the limited information in job ads to decide where to apply—often choosing jobs in their specialization, desired location, and sometimes with large companies, ones they saw as high status.[18] They did not have enough information to make more specific decisions. So, within these criteria, they applied widely to any job that fit their broad criteria. Jim, for instance, was typical of class-advantaged students who first applied to particular positions. He explained how he next decided where to apply: "Entry level, big company, supply chain–oriented job, a job maybe in [city]." Asked how he narrowed it down within those criteria, he replied that he did not: "My whole thing is just to apply to positions and hope that someone will accept me." Asked where she would apply, Kathy (class advantaged) also kept it broad: "Really anything marketing." Asked if he had any preferences besides a job in operations and logistics, Dylan (class advantaged) maintained: "Absolutely none." John (class advantaged) stated: "I wasn't very picky in what I wanted, so I was pretty up for anything." Logan (class advantaged) maintained: "If it's there, I apply to it." Sally (class advantaged) set her sights on a particular consulting position, but when she did not receive it, she claimed: "I applied to everything."

Class-advantaged students were also forced to guess how to impress their evaluators. They were not used to this approach. They grew up with great resources and in families with authority. They were used to controlling situations and planning for them, not having to quickly guess how to please others.[19] They found it challenging to adapt. Carter (class advantaged) said he did poorly in interviews because he could not predict the questions: "He asked me a couple of questions that threw me for a loop, and whenever questions threw me for a loop, I got off my game." Ryan (class advantaged) said he reacted poorly to unexpected events too: "At the beginning of the interview I seemed like a deer in headlights just because I wasn't expecting his personality." Alice (class advantaged) reported feeling uncomfortable winging interviews too: "I was asked a very trick question and it just totally threw me off." Josh (class advantaged) added: "I didn't really expect those questions so it caught me off guard."

Class-advantaged students routinely found themselves caught off guard. They were asked questions that were not on lists of most-asked questions and that no one had told them they would need to answer. In this sense, they were unlucky. They applied for jobs without any information about what key they needed and found they had the wrong one. Tyler (class advantaged), the son of a financial analyst, knew that to receive one finance job he would need to pass a written test of his financial knowledge. He did not know what would be on it, claiming: "They're very secretive about their questions, and they don't like to release them or let anybody know what they're going to be." He studied for the test but found he studied the wrong material. The material on the test, he said, "was stuff that I hadn't really seen before." Likewise, Nathan (class advantaged), the son of a businessman, was asked highly specific questions which he could not answer. An interviewer asked him to explain the acronyms MRP and SEM. Nathan had never heard of them. He did not receive the job. Claire (class advantaged) was asked a different version of the question "why do you want to work here" than she had heard before: "Why do you want to work for a young and upcoming company [like us] as opposed to those more established names?" Claire hadn't prepared an answer to that version of the question, stumbled while answering it, and did not receive the job.[20]

Class-advantaged students also had to guess evaluators' hiring criteria. Some were unlucky; they guessed incorrectly. An interviewer asked Andrew (class advantaged) to talk about himself. He described himself as a people person and a team player. The interviewer then told him that the job was to sit by himself at a computer all day. He was not offered the position. Mason (class advantaged) was dismissed using criteria that he did not know he would be evaluated upon: the hiring agent told him he was rejected because his answers were not long enough. Grace (class advantaged) answered a question about what brands she worked with in her last internship. Grace didn't know why the hiring agent disliked her answer but noticed that the tone of the interview changed dramatically after she replied. Norah's (class advantaged) interviewer criticized her for not participating in on-campus extracurricular activities, though she participated in off-campus ones.

Of course, as for class-disadvantaged students, class-advantaged students could keep applying for jobs until they happened to have the experiences, skills, and styles that particular employers rewarded. This worked for Tyler. After failing the finance test, he received a similar job with a company in the same industry and of similar prestige after being asked very different questions: "[They asked] a lot about my work history, a lot about where I was headed, why I was interested in their job, how I handled myself in different situations, more behavioral stuff than actual problems. I don't think I had a single actual problem." It worked for Nathan too. After being denied a job after admitting to not knowing what certain acronyms meant, he applied for and received a similar job in a similar industry. This time, he was not asked about acronyms but about teamwork, coursework, problem solving, and Excel. Andrew did not get the job he applied for—one that did not require teamwork—but he was hired for another job at the same company in which he would work on a team.

Other class-advantaged students—like most class-disadvantaged students—found jobs after being asked only questions that the university had prepared them to answer. For instance, Ryan (class advantaged) described the interview that led to a job offer: "They asked if I was okay with the long hours, why I wanted to work at [company], why I thought I would be a good fit at the company, what kind of experience I've had in the past." For a job she was offered, Caroline (class advantaged) was simply asked about her internship project—something she could easily talk about. For the job she accepted, Claire (class advantaged) remembered being asked the behavioral questions that SSU courses and clubs had reviewed: "A lot of the questions were 'tell me about a time when'" questions, ones "I've gotten in so many interviews that I make sure that I have a defined, perfect memorized answer for." Elena (class advantaged) barely had to show any skills at all: "It was about a half an hour. Mostly they told me about the job and asked questions about how my skill set would apply to working with them. Then really they just talked about the job."

And, as for class-disadvantaged students, class-advantaged students sometimes just happened to have the right key. Without preparation or intent, they said the answer the hiring agent wanted to hear. One of these students was James (class advantaged). The CEO who interviewed James asked him to describe the account manager he had met earlier. James did not know what the CEO was testing. He decided to reply honestly rather than to follow the rule he had been taught: to remain positive in interviews. He criticized the account manager: "He was self-centric and he wasn't always focused on customer solutions. And he's not the best listener." The CEO told James that his answer was perceptive and that it was exactly the answer he wanted to hear.

It took class-advantaged students an average of three interviews to find a job—the same number as it took class-disadvantaged students. Most students received the jobs they did through luck: they applied to any jobs that fit their broad criteria, guessed how to prepare, and were offered a job when hiring agents asked only questions the university had prepared them to answer or, sometimes, when students just happened to say the "right" thing.

For most students, the role of luck would continue. They did not know in advance what pay they would receive if offered the position; luck would determine if they happened to be offered a high-paying position for their subfield. Class-advantaged students had to guess what jobs paid, too, because the information they sought about pay tended to be incomplete or inaccurate—an unsurprising fact since employers did not tell their employees what other positions paid. Cody (class advantaged), for example, received inaccurate information. A contact told him that the job he applied for paid $45,000 a year. Only after receiving the offer did he discover that it paid less: $18.67 an hour. Working forty hours a week for fifty weeks a year, he would earn about $37,000 and become one of the lowest-paid students who entered his field. Ryan (class advantaged) asked his father and internship mentor which industries and jobs paid the most. He accepted a sales position that paid $53,500 a year plus commission. He only found out after taking the job that he would not receive the commission he expected; at his company, employees only averaged one sale every two years.[21] Other class-advantaged students simply could not find the pay information they sought; it was hidden from their view and their contacts' view too.[22]

Students also did not know which of their connections could find them high-paying jobs, and many approached people who shepherded them into a low-paying position. This was not purposeful on their contacts' part. These contacts were unlikely to know what students would be paid for entry-level positions at their own workplaces and certainly did not know what students would be paid if they obtained similar positions at other companies. Grace (class advantaged, mentioned in chapter 4) was one of the students led into a low-paying position. Grace's roommate's mother, sorority sister, and friend's friend all worked at the same company. Each helped her receive a job at their firm—a job that paid $40,000, or $28,000 less than the top marketing student, less than all class-disadvantaged marketing students, less than marketing students with far fewer internships, and less than she hoped. This was not even a job she particularly wanted; she only applied after the company where she interned told her they would not have the funds to hire her full-time. Natalie (class advantaged) found a job through her college roommate's mother. The job paid $35,000 a year—only about half as much as the highest-paid marketing student I followed. Owen's (class advantaged) approach of reaching out to strangers never worked, but he did receive a position at his internship supervisor's brother's firm. The offer was for sufficiently little that Owen was not sure he would be able to make ends meet.

Of course, other class-advantaged students found jobs through applying to jobs on their own while knowing little about the job's pay. Just as for class-disadvantaged students, some then lucked into high-paying jobs and others received low-paying positions. Jill (class advantaged) looked for a job with a résumé that included one human resources internship, several years in a leadership club, the director of her sorority's

rush, and leadership experience on the executive board of her university's
Pan-Hellenic council. She attended a career fair and approached the representatives of the company she would eventually work for because "I
was looking for another employer to talk to." She talked to the recruiter
and then decided to apply: "He described it as more of a generalist role
for HR, which is what I was starting to look for." She went through a
lengthy interview process that involved her repeatedly saying why she
was interested in the job and talking about her leadership experience.
She received the job. It paid $40,000 a year, $10,000 less than Christina
(class disadvantaged) and Karen (class disadvantaged) for doing similar
work in similar cities and after all of them applied with little information about pay.

Ethan (class advantaged) would also go on to earn $10,000 less than
Seth (class disadvantaged)—a difference attributable to luck. Ethan and
Seth were both clean-cut white men who applied to college knowing
they wanted to be business majors, and each figured out early in their
college careers that they wanted to specialize in finance. By their junior
years, both Ethan and Seth had completed multiple internships: both had
interned at financial advising companies as well as at small companies in
positions unrelated to finance. Seth also had a third internship at a bank,
while Ethan took on leadership roles in his business fraternity and social
fraternity. Ethan and Seth also spent years in the business school's leadership clubs and prided themselves on their math skills. Their résumés
were highly similar.

Ethan and Seth each wanted a job in finance with a big bank. Both
applied to every bank that recruited from Southern State University, attended the banks' information sessions, introduced themselves to recruiters, and tried to appear personable. Both men received interviews
from multiple banks, including three of the same ones. At the bank
where they accepted offers, both men remembered being asked similar
questions.

ETHAN: They asked me if you're a member of a team, this happens, how
would you handle it? These questions were more just tell me about a time

where you led, tell me about what you did in this organization. We talked a lot about my past internship experience.

SETH: They really wanted to know how I worked on a team. So it was a lot of examples of a team environment, both academic classes but also in my work experience. They also asked me about my leadership experience, how I changed somebody's mind one time. They asked me why I thought I would do well in that position, and what I liked about the company, if I saw myself in [city], which is where they were from.

Ethan and Seth both received internship offers from two banks. Ethan received offers from the bank where he accepted the position and the bank where Seth previously interned. Seth received offers from the bank he would eventually work for and the bank that offered Ethan a position. The two men selected different offers for internships. They each knew that the internship could lead to a job, but they did not know in advance what jobs would be available at each bank or how much they would pay. At the end of the summer, Ethan and Seth each received offers to work in rotational programs for the banks they interned with, each in similar southern cities. It was only then—at the end of the summer, long past when they initially interviewed—that they learned what they would be paid as full-time employees. Ethan (class advantaged) was offered $43,000 a year while Seth (class disadvantaged) was offered $53,000. Without knowing the prize behind each door, Ethan selected the wrong one.

The degree that luck was involved in students' outcomes could also be viewed by comparing students who were less similar. Kathy (class advantaged) and Bethany (class disadvantaged) both specialized in marketing, but they had very different résumés. Kathy scoffed at students who spent their summers scooping ice cream rather than interning. She thought they were throwing away their futures. Accordingly, she completed three internships by the time she graduated and led what she said was one of the largest clubs on campus. She then contacted her friend's Facebook friend to ask how to find a post-college gig at an entertainment center. She received the job. Six months later, she was ready to look for a more permanent position and applied to any jobs related to marketing in her geographic area. She went to an interview and immediately noticed that the building was decorated with themes from the entertainment center where she had just worked. She and the CEO talked about the entertainment center for most of the interview. Unintentionally having had an experience the hiring agent rewarded, she received the job. It paid $34,000 a year.

Bethany (class disadvantaged) was one of the students Kathy had looked down upon. She had never interned, though she did have work experience. She sold T-shirts and worked as a campus brand ambassador where she handed out flyers to students. Like Kathy, she also wanted a marketing job but felt she shouldn't be too picky so applied to sales jobs as well. Bethany applied widely online and also to a position with the company where her aunt worked. Her aunt's colleague told Bethany what kind of people the company typically looked for, though offered no insight on what questions she would be asked. Either her aunt's colleague's advice paid off or Bethany's own luck and abilities did. She received the job and would be paid $68,000 a year, twice as much as Kathy.

Of course, class-advantaged students were not uniformly unlucky—some lucked into applying for high-paying jobs too. Levi (class advantaged) applied to a position after literally bumping into a recruiter at a career fair. Levi was a large man; bumping into the recruiter sent the recruiter's papers flying. Levi bent down to help collect the papers and started talking with the recruiter as he did. The recruiter encouraged Levi to apply to the position, one Levi had no intention of applying to before. Levi applied and received the internship that led to the job. He received a salary of $60,000 a year, making him one of the highest-paid marketing students in the sample. John (class advantaged) applied to a job because the application was easy. He then answered questions about teamwork, diversity, and basic software programs—ones he knew to expect due to his university's training. He was offered a job that paid $64,000 a year. Jenny (class advantaged) was nervous about attending the career fair. As she was advised, she calmed her nerves by talking to company representatives about a position she did not want. They convinced her to apply. She later accepted their internship offer and then job offer. Without having ever planned to apply, she received a position that paid well: she received $58,000 a year.

Whether they received a low-paying offer or a high-paying one, class-advantaged students, too, tended to take the first offer they received. That is, only 11% of class-advantaged participants turned down an offer for a professional business job when they did not have another offer in hand. They also tended not to negotiate. Like most class-disadvantaged students, they did not think they were allowed to negotiate, didn't think to do it, or were grateful for the offer they received.[23] They also had to decide whether to accept an offer in one day to two weeks—rarely enough time to receive other job offers and to gain leverage with which to negotiate.

But why did class-advantaged students accept low-paying positions? Like class-disadvantaged students, they did not all know that their offers were low. But even for those that sensed this, a low offer seemed better than no offer at all—a risk they took by turning down a position. They searched for jobs as headlines documented the phenomenon of college-educated baristas, the return of college-educated children to their parents' homes, and the rise of downward mobility. Not having a job meant that they could be in any one of these categories, and that their friends and family would know. Certainty of a professional job, even with an undesirable salary, was better than risking finding no job at all.

Along the same lines, being in an undergraduate business school meant learning a particular definition of success. The flyers on the walls, the regular presence of hiring agents, the high visibility of the career center, and the importance of career fairs signaled to students that to succeed was to find a professional job and to fail was not to have one. And who succeeded was visible. Students swapped stories about who found a job; they knew who "succeeded." Taking a job that signaled success was far better than ending up without a job at all, even if the job did not pay as well as they wanted.

Students' decisions to take low-paying jobs were also fueled by false beliefs. Some rationalized that their low pay would not matter for long as they could get another job soon. They did not know the results of social science research: that first pay follows students for years.[24] Their parents also encouraged them to take the positions, though they, too, may have been guided by false beliefs. American adults estimate that the unemployment rate for new college graduates is 20% to 30%.[25] It is usually far lower, closer to 5%.[26] Career center staff also did not dissuade them from taking these jobs; they saw their role as helping students meet their own goals, not using a heavy hand to persuade them to take or turn down any particular job.

In addition, the process of finding a job made it difficult for students to feel like maximizers rather than satisficers.[27] Maximizers vie for the best possible outcome while satisficers vie for good enough. Students of all class backgrounds could not know what counted as the best possible outcome. They did not know what other jobs would become available, be offered to them, and pay. Even after receiving an offer, many also still did not know what tasks they would do, and they certainly did not know what their job tasks could be at other firms. It was hard to feel like they wanted the best possible outcome rather than a good-enough one when they did not know what the best could be.

Furthermore, some employers hire for some jobs seasonally, so turning down a suboptimal job for the chance at a "better" job could mean waiting a year until the hiring season returned. If they waited a year, they would have little to add to their résumé in the meantime, giving them little confidence that they would receive a better job later. All that was guaranteed was that they'd have less of the CoB's institutional support to find a job—less access to networking events and career fairs, less ability to run into a hiring agent in the business school's halls, and less help from the career center. Moreover, they'd need to come up with a story to tell hiring agents about why they did not find or accept a job the previous year,[28] and convince them to depart from their usual practice of hiring college seniors. None of this would be impossible, but research suggests that job search intensity is unrelated to the quality of the job people receive[29] and that employed workers receive better job offers than unemployed ones.[30] Students may have rightly assumed that continuing to search for a job may not yield better results, and that turning down job offers was a bigger risk than taking a low-paying job and then applying for a higher-paying job later.

To turn down a guaranteed job for an unknown possibility then seemed like a terrible risk. Most students of all class backgrounds accepted the first offer they received for a job in their field, cementing the role that luck played in who opened which door. And luck evened out inequality, at least in terms of pay. Despite their unequal class backgrounds, students of different class backgrounds would earn about the same amounts: on average, $48,000 for class-disadvantaged students and $45,000 for class-advantaged students.

The Limits of Luck

Luck did not matter for everyone. Students who did not meet employers' low bar of employability were pushed out of professional jobs and into lower-paying positions.

Alice (class advantaged) was one of these few students. Though she was the daughter of two doctors, she still had trouble enacting professional norms. She could recite the lessons that the university taught: in résumés, avoid spelling errors, follow formatting guidelines, and match your skills and experiences to the job; in interviews, be early, prepare to answer behavioral questions in the STAR format, avoid fidgeting, and follow up with a thank-you note. However, she said that she struggled to enact these lessons. She would get to interviews late, forget her résumé, show she was flustered, forget to write thank-you notes, and go on long tangents—ones that her friends told her made her sound crazy. In our own research interviews, she also arrived late and engaged in long tangents, often talking at length about her workplace anxieties rather than answering the question directly. She also fidgeted throughout her research interviews. She picked at her fingernails, draped the end of her ponytail over the top of her head and into her eyes, pulled at her mouth and eyelids, did not cover her mouth while yawning, and avoided eye contact. She did not meet hiring agents' bar of employability and was not offered a professional position. Instead, she started her post-college work life paid to stand on street corners and ask people to donate to charity.

Other students met the bar but opted out of professional jobs. Eli (class disadvantaged) was a college athlete. He went on a few job interviews but ultimately rejected any job that required him to sit all day. He chose to become a personal trainer instead—at least until, months after graduating, he found a professional job that allowed him considerable time on his feet.

Conclusion

Luckocracies are created by the even suppression of information coupled with class-neutral hiring criteria. Together, these factors tore asunder the typical ways that inequality is reproduced. Class-advantaged students tried to get an informational edge but could not gain information that benefited them. They displayed classed status symbols, but employers ignored them. They had more professional contacts than class-disadvantaged students and networked more, but their connections did not confer an advantage. Instead, these professional contacts gave advice that was not useful and led students into low-paying positions just as often as high-paying ones. Both class-disadvantaged and class-advantaged students then had to guess where to get ahead and how to present themselves, and they would be judged in class-neutral ways. Thus, the luckocracy put students from each class in the same position, where their earnings would be determined by luck.

PART III

THE
CONSEQUENCES AND
CONTINUATION
OF THE
LUCKOCRACY

The Consequences of the Luckocracy

When Chona lost the *Let's Make a Deal* game, she simply went home empty-handed. Students, instead, continued to be affected by the outcomes of their job search. A year after they received their jobs, their paychecks were still shaped by the luckocracy and so were their professional lives. Students' workplace responsibilities, opportunities to build new skills, and ability to receive mentorship were all determined by which door they happened to walk through. And because these facets of their work were determined by luck, they did not relate to students' class origins.

The Consequences of Hidden Information about Jobs

After students found a job, they could peer behind the door and learn what prize they had won. For many, it was not the prize they expected.

UNEXPECTED PAY

Students' starting salaries were not always what they seemed. The pay information that students received in their offer letters could be deceptive and subject to change.

Chloe (class advantaged), for example, wanted a high-paying position. In addition to applying for other jobs, she also applied for a job that listed its wages in the ad. She knew people at the firm as well and asked them general questions about the pay. She then followed up, reviewing Glassdoor's salary information online. Still, after starting her job, she learned that the pay was not what she expected. The earnings listed in the job ad was based on an hourly calculation rather than an annual salary, presumed she would work over forty hours a week, and made assumptions about the size of her team-based performance bonuses—bonuses that were not guaranteed. Despite her in-depth research, she was not given the information she needed to understand what she would be paid. If she worked forty hours a week, she would earn less than the pay listed in the job ad. She felt deceived.

Other students entered the workforce as their company's salary policies shifted. Dylan (class advantaged) was promised bonuses of up to $25,000 a year. After he started, the company eliminated bonuses and boosted his salary by just $2,500 instead, far less than Dylan thought he would receive. For Avery (class disadvantaged), salary shifts went her way. Before she started working but after she accepted the position, the company's compensation policies changed. She was given a $3,000 raise before working a single day. In a low-information and dynamic system, there was no way for students from any class background to successfully strategize to receive the highest pay.

UNEXPECTED RESPONSIBILITIES

Students routinely accepted jobs without understanding their future responsibilities. This was not the students' fault—employers did not always know either. They hired in the fall and spring for positions that began in the summer and did not always know what work they would have months later. In that time, the company could gain new leadership, change directions to respond to a competitor, merge divisions internally, see employees leave, and hire other employees. Any of these factors could change what work they assigned new hires.

In addition, some employers brought in multiple students for similar positions and assigned them to different teams. Each team might have different responsibilities and opportunities; students would only learn theirs after starting the job. Students could then easily be misled when hiring agents talked about experiences other teams would have but that the students themselves would not. Employer 28 (technology, procurement), for instance, admitted that the job he hired for explicitly listed 25% travel time in the ad. During job interviews, current employees sold the job by regaling interviewees with stories of their company-sponsored travel. However, new employees' opportunities for travel depended upon the accounts they were assigned. Some were assigned to local accounts and would not travel at all. To them, the job ad and stories were misleading.

Thus, it was not surprising that a year into their first jobs, a majority of respondents from all class backgrounds said that their job did not meet their original expectations. This outcome, however, was not due to the savviness of some students over others; students from all class backgrounds could not foresee what they would be expected to do. For example, Ben (class disadvantaged) thought he would be a project manager who allocated tasks and kept a team moving. Instead, he became an analyst who spent his days working in Excel. Similarly, Chloe (class advantaged) received her first-choice job; one in which she thought she would learn to design ads. Instead, a year into her job, she rarely designed ads:

> On a day-to-day basis I'm really just looking at numbers. It's not as creative as I thought it was going to be. We look at different metrics that are associated with our advertisements. So, how many people clicked on the ad? How many people saw the ad? How many people purchased off the ad? It's very analytical and they definitely didn't advertise that going into the role.

Natalie (class advantaged) also ended up taking on different responsibilities than she expected. She explained: "The position's official name was marketing and development coordinator. When I heard that, I really thought it was going to be more marketing based, but we actually outsource our marketing to this lovely woman in Florida. She's great, but I really thought I was going to have a little bit more control on that."

Julie (class advantaged) also found herself surprised by what her job entailed. She moved six hundred miles from home to become a visual merchandiser but instead straightened shirts in a retail store. She recalled what happened:

> When I interviewed for the job and when I applied, they had made it seem like I would be going to multiple stores, doing visual merchandising. That I would manage inventory and that I would go into one store one day, do a little in-service training, set the floor, and then leave. Then the next day, I'd do the same thing but at a different store. Well, I got there and they had taken us to [city] for a week for training. They hyped up the job. It seemed awesome.
>
> I got there on my first day of the job and one of the managers on my team came up from New York to train me. He said, "Just so you know, that is not what you will be doing." Pretty much, [the company] hired a bunch of us at the beginning of November so they would have people in place in high volume [retail stores] to help increase sales over the holidays. And so, I was pretty much told, "Until the end of the first quarter, the end of January, your primary focus is going to be sales. You're gonna be in the store five to six days a week, eight hours a day, solely in the [company] section, straightening the sections and selling [company products]." So it was just very different from what I had expected and what they had made the job out to be.

The company's updated assertion that she would straighten shirts only until the end of January also proved untrue. In March, Julie concluded that the company would never teach her to become a visual merchandiser or teach her any related skills.

UNEXPECTED ROADBLOCKS TO BUILDING NEW SKILLS

Most students I spoke to hoped that their job would help them build new skills. Some students found this to be true while others did not. Since students rarely knew—and sometimes *could not* know—what they would do, those who found themselves in jobs that built their skills was largely a matter of luck, not class origin.

Some recent graduates had few opportunities to build new skills because they were barely assigned any work. For instance, Andrea (class disadvantaged), who was paid around the median amount of the students I spoke to, did less work than most. She explained that her job was not demanding: "Sometimes I'm done with everything by ten o'clock in the morning." Connor (class disadvantaged), who was tied for the fourth highest-paid student in the sample, said of his job: "I would spend maybe forty percent of the day with issues to work on and then maybe sixty percent just waiting around." He started spending his time reading fiction since he had little work to do. Claire (class advantaged), a highly paid respondent, said she sometimes had little work to do as well: "There were times when it was two-thirty p.m., three p.m., and I was like, 'Okay, I'm done with my group project stuff, and I'm done shadowing people for the day. I just don't know what I'm supposed to be doing right now.'"

Other students worked regular hours but felt that their tasks left them little room to grow. Shawna (class disadvantaged) took a job with a prestigious and high-paying firm, which advertised that its employees would always be challenged and never be bored. She believed them. Instead, she found herself bored, not challenged, and not positioned to develop new skills:

> A lot of it is just project management, which is fine. But it's the same work every week. So I was really struggling with staying focused or staying involved in it. It just became robotic for me. It's like okay, it's Monday, I have to push this out. Tuesday, collect this. Wednesday, do this. The work was not what I thought it was going to be.

For her "robotic" work, Shawna earned $72,500 a year, making her the highest-paid student with whom I spoke.

Nathan (class advantaged) was also highly paid, earning $60,000 a year. He found a job related to his specialization and in the same large company that employed his father. When he accepted it, the job seemed to be exactly what he wanted, but he soon found it offered him less room to develop his skills than he anticipated. Instead, he spent much of his time on data entry: "It can get monotonous. Putting in those same numbers. Once you do a couple hundred of them, you don't want to do another hundred more in the same day."

Some students also learned new skills, but their skills would only help them if they remained with their current companies. These students learned how to navigate their own workplace but not how to navigate others. Rebecca (class disadvantaged) recalled what she learned over her first year at work: "I learned a lot of [company-]specific processes. [Company] uses certain programs for certain things like payroll, there's a certain way to do it for [company], and I learned how to do that quickly. There are certain reports that you have to learn. You have to learn how to do them a specific way. A lot of what I learned was all [company] specific." Similarly, Jenny (class advantaged) mostly learned skills that were useful at her company: "I got exposure to internal tools which wouldn't be a universal experience at every position I went into, but I'm sure every company has its own internal tools that you have to get accustomed to using."

Of course, other students spent more time working, were challenged, and learned new skills, including ones that they could use no matter where they worked. But as students of all class backgrounds could not know what they would do in advance, they also could not know if they would have the opportunity to learn new skills. The ability to do challenging work or to be paid for doing little work was distributed by the luck of happening to apply to and receive a job that offered it. It was not distributed by social class.

UNEXPECTED MENTORSHIP

Before they began their jobs, students did not necessarily know if they would be assigned a mentor. Some were and some were not, and the difference was another unanticipated outcome of the luckocracy. Which students found mentors had to do more with the company's policies and size than students' class origin.[1]

Some respondents were assigned mentors and required to meet with them frequently. Through no initiative of their own, they were connected with someone whose job was to help them. Lucas (class advantaged), for example, was assigned a helpful mentor:

> This guy, Greg, who's the middle-level manager between me and the owners, he's my mentor. We've had weekly meetings for a half hour for almost a year now. And so if I ever have any trouble, I'll talk to him about it and he gives me lots of advice. And he's just extremely good. He's like the best employee that someone could ever imagine. . . . So I get a lot out of our discussions.

Connor (class disadvantaged) was also assigned a useful mentor: "I do have a mentor who sits right next to me. He's been specifically chosen to be my mentor. So if I have general questions about project management or how I should approach this issue or what's the best way to tackle this problem, I have my mentor who sits right next to me to help me out." Ben (class disadvantaged) was assigned a useful mentor as well: "She is always willing to teach. She's been at [the company] for about twenty years, and she knows literally everything in the company. It doesn't even make sense how she knows so much." Connor (class disadvantaged) and Ben (class disadvantaged) had not reached out to many new people when searching for jobs. Yet by being assigned a mentor, they were in the same position as Lucas, a class-advantaged student who was more comfortable networking.

Opportunities for mentorship was also related to the size of the company or team. In some workplaces, students were not assigned a mentor, and there was no one available for them to approach. Owen (class advantaged), who reported calling over one hundred people to find a job, did not find a mentor at work. Owen worked in a small firm in which most employees were only a few years older than him. Because of this, he thought there was no one available to serve in a mentorship role. Chloe (class advantaged) also reached out to many people during her job search but was unable to find a mentor at work. She had a weekly meeting with a supervisor but found the meetings useless. She otherwise worked with colleagues who were also new to the company, and her other supervisors discouraged her from asking them questions. In a small department, no one else was available to serve as her mentor. Christina (class disadvantaged) and Amy (class disadvantaged) both worked alongside their supervisors as the only human resource specialists in their plants. Their supervisors could help them, but there was no one else at their location who was available to serve as a mentor. Similarly, Eli (class disadvantaged) eventually found work as a manager of a warehouse. There had not been a previous manager, and there was no one else at the warehouse who knew enough about his position to ask for advice. Even if he had felt comfortable reaching out to others, there was no one to approach.

Peers could also serve as mentors in a new workplace. Having helpful peers was again an unexpected part of the job, which some students lucked into and others did not. Some students were placed in cohorts of new employees. Regardless of their approach to networking, they met many peers they could turn to for help. John (class advantaged), for example, entered his company alongside about forty other college graduates, then went through a five-month training program with them. A year into the workforce, he still turned to them for advice. Keri (class disadvantaged), who had done little networking in college, also had a cohort of peers to rely on: "I'm part of a management training squad. We try to support each other. So that was really great because if there's something that I wouldn't talk to my boss about, I have a peer to talk to." Avery (class disadvantaged), who called networking "my extreme weak point" during her job search, also was surrounded by peers she could turn to at work: "I am on a team of eighteen people, so right there you know eighteen people and your manager. So I could really just be on the way to the bathroom or in the bathroom and find somebody that I'm able to get tips from."

Not all students were so lucky to have peers at work. In some workplaces, there were no peers for recent graduates to meet. Caroline (class advantaged) and Nathan (class advantaged) were both the only members of their teams in the city where they worked. Some of their colleagues were in different states or countries. They did not have peers to whom they could easily turn. Likewise, Rebecca (class disadvantaged) was the only person in human resources at her entire plant. Though she disliked networking, even had she liked it, there was no one around she could turn to for advice. Similarly, Ben (class disadvantaged) worked from home and only had conference calls with his mentor and colleagues. He did not have peers he could ask for help, whether he wanted to or not.

Some jobs, on the other hand, were organized in ways that enabled new hires to meet many new people—those who could mentor them or open doors for them in the future. For example, Andrea's (class disadvantaged) desk was positioned right outside of the company vice president's office, so she was able to meet many other employees because of her location. Katelyn's (class advantaged) workplace had an early career program that she found helpful where she regularly met the executives at the firm. Owen's (class advantaged) job entailed "communicating with some of the most powerful institutional investors in the world on a daily basis." He hoped they would help him in the future. Notably, these opportunities to meet new people had little to do with students' social class or propensity to network. Instead, they related to how their jobs were structured.

Conclusion

The luckocracy suppressed information about the job and pay structure for students from all class backgrounds. The lack of information available to job seekers continued to affect them during their first year at work. Even after they signed contracts, some students still discovered new information about their pay. And as new hires, they entered their jobs with little knowledge of what their responsibilities, skill-building opportunities, and mentorship experiences would be. Importantly, these were determined more by the workplace than the individual. As students could not know ahead of time which jobs would give them which opportunities, the distribution of these opportunities related more to luck than to class origin.

The Luckocracy, Redux

Chona played the game just once. A year after graduating from college, students would play the game again. When searching for a promotion, raise, or job at a new company, students would again confront a luckocracy, a labor market structured by evenly hidden information and class-neutral selection criteria. Remarkably, then, earnings equality would continue.

Hidden Salaries

Most employers I spoke to said that new hires would not be able to know how much they would be paid if they took a different position within the company. Employer 20 (energy, hourly trader) spoke of what employees knew about internal pay: "The employees see what level the position is. So, for example, a senior hourly trader is a level six. But they would not see the detailed pay range. All they would know is if there's an open position that's been posted." I asked Employer 22 if new hires would know the salary of the positions that they could receive through promotions. Employer 22 (healthcare, many business roles) responded: "No. We don't share that." Employer 25 (research, sales) agreed that new hires would have little information about what they would be paid if they were promoted: "The compensation structure is not known knowledge across the company. It's kept more confidential." New hires would also not necessarily know how much they could receive from a raise without a promotion. Employer 27 (finance, HR, and finance) said of raises: "I think we catch people by surprise."[1]

Uninformative Job Titles

New hires would also not be able to use job titles to understand what potential new jobs would pay. Employer 21 (energy, many business roles) said of job titles for non-entry-level positions at her firm: "For most of our jobs we don't include the level either. Unless it's intern. But other than that you can look at our job postings and you wouldn't know if it's a senior-level role, except looking for the years of experience. We don't say level one, level two, level three. We keep that vague as well." Employer 12 (manufacturing, many business roles) also thought that job seekers would not be able to read the employer's job titles for advanced positions and understand them. She said they used a job title that sounded like a senior-level position but was a low-level position. According to her, many people got through the interview process and then were disappointed by the job and pay. Employer 28 (technology, procurement) also indicated that job titles could be a poor proxy for level or pay. He said that his company recently revised their job titles because employees wrongly assumed that some job titles indicated higher pay and more responsibility. Students looking to increase their pay by switching jobs—either within their firm or outside of it—would know little about that possibility from a job title alone.

Vague Job Descriptions

If new hires decided to look for a different job, they would still have little information about what it entailed. They would no longer be able to search for jobs on university websites, having to rely on national job boards and company websites. These sites also included vague descriptions of the company and job. A study of job ads on Monster.com found that "most organizations fail to differentiate themselves in any material way from their competitors."[2] Other studies found that most job ads described their company as successful, growing, and global but included little about what candidates could expect in terms of their training or potential for advancement.[3] Career pages on company websites were typically no more informative, instead focusing on the history, products, mission, and "lofty descriptions" of the firm.[4] Moreover, the skills listed in the job ads did not necessarily reflect the ones candidates needed or would use—managers still did not always know in advance what the job would entail. Job descriptions and information about necessary skills were also prone to be incorrect due to members of the hiring team disagreeing about the type of candidate they wanted.[5] Job descriptions, again, told candidates little about the position.[6]

Hidden Promotional Structures

If new hires preferred to stay with their company, they would not necessarily know what career trajectories awaited them. Large companies that hired many college graduates often had transparent promotional structures or mentors who helped them learn the next steps. Other companies were less likely to have a set promotional structure that new hires could know and follow. As Employer 18 (e-commerce, sales) told me: "There's no set structure. It depends on what your role is, what organization you're in, and the business need." Employer 24 (technology, many business roles) said that it was up to new hires to navigate the internal promotion structure at her large company: "I don't think there was, 'Hey, here's a map if you wanna take this.'" When I asked Employer 28 (technology, procurement) if new hires would know how to be promoted, he said that they would not. Even he did not know: "That is an area that is continuing to be developed, and even for someone like myself who has been here for some time, that's a question that continues to come up. A lot of work is being done to help develop that road map, but as a new hire, I guess the answer would be probably not right away."

Any information new hires did receive about their company's promotional structure might also change. Employer 21 (energy, many business roles), for instance, described a substantial change at her firm.

EMPLOYER 21: We have a new CEO and a new VP of HR. Part of their strategy is to fill at least forty percent of positions with internal talent, which has really opened up this door for upward personal mobility.

JESSI: So what was it like before these new policies were implemented?

EMPLOYER 21: Basically you had to get your manager's approval before you could apply for a position. That led a lot of people to not asking for approval because they didn't want to tell their boss, "Hey, I'm interested in working in another area." Or, if they did ask, their manager would say, "You're too crucial for our company in this position so we really can't afford to lose you to another team." It's definitely a 180 from where we were before.

Employer 22 (healthcare, many business roles) also said that the promotional opportunities at her firm expanded recently: "Over the past five years, we've grown from 250 people to 1,200. So we had a rapid growth in a really short period. . . . We're in the process of building out career maps or career families for people to be able to navigate their path here." In Employer 25's (research, sales) company, the promotional structure was changing too. In her case, the company split into two, creating different career opportunities for employees. As Employer 18 (e-commerce, sales) summed up about promotional structures, "A lot depends on the company because the role may be changing as the company is growing quickly or changing."

New Hires' Perspectives

Unsurprisingly given companies' opaque policies, most students I spoke to didn't know how to increase their salary or what job they would fill if they were promoted. Not wanting to ask about seemingly taboo topics, students from all class backgrounds now accepted what they believed they could not change—that they had to operate with little information.

Asked how much they would earn if they received a raise, new hires regularly said that they did not know. I had the following conversation with Katelyn (class advantaged):

JESSI: Do you mind if I ask how much your raise will be?
KATELYN: No, I actually don't know.
JESSI: Do you have a ballpark?
KATELYN: I have no idea to be honest. I haven't asked other people.

Similarly, Jenny (class advantaged) did not know how much money she would be paid if she stayed at her firm for another year: "I want to say [the raise would be] upwards of ten percent. But I'm not really sure. I could reach out to someone and ask, but I've never really done it. I would say that it's probably upwards of—I don't know. I really can't tell you." Connor (class disadvantaged) also did not know how much he could expect to earn in the future. He explained: "I'm not sure how that works right now." Avery (class disadvantaged), too, knew that there were possibilities to receive bonuses, but she had no idea how much she could receive. She explained: "I have no idea [how much bonuses can be]. I really don't know, because my boss was so hesitant about showing me my bonus [this year], but inside I was ecstatic. But I know that we're in two different places in our lives. But I don't know, I have to imagine it's in the thousands or at least one thousand something. Because if my bonus was terrible, then I don't know what the good ones look like."

Even respondents who had received bonuses or raises often did not know how they were awarded. Kathy (class advantaged) was surprised to receive a $2,000 raise a few months after she began her job: "And then when they gave me my raise, I wasn't really expecting it. I just took it with open arms and was thankful." A month after she started, Andrea (class disadvantaged) received an $8,000 raise; she was not expecting it, was not told why she received it, and was not told if she would receive a raise again. While they were grateful for the extra money, the lack of information surrounding their raise made it difficult for them to know how to receive another.

New hires who did not work at companies that regularly hired large numbers of college students reported having little information about how to be promoted, too. Asked about opportunities for promotion, Andrew (class advantaged) said: "That's something I honestly don't know. Because there's no specific promotion [process]. I'm not sure if I stayed another year if they would have someone else come in and then I would shift over to sales and get commission. There's no really set outline for me, so that is something I honestly don't even know." Owen (class advantaged) also worked for a company without a transparent or standard promotion process, leaving him uncertain about if he could be promoted or how: "I don't know what my path would be and that's something that sticks out, right? That's something that that makes you think. I can't formulate a good path where I am now. I mean, there certainly are promotional capabilities. The people that have been at the company prior to me joining it, they've risen up the ranks. But it's so entrepreneurial. Certain parts of the company grow or there's a new part of the business added. You don't know until you're on the fly and something happens. So it's just up in the air in terms of where you would land." Without knowing the possibilities for promotion, let alone how to achieve them, Owen did not know if it was best for him to stay with his company or leave.

Keri (class disadvantaged) also said that it was hard to plan her future trajectory. Like Owen, she thought there was not a standard promotional process, but one subject to change as the company changed: "[The company where I work] is in the process of acquiring one of our competitors. So I'm thinking maybe there's something with that I can do. And the timeline for the position I'm in right now is two years because of the way the benefits work. But if they can offer more, I'm thinking maybe—I don't really know. It's hard to plan. They have a lot going on."

Similarly, Ben (class disadvantaged) said that the promotional process was opaque, making it difficult for him to know how to plan his future. He worked as an independent contractor for a large technology company. He was originally told that after working for a short time as an independent contractor, he would be promoted to a full-time employee and receive benefits and higher pay. However, he was given little information about the process: "I don't understand many things about the conversion process, and nobody seems to have answers. I was told back in December, January that very soon we were going to be converted, and that hasn't happened yet. I don't know many things about it. I've asked multiple people. I'm just trying to understand what the holdup is, and most of them don't know themselves. It's all pending on people above them it seems. So the big thing that's driving it is in October, the Affordable Care Act, some revision of that is cutting the amount of time that contractors can work to eighteen months, so that's what's driving their decision to convert some people and let some people go. I'd love to have a more specific answer for you [about the promotional process], but I don't know myself."

Class-Neutral Criteria

Employers not only used class-neutral criteria to hire students but also to evaluate them once they were employed. I asked hiring agents what made new hires stand out after a year on the job—both in negative and positive ways. The negative answers were simple: bad hires were those with a low level of professionalism or skill.

Employer 13 (government, auditors) gave an example of lacking professionalism, which had little to do with class for college graduates who had been socialized by a business school: "Just punctuality, are they coming to work on time?[7] Are they professionally dressed? Are they remembering to attend whatever meeting they're supposed to be at?" Employer 32 (transportation, management) said the same. Those she regretted hiring were employees who did not do the basics: "Coming to work on time and being ready to work for the day. Setting goals and working hard." Employer 22 (healthcare, many business roles) also noticed the same mistakes: "They're not showing up for meetings, not responding to calendar invites, just not being professional with attire and language."[8]

Employers also examined whether new hires completed their tasks.

Employer 19 (technology, many business roles) said she evaluated: "Have you produced something yet? And if not, then why not?" Employer 28 (technology, procurement) also examined whether new hires completed their work well, asking: "What is their work product like?" Employer 21 (energy, many business roles) said that new hires made mistakes when "they are not meeting all of the goals of the project—not only meeting, but exceeding those goals."

Employers also wanted new hires who took initiative. Employer 18 (e-commerce, sales) shared that good hires "have a bias for action. People that don't just sit there and wait for you to tell them what to do." Employer 25 (research, sales) raised the same theme: "I'd say the individuals that we find to be most successful are the individuals that are self-motivated and take initiative and are able to drive their own learning." Employer 6 (healthcare, consultants) agreed: "Are they self-sufficient? Are they able to work independently and become a problem solver? Versus them just wanting to sit on their hands and be given the answers to everything?"

Some of these criteria were class neutral because students of all classes could meet them. They could all show up on time and work to meet goals. With training from the CoB, they knew what counted as professional attire, and they received paychecks that allowed them to buy it. However, employers' desire for workers who took initiative was different. This criterion was also class neutral because both groups struggled to meet it.

It was no wonder that recent graduates found it challenging to take initiative in the "right" ways. They had to balance taking initiative with fitting into their company's hierarchy. They had little experience doing this. They had spent much of their lives in school, where there is a clear hierarchy with teachers and professors who had more power than students. In making a switch into organizations with more complicated hierarchies, new hires were not clear how to proceed.

Although class-advantaged and class-disadvantaged students both reported having difficulty showing the right kind of initiative, they struggled in different ways. Reflecting on their first year at work, class-advantaged students often thought that they took too much initiative—disregarding company hierarchies when they did.[9] Claire (class advantaged) relayed her mistake:

> I reached out to their boss and he wasn't responding, and I had a really good relationship with his boss's boss. And so I reached out to him and I said, "Hi, could you reach out to so-and-so and see if you could get me this report?" And apparently that wasn't a good thing to do, going up three levels. I didn't realize that at the time.

Likewise, John (class advantaged) did not initially recognize that he needed to consider the company's hierarchy. He reflected on what happened during his first few weeks at work: "There was a [training] class that I was in that I thought was really stupid, and I didn't want to be in it. I thought I could learn better through another route, so I sent an email to the director." The director stormed into the class, believing that something was seriously awry if a new hire was emailing her. Once it was clear that nothing was amiss, the director communicated that John had wasted her time and that he needed to follow the standard training procedure. John believed he lost the director's respect.

Similarly, Cody (class advantaged) initially did not consider his company's hierarchy when interacting with his colleagues. He learned the hard way that he needed to take this into account. He recalled: "I realized you have to know your position within the company. You can't really challenge people. And, like I said, you have to learn to bite your tongue." Nathan (class advantaged) also learned that he could not take as much initiative as he originally thought in a hierarchical setting: "I'm not going to be throwing out any company-changing ideas. . . . I realized that this is not a position [where] I change the world. This is a position that I learn and grow [in], get some good experience, and show that."

Class-disadvantaged students also struggled to take initiative in a hierarchical setting. To them, the problem was different: they had been overly deferential and needed to make more decisions on their own.[10] For instance, Sean (class disadvantaged) said he learned to take charge more: "[My mentor said] if I act like my time is just as important as theirs, then that's how they're going to feel about it. That was really big for me because I felt like I was being a nuisance to people I needed to work with. But I now feel that that is not the case, and so I have no problem calling 18,000 people a day and being like, 'Please help me right now.'"

Likewise, Andrea (class disadvantaged) learned to take more initiative around experienced colleagues:

I didn't like bothering people and I didn't like asking questions too much. I just didn't like to talk unnecessarily. Now, I open my mouth a bit more, 'cause communication is a key part. It's not that I didn't want to communicate but being new you don't want to ask a whole bunch of questions to people who you know are busy. They're directors, they're not just people who are just working. They have to be on it 24/7.

Thomas (class disadvantaged) learned to take charge in a hierarchical setting more, too.

I came in not knowing what to do and now I'm a little more assertive. When I need something I say, "This is what I need to be successful, and here's when I need it" and calling it out. If you say you are going to do this thing and you don't do it, pulling them aside and saying, "Hey, this is something I need done by this time."

Thus, some of employers' criteria for good hires were class neutral in that students of all classes struggled to meet it. They just struggled to meet it for different reasons.

Conclusion

At the end of their first year in the professional workforce, students from different class origins felt the impact of a luckocracy. Some were lucky to receive high pay, promotions, or opportunities to build their skills. Others were unlucky not to have any of these. As they moved on in their careers, luck would continue to matter. They still might not know how to earn more within their firm or with different companies, and, for the time being, employers still judged them in class-neutral ways. As long as they remained in a luckocracy, students from different class origins would continue to earn similar amounts. Like Chona, they were still playing a game in which luck, not class origin, determined the prizes each person won.[11]

Should We Keep America's Best Equalizing System?

Class-advantaged children tend to grow up with parents who have more resources than the parents of class-disadvantaged children. With more money and education, their parents teach them more words and other academic skills,[1] enroll them in more enriching activities,[2] provide them with more nutritious meals,[3] and are better able to shield them from traumatic events.[4] These inequalities follow children into school, where the cognitive scores of class-advantaged kindergarteners eclipse those of class-disadvantaged students.[5] Schools maintain these inequalities,[6] and they later explode: just one in five children of parents with high school degrees at most earn a bachelor's degree while four in five children of two college-educated parents do.[7] And even students from different classes who matriculate at the same four-year college experience life unequally. Given their greater resources and opportunities, class-advantaged students talk to more professionals, have higher GPAs, engage in more high-status cultural activities, and incur less student debt.[8]

Each of these forms of class inequality are well known, and many policy makers, philanthropists, and institutions have tried to end them. Indeed, combining public and private efforts, the nation has spent billions of dollars on these issues.[9] But despite noble efforts, deep pockets, and many attempts, we still live in two Americas, with wide inequalities on each of these measures.

Yet, without intent, investment, or recognition, a silent system has been creating a form of class equality. This system is a luckocracy, which distributes earnings by luck and without regard to college graduates' class origins. And it's likely that this system is all around us, operating not only for students who graduate from the same university but any non-elite university, and operating not only in the mid-tier business labor market but in other mid-tier labor markets with opaque earnings, hidden hiring criteria, and little incentive to care about classed tastes—ones such as the mid-tier healthcare, technology, science, and engineering labor markets. Importantly, the luckocracy also structures workers' opportunities for many years, equalizing earnings for graduates from different classes even after they enter the professional labor force.

What are we to make of this newly recognized system? First, we can admire its awe-inducing feat, erasing a major form of inequality between some class-advantaged and class-disadvantaged college graduates. But it's hardly a flawless system, and so we must weigh its advantages against its disadvantages and compare them to those in other opportunity structures. With this information, the question becomes: Should we keep America's best equalizing system?

The Luckocracy's Advantages

The luckocracy has advantages and disadvantages, and some of its elements are advantages in one light and disadvantages in another. Let's review the advantages first.

IT'S EFFECTIVE

As a nation, we've tried many ways of erasing inequality, even among narrow groups of students. To address the class achievement gap that concretizes before children begin kindergarten,[10] we've tried giving some class-disadvantaged families access to free preschool, books, food, healthcare, and parenting classes. At most, these programs have held the class achievement gap steady against threats to widen it; they have not erased the gap.[11] To address class gaps in college attendance among students who graduate from high school, we've tried college promise programs that offer free tuition to students in some school districts, guaranteed free tuition for disadvantaged students admitted to some colleges and universities, made financial aid easier to access, and mailed messages that encourage students to apply.[12] Still, class-disadvantaged students attend college at lower rates than class-advantaged students.[13] To address class gaps in college completion among students already attending, universities have texted students reminders about financial aid deadlines; offered tutoring, mentoring, and leadership programs; established emergency grant funding; and formed first-generation and low-income student groups. Still, class gaps in college completion persist.[14]

The luckocracy succeeds where other tactics have failed. It is one of the few systems that creates a form of equality, not only reducing but erasing earnings inequality among a subset of class-advantaged and class-disadvantaged students.

It's also clear that the luckocracy is responsible for earnings equalization, not other mechanisms. Earnings equalization doesn't happen because the class-advantaged and class-disadvantaged students who graduate from college—even the same one—are basically the same. Instead, they're different: class-advantaged students have slightly higher GPAs, complete slightly more internships, enter college knowing more about the professional labor force, conduct more informational interviews to learn more, attend more networking events, participate in more high-status activities, and come from families with more money. Earnings equalization also does not occur because hiring agents actively favor class-disadvantaged students or show bias against class-advantaged students. Instead, they use either class-neutral or class-balanced hiring criteria. Earnings equalization also doesn't happen only because employers see most students as interchangeable for another. If wages weren't hidden, class-advantaged students would use their networks to obtain the highest-paid positions. And earnings equalization doesn't occur because class-disadvantaged students favor high-paying roles while class-advantaged students favor low-paying roles or leisurely gap years. Instead, students from each class prefer areas of business that pay similar amounts, typically want to work at big firms, and enter the professional labor force soon after graduating. Contrary to these explanations, earnings equalization happens because of the opportunity structure students enter, a luckocracy that allocates earnings based upon who makes the most fortuitous guesses.

IT'S FREE

The luckocracy requires that employers do not post or reveal their wages, tell applicants their hiring criteria, or use class-biased hiring processes and criteria. None of these cost money.

IT'S SELF-SUSTAINING

The luckocracy is likely to last.

For the luckocracy to continue, employers must hide information about how to get ahead from students of all classes and use class-neutral hiring criteria. If they fail to do either, the luckocracy unravels. But it's in their interest to do both, and so they are likely to sustain their equalizing system.

Luckocracies force luck to matter by suppressing information about where students can get ahead, requiring all students to guess. This aspect of the luckocracy is secure as employers pay employees more when they post wages than when they don't.[15] Absent a stronger legal push for wage posting than currently exists, they have little incentive to alter a system that's working for them.[16]

Luckocracies also make luck matter by hiding varied hiring criteria, forcing students to guess how to get ahead. This aspect of the luckocracy also benefits employers, ensuring its longevity. If hiring teams can avoid announcing their hiring criteria in advance and coming to an agreement about how to hire, they can avoid long meetings, sidestep potentially ugly conflicts, and flexibly adapt to each new pool of candidates. Companies also compete with each other, so it's not in their interest to coordinate their hiring. It's also potentially illegal.

The varied, contradictory, and non-systematic ways that employers hire is also built into the process and therefore likely to be sustained.

Using the garbage can model of decision-making, management scientists find that workers often make decisions under conditions of "organized anarchy":[17] times when problems and processes are not clearly defined, there are personnel changes, and time and attention are constrained. Under these conditions, decision makers discover their preferences while making decisions, satisfice by selecting good-enough solutions, and take action in inconsistent and irrational ways.[18] These conditions characterize the hiring process. Hiring agents post job ads without knowing what type of person they want or what hiring processes to use, rotate on and off hiring teams, and hire while distracted by the demands of their usual work. Because hiring agents often make decisions under conditions that produce inconsistent, contradictory, and satisficing choices, we can expect the luckocracy to continue. Hiring criteria will be hidden because hiring agents cannot articulate it in advance, and a degree of class neutrality will be enforced as hiring agents use lower-than-needed hiring bars.

Luckocracies allow luck to matter equally for people from different classes by relying on class-neutral criteria. In the mid-tier business market, employers keep their processes class neutral by using a low bar of employability and ignoring how far above the bar students rise, disregarding where students gain their skills, defining traits like "polish" and "fit" in ways that students from all classes can meet, and turning a blind eye to status signals. These preferences align with employers' mission of hiring people who can competently complete a job. Whether a job seeker has a 4.0 GPA rather than a 3.5, has interned for two summers rather than one, led a shift at McDonald's or at a country club, traveled to Europe, or knows how to sail has little to do with whether they can properly fill in a spreadsheet, calculate a profit margin, sell a product, or explain the company's healthcare benefits to employees. Why change their hiring criteria to be less relevant to the job?

Other processes limit students' access to information and enforce class neutrality, and they are likely to endure for the same reasons. Employers distribute job offers to interns soon after the summer ends and tell students they must accept or reject their offers quickly, before other companies have time to hire them. They distribute job offers to non-interns later, when more companies are hiring, and usually give students one day to two weeks to decide whether to accept the position. These practices limit students' ability to learn what other jobs pay and enforce class neutrality by blocking leverage that class-advantaged students are more likely to use. They are likely to remain in place as they increase the odds that students accept employers' first offer and do so without having another job offer to negotiate for higher pay. Again, these processes are likely to persist because they are in employers' interests.

Not only is the luckocracy stable because it meets employers' needs, but also because it blocks class-advantaged students' parents from advantaging their children. These parents can obtain internships for their children, but internships created as favors often come with little work and few future employment opportunities. This makes it necessary for students to seek new employers later and hard for them to announce their accomplishments—if they even talk to employers who care. Class-advantaged students' parents help their children revise their résumés and prepare for interviews, but they cannot know what each hiring agent looks for in a résumé, what interview questions they will ask, or how they will evaluate students' answers. Class-advantaged students' parents can land their children interviews, but they cannot prepare their child to meet specific hiring agents' expectations. Some advantaged parents can convince employers to hire their child directly or do so themselves, but these parents cannot know if the job pays well or poorly compared to similar jobs at different firms. So these parents risk easing their children into low-paying positions, not giving them an advantage at all.

The luckocracy is also stable because it doesn't rely on goodwill. Goodwill is hard to sustain, not always easy to act upon, difficult to generate when it's lacking, and competes with other causes even when it's there. But the luckocracy does not require that employers care about class equality. Earnings equalization by class origin happens in the business sector, whose reputation rests upon helping people become or stay rich, not advancing equality. And while some hiring agents told me about their projects to tackle racial or gender equality, none mentioned that they tried for equality by class origin. But in a luckocracy, this doesn't matter because the system doesn't run on goodwill. Employers can look out for themselves, look askance on equality, and equalize earnings by class origin anyway.

Luck slinks into the hiring process beyond the ways the luckocracy generates itself, reinforcing the role that luck plays in allocating earnings. Luck shapes students' outcomes since some employers post job ads at unpredictable times, so that students who don't check the job boards every day miss some openings while candidates already matched to other positions are unlikely to pursue new job leads. Employers hire for different numbers of positions each year, and each year the applicant pool changes size, so some students luck into little competition while others face much more.[19] Employers' initially chosen applicants also sometimes pull out and existing employees sometimes unexpectedly leave, allowing others to luck into their spot.[20] Sometimes firms change locations, and students luck out that a high-paying employer for a particular position is now eager to hire students from their school.[21] And luck slinks in on the students' side as well. Students may receive good or bad news right before a job interview; students who just received an unexpected high grade may show a pep in their step while those who just experienced a breakup, car accident, health issue, or death in the family may struggle to keep it together. These and other forms of luck slide into the process when students apply to their first jobs and their next ones, too, strengthening the ways that chance allocates outcomes.[22]

Finally, the luckocracy is likely to keep equalizing earnings because of the actions of employers in elite labor markets. These employers define themselves as elite partly by hiring graduates from elite universities.[23] By excluding even advantaged students from non-elite universities, they force most to stay in the luckocracy—in a system that equalizes earnings.

IT DOESN'T REQUIRE CULTURAL ASSIMILATION

Some programs that try to equalize outcomes for students from unequal classes focus on changing the tastes, styles, and approaches taken by the class disadvantaged. These programs rest on one of two assumptions: that since the class advantaged are succeeding, they must be doing something worth emulating or that gatekeepers value the ways class-advantaged people do things so it's a necessary evil to emulate the advantaged.[24] There are several issues with these approaches. Some wrongly identify cultural styles as the primary cause of economic success;[25] some wrongly assume that people can easily mimic people from other classes;[26] others wrongly assume that the tastes, styles, and approaches of the class advantaged are more morally righteous than those of the class disadvantaged;[27] and some fail to acknowledge that the diversity of approaches taken by people of different classes can strengthen workplaces.[28] The luckocracy has the benefit of not demanding that the class disadvantaged assimilate into the upper-middle class, allowing them to remain as they are.

IT LESSENS OTHER INEQUALITIES

The luckocracy equalizes earnings by class origin, but it does not equalize earnings by race or gender. This is because a luckocracy is predicated on gatekeepers using class-neutral criteria, not race- or gender-neutral criteria, and because there are race and gender differences in the types of jobs students want and what they pay.[29] Still, if some elements of the luckocracy vanished, race and gender inequality would be worse.

The luckocracy hides information about where and how to get ahead from everyone, and that's as true by race and gender as it is by class. White people tend to have more ties to college-educated professionals than people of color,[30] and men tend to have more ties to professionals and to benefit from them more than women.[31] If everyone could know how much each job paid, white people and men would use their networks to obtain the highest-paying positions—and this would work in fields with substantial wage variation for similar work at different organizations. So while the luckocracy doesn't stop hiring agents from discriminating or using race- and gender-biased hiring criteria, it does block some channels that could make race and gender inequality worse.

IT ENCOURAGES BALANCE AND COMMUNITY

In luckocracies, gatekeepers look for good-enough candidates. They communicate this to students indirectly. They tell students what not to do, and the bar is so low that nearly all students can pass it: they should not chew gum, swear, wear ripped clothes, demean others, or have an email handle that refers to alcohol or sex. Some quip that they hire on what their mothers should have taught them—basic social skills—and not any skills specific to the job. And, in a luckocracy, there's no guarantee that students with more skills will receive more money. By dint of bad luck, they may apply to and receive only positions that pay little. This dampens students' incentive to gain as many skills as they can.

The luckocracy then encourages students to become good enough, not to acquire as many skills as possible. This system has advantages. Students don't need to center their lives around preparing for work; they can live a balanced life full of friends, family, and leisure while still meeting employers' hiring bars. Without trying to be the best workers, they have no reason to view peers as competitors and can instead cooperate with them as companions. The class neutrality of the system also gives class-advantaged students no extra reason to distinguish themselves from class-disadvantaged students. Everyone can relax together.

IT ENCOURAGES COLLECTIVE ACTION

Learning they are in, may be entering, or know others in a luckocracy may spur action to raise working conditions for all. If individuals foresee entering a luckocracy, they foresee that they may be unlucky; it becomes in their interest to work on behalf of the collective good to ensure that all jobs meet standards they'd accept.[32] They might advocate for mechanisms that allow for this, such as more workers' voices on company boards or more unionization, or for particular outcomes, such as guaranteed maternity and paternity leave or other high-quality benefits. If Americans realize how much luck matters for college graduates' earnings, they may also start to question how much luck matters in other aspects of their lives too. They may question what we owe other unlucky groups: those born to poor parents, with health issues, or in places that provide few opportunities.

If people realize their earnings reflect their luck, feelings that some people deserve high pay and others deserve low pay fade away. Smugness at one's large paycheck is undermined when it's known that wages are allocated by luck, and shame at earning little becomes nonsensical when one acknowledges that they just lost a game of chance. The luckocracy may help us stop seeing ourselves and others as deserving or undeserving more broadly, and to work toward creating a tax code, safety net, justice system, and educational system that are fair to the lucky and the unlucky alike.[33]

In sum, the luckocracy has several notable advantages. It's our only system that equalizes an important outcome among people from unequal class origins. It's free, self-sustaining, and doesn't call for cultural assimilation. It also lessens inequality by race and gender and allows for cooperation, community, and balance, all while encouraging collective action to ensure that the unlucky aren't too badly off.

The Disadvantages

The luckocracy has shortcomings too.

The luckocracy comes with two types of disadvantages: those that are inherent to the equalizing process and those that are not. Change the former and we no longer get earnings equality. Change the latter and we get a better equalizing system.

INHERENT DISADVANTAGES

The luckocracy equalizes earnings through hidden information and class neutrality. Each of these creates their own problems.

Hidden Information Limits Job Seekers' Control

In a luckocracy, job seekers lack the information they need to control their earnings and choose their work. Mostly this is because wages and hiring criteria are hidden; sometimes it's because employers are misleading or dishonest. Either way, without detailed and accurate information, some job seekers end up in positions and with pay they would not have taken had they known more. This downside is profound; many job seekers crave more control over their careers. And because opacity helps create earnings equality, we cannot remove it and expect earnings equality to continue.

Hidden Information Creates Market Failures

The luckocracy limits workers' information about jobs. Some then select into jobs that are misaligned with their interests and skills. This is a form of a market failure since it creates inefficiencies and problems. Mismatches between workers and jobs can decrease productivity, increase turnover, produce worker alienation, and lower economic growth.[34]

Of course, some employers may see these market failures as offset by the benefits the same system produces. As mentioned above, limiting the information students receive allows employers to avoid internal conversations and potential disputes, remain flexible in who and how they hire, and pay workers less. Seemingly, employers have decided that this trade-off is worthwhile. Job seekers are likely to feel differently.

Hidden Information and Employer Power Limits Job Seekers' Pay

The luckocracy is built upon a power imbalance between employers and job seekers, one that limits workers' pay. Many employers hide wages, issue exploding offers (ones they retract if not accepted in a short time period), and refuse to negotiate. These practices depress workers' wages by limiting competition, constraining workers' ability to gain leverage, and increasing the chance that workers accept low-paying positions. Earnings equality by class origin then comes at the cost of lowering both class-advantaged and class-disadvantaged students' wages.

This disadvantage may not be as bad as it first seems. At age twenty-two, most graduates who enter luckocracies find jobs that do not require long hours or great skill, and do not risk their health or break their backs with physical labor. They still get paid more than the median American worker, including those who have been in the workforce for much longer. They also get paid more than 99% of adults worldwide.[35] Employers' power relative to employees also depresses college-educated workers' wages, which in turn depresses wage inequality between college-educated and non-college-educated workers. The gap between college-educated and non-college-educated workers' wages is already large.[36] Thus, while some may see practices that limit college-educated workers' relatively high wages as problematic, it may also spare us from the social and political fallout of allowing a large gap to grow even larger.[37]

The Low Skills Bar Disincentivizes Hard Work and Skill Development

The luckocracy uses a low bar for employment, ensuring that those with varied levels of resources can meet it. But a low bar does not incentivize hard work and skill development. And our society benefits from hard workers who are highly skilled.

For mid-tier business jobs, and possibly other mid-tier jobs as well, this disadvantage is also not as compelling as it may seem. In this labor market, jobs include data entry, processing accounts payable and accounts receivable, monitoring payroll, checking the performance of an ad campaign, creating pivot tables, researching investments, managing projects, talking to clients, organizing events, and selling products. Recent graduates completed these tasks without devoting themselves to work, and some had little work to do at all. For these jobs, there was no need to incentivize hard work and high skills. But for other jobs and for the same workers' future jobs, these incentives can be costly.

It Cannot Serve as a Model for Equalizing Other Outcomes

Luckocracies cannot exist outside of markets as they are predicated upon what happens in one. Thus, their logic doesn't reveal how to reduce inequalities in non-market spheres. Knowing how to create a luckocracy does not tell us how to address the class achievement gap, since this gap is created by the differential investments that parents make when acting outside of a market. It cannot tell us how to solve the class wealth gap, as many wealth transfers occur between parents and children, outside of a market.

Luckocracies won't work in all markets, either. To form a luckocracy, markets must be large enough so that individuals cannot learn about each opportunity, leaving people from all classes blind to how each opportunity compares to others. Local education markets will never be luckocracies because there are a small number of schools in each location, allowing parents to learn about each. Luckocracies also use class-neutral selection criteria, so any market in which opportunity seekers trade money for rewards cannot be a luckocracy. The higher education, housing, healthcare, and consumer markets cannot act as luckocracies since they include the exchange of money for services and products. Only labor markets allow for luckocracies, and we cannot learn from luckocracies in labor markets how to create equality in situations outside of them.

NON-INHERENT DISADVANTAGES

The luckocracy equalizes earnings through hidden information and class neutrality. Any disadvantages unrelated to these factors are not inherent to luckocracies' equalizing mechanisms. They can be changed while still producing earnings equality.

The Luckocracy Has a Limited Reach

Not only does the luckocracy not equalize a wide array of outcomes, but it does not reach as many people as it could. While the luckocracy equalizes earnings for a large share of the college-educated population, it excludes most people without a bachelor's degree. Most students from disadvantaged backgrounds do not receive bachelor's degrees,[38] limiting the luckocracy's equalizing potential.

It Creates the Need for an Expensive Degree

As it currently operates, the luckocracy mostly admits people with bachelor's degrees. This tendency is not based on strong evidence that students need to graduate from college to meet mid-tier employers' skills bar. To the contrary, some mid-tier business employers tell students that they do not hire on the skills they learn in the college classroom.

Instead, mid-tier business employers emphasize skills they believe students learn in their extracurricular and informal activities: leadership, teamwork, and communication. But even if these are the places where students learn these skills, there is little evidence that it takes four years in college to acquire them. Many college students participate in extracurricular activities for much of their lives;[39] they may already have these skills. Selective colleges admit students partly based on their extracurricular activities;[40] if students learn skills through these activities, they are likely to have them before entering college.

And given that hiring agents also tell professors and undergraduate business school administrators that they do not hire based upon classroom learning, there is little reason for undergraduate business schools to demand that their students learn many skills either. Indeed, several students told me that they did not apply to jobs that required cover letters because they could not write a few paragraphs well, and several students bragged about their ability to complete a VLOOKUP in Excel—a technique they could learn by watching a short YouTube video. Moreover, other research on undergraduate education confirms that business students learn less than students in other majors.[41] Of course, this is not to suggest that business students learn nothing in college—some do. They just are not incentivized to maximize the amount they learn or to prioritize learning difficult skills.

Thus, mid-tier business employers require undergraduate business students to have a bachelor's degree but not the skills often associated with a bachelor's degree. This creates a system in which a college degree is little more than an expensive piece of paper, disadvantaged students who cannot afford college are excluded, and other students are stripped of tens of thousands of dollars to complete a degree unnecessary for the type of work they will later do.[42] It also delegitimizes a college education in some people's minds, leaving some to wonder why going to college is important. Additionally damaging, the practice of only hiring college graduates allows those without college degrees to believe that graduates are hired for their specialized skills when instead they are hired for meeting the same standards as low-wage workers: possessing soft skills, the ability to complete work that many can do, and meeting employers' idiosyncratic preferences.[43]

It Includes Dishonesty

The luckocracy hides information from students from all classes, but in its current iteration, it also includes employers who give dishonest and misleading information. This leaves some students taking jobs that they believe pay one amount and require certain tasks to only later discover that they have been deceived. Though this is currently part of the luckocracy, it doesn't need to be.

Thus, the luckocracy has many advantages but also many disadvantages, some of which are inherent to its equalizing process and some of which can be fixed. But to know if we should keep a luckocracy, we need to consider more than its advantages and disadvantages. We need to know the advantages and disadvantages of systems that would replace it—ones that equalize earnings and ones that do not.

The Alternatives

MERITOCRACIES

As table 3 shows, there is another potentially equalizing opportunity structure: a meritocracy, as it operates in theory. This system uses class-neutral selection criteria and gives opportunity seekers of all classes high levels of information about where and how to get ahead.

In theory, meritocracies equalize earnings for people from different class backgrounds, giving everyone the information they need to strategize about how to get ahead. And since meritocracies use class-neutral criteria, they allow equal opportunities for those strategies to pay off. However, in practice, this is not what happens. In practice, as table 3 indicates, meritocracies are weak class-reproduction systems.

A meritocracy fails to live up to its equalizing potential for two reasons. First, meritocracies never offer true class neutrality. Meritocracies do not reward people who pass a low bar; they reward those who are the best of the best or those who meet a high bar. And it often takes money,

TABLE 3: Opportunity Structures

		INFORMATION ABOUT HOW TO GET AHEAD	
		Equally Available by Class	*Unequally Available by Class*
GATEKEEPERS' SELECTION PROCESSES AND CRITERIA	*Class Neutral*	No Class Reproduction Low Levels of Information: *Luckocracy* High Levels of Information: *Meritocracy, in theory*	Weak Class Reproduction
	Class Biased	Weak Class Reproduction High Levels of Information: *Meritocracy, in practice*	Strong Class Reproduction

time, and mentorship to become the best of the best or to reach a high bar. Who has the most money, time, and mentorship? The class advantaged.

Second, meritocracies do not block class-advantaged job seekers from using their other resources to outearn the class disadvantaged. Class-advantaged students have more ties to professionals.[44] They also tend to grow up around more professionals, feel more comfortable around them, and then reach out to more professionals they haven't yet met.[45] In a luckocracy where they do not know which jobs pay the most, the help they receive from their connections just as often leads them into low-paying jobs as high-paying ones. But in a meritocracy where everyone knows which jobs pay the most, the advantaged would use their greater networks to target and receive more highly paid positions.

Thus, in practice, a meritocracy produces inequality rather than equality. But to know whether we want to replace the luckocracy with a meritocracy, we need to consider more than its equalizing potential. Doing so, it becomes apparent that the meritocracy's advantages are the opposite of the luckocracy's disadvantages. Whereas the luckocracy delivers equality via opacity, the meritocracy creates inequality through transparency. And whereas the luckocracy uses a class-neutral low skills bar, the meritocracy uses a class-biased high skills bar. Transparency and a high skills bar do not produce equality, but they do offer what a luckocracy does not: control over the job search and incentives to work harder to build more skills.

But meritocracies come with their own downsides—ones that luckocracies lack. They promote a false idea: that everyone has the same opportunities to show merit, and so it is the most skilled and strategic who get ahead.[46] Some then falsely assume that their place in the earnings distribution is due to their own talents and savvy, not to a system that is biased toward those born with class advantage.[47]

Meritocracies also promote the false belief that we can measure merit. But as we've seen, hiring agents' views of merit are varied and contradictory, undermining the idea that they can objectively identify the best candidate for any job.[48] A meritocracy also assumes that only merit is considered in the selection processes, but this isn't true. Not only are high skills bars easier to meet for the class advantaged, but other biases enter the process as well. For instance, one study finds that white applicants receive 145% more job offers than minority applicants who use the same résumé and who interact with employers in similar ways.[49]

The idea of hiring the most meritorious candidate comes with its own downsides. Those who try to become the "best of the best" enter a rat race. Each person is incentivized to revolve their life around work and to push relationships, community, and leisure aside, even to the point that some forget how to play.[50] The competition to be the best never stops, instead requiring the temporary winners to keep looking over their shoulder, fearfully checking if someone might knock them out of their spot. It also encourages everyone to view others as competitors rather than allies united in pursuit of collective goals. The "winners" gain status and money but sacrifice so much else. Many become isolated, anxious, one-dimensional people, unable to fully enjoy their spoils.[51]

Moreover, it's not clear that these costs are worthwhile. In entry-level mid-tier business jobs, there is no need to hire the "best of the best" or even to use a high skills bar. Indeed, as the jobs can be conducted by many people, it would waste company resources to seek the best of the best. Overqualified workers may also feel disenchanted if their skill set outstrips the tasks they are asked to perform, and this contributes to low morale.[52] While some may value incentivizing hard work and skill development for their own sake or for their unknown future use, they must also note that in some labor markets, seeking the best or imposing high skills bars can be unneeded or even detrimental.

Replacing a luckocracy with a meritocracy would come with costs and benefits. It creates earnings inequality rather than earnings equality. It corrects some of the luckocracy's flaws while producing its own.

OTHER WEAK CLASS-REPRODUCTION SYSTEMS

Another option is to replace the luckocracy with other types of weak class-reproduction systems.

One type combines class-biased selection processes with low levels of information about how to get ahead—ones that, like real-world meritocracies, fit in the bottom left corner of table 3. The class bias can be a high bar for employability, one that the class advantaged have more resources to meet. The strengths and weaknesses of the high bar in a low-information system are the same as in a meritocracy: it incentivizes hard work while creating a rat race, and in a mid-tier market, it's unclear that a high skills bar is needed to complete the work. But in a low-information system, job seekers would know that standards are high but not what they entail or which jobs pay the most for meeting them. This creates inefficiencies as job seekers invest in skills that may not be needed, though some also become more well-rounded. It also still strips workers of control; they cannot know where to apply to meet their monetary goals or how to use their resources to invest in rewarded skills. At the same time, it is a weaker class-reproduction system than a meritocracy. With little information, some class-advantaged students who meet high bars will opt into companies that pay little for their skills, and some class-disadvantaged students who do not meet the high bars will luck into positions that pay well without requiring such high standards. And so this system comes with its own trade-offs, repeating some of the luckocracy's and meritocracy's flaws while creating less earnings equality than the former and more than the latter.

There is a second type of class-biased criteria these systems could deploy: hiring based on classed signals that are unrelated to completing job tasks. This includes hiring based upon status symbols and networks, or paying more to those who negotiate more aggressively or effectively. There is little good reason to use these class biases. Some suggest that hiring people with the same tastes and experiences makes work more fun or produces smoother interactions,[53] but trading equality for collegiality is dubious, and workers can find ways to connect with their coworkers who did not grow up like them.[54] Hiring based on networks is also efficient during the hiring process but inefficient if it does not result in hiring good workers. Paying more to those who negotiate better—not necessarily to those who work better—has clear downsides as well. Since this system introduces class biases that do not serve a broader purpose, it is not a strong contender to replace a luckocracy.

There is also another type of weak class-reproduction system—one shown in the top right cell of table 3 and that is created when class-neutral hiring criteria is combined with allowing class-advantaged students more information about how to get ahead. This type of system would exist if information about where or how to get ahead was available only through networks or by paying for it. This system would allow more class-advantaged students greater control of their work lives. But many class-disadvantaged students would still lack control of their outcomes, and with less information they would typically earn less than their class-advantaged counterparts. Colleges would also lose some of their legitimacy as they could no longer claim to be "the great equalizer," even if it's luckocracies that deserve that title more. And so these types of weak class-reproduction systems do not resolve the luckocracy's problems and come with their own. There is little reason to replace the luckocracy with them.

QUOTAS

It is not only the structure of labor markets that can equalize earnings; some policies have this potential too. One such policy is a quota system. In quota systems, employers reserve slots for members of certain groups, such as the class disadvantaged. There is precedent for such a system. In India, a large number of public jobs are reserved for what they call "backwards" classes.[55]

Of course, the downsides of this approach are obvious and many. In the United States, quota systems are often struck down by courts and have little public support.[56] A class-origin quota system would produce conflict: no matter how the government defined disadvantaged class origins, people who benefit from a different definition would fight to include themselves. Others would argue that coming from a disadvantaged class background isn't the only hardship in life, and so some would advocate for quotas based upon other statuses—creating fights over which quotas are most deserved. Others would lie about their class origin, claiming to be more disadvantaged than they are, thereby undermining quotas' ability to create equal outcomes. Tensions between the classes would flare as some of the advantaged would resent the disadvantaged for being handed what the advantaged believe they earned. Given this, it's possible that not all members of advantaged groups would follow the law and fulfill the quotas. Quotas would then create limited progress on earnings equality while also creating many problems.[57] They are not a viable candidate for replacing luckocracies.

EQUAL PAY FOR EQUAL WORK ACROSS COMPANIES

Another policy that creates earnings equality is ensuring that workers who do the same jobs at different companies earn the same amount. This is effectively what aspects of the public sector do. For instance, there is little wage variation among public school teachers who work at different schools in the same location.[58] With little wage variation, there is also little wage inequality by class background.[59]

However, this "fix" also has several disadvantages. It is feasible in the public sector, where there is centralized control of salaries. But in the private sector, there is no entity in charge of setting pay across firms, and arguably there should not be one either. If rules forced companies to pay workers a specific salary for a specific type of work, they could not raise wages for positions they see as more central to their organization, hike salaries when they need to hire in a hurry, or lower salaries when they face a budget crisis or recession. Not backed by public money, private companies need to be able to adjust their salaries to keep their services running and to stay afloat. So this "solution" will not suffice. It's impractical and undesirable.

JOB LOTTERIES

One can imagine setting up a system in which employers use a lottery to select new employees. Many different versions of lotteries could be created: ones where employers reveal the earnings and job tasks in advance or don't; where all recent college graduates in certain majors and geographic locations are enrolled in each job lottery automatically or students opt in; where students must first past a test to enter certain job lotteries or not; where students must take their first match or not—and, of course, many combinations of these. Some of these systems would equalize earnings for students from unequal class backgrounds, and others would create weak class-reproduction systems. But all would be logistically complicated as multiple firms and thousands of job candidates would need to coordinate. Moreover, many of these systems would not give students more control over their job outcomes, and all would give employers less. It is thus not worth replacing the luckocracy with a lottery that also allocates outcomes by luck.

And so none of the luckocracy's potential replacements are flawless either. We must choose between imperfect options.

How to Keep or Replace the Luckocracy

The luckocracy is America's best *equalizing* system, but not necessarily the best overall system. Deciding which system to keep or install depends upon one's values. Those who value earnings equality over transparency and a high skills bar will want to advocate for improving, maintaining, and expanding the luckocracy. Those who value transparency and a high skills bar over earnings equality will want to replace the luckocracy with an improved meritocracy. Those who are ambivalent will want to consider middle grounds.

LUCKOCRACY ADVOCATES

Some people deeply value earnings equality and will prefer a luckocracy, even with its costs. They can improve the luckocracy and guard against forces that threaten to tear it down.

Improving the Luckocracy

Luckocracies equalize earnings for a narrow group of people and incentivize students to spend tens of thousands of dollars on a degree that is unnecessary for mid-tier work. These issues can be fixed simultaneously: mid-tier employers can hire more students without bachelor's degrees.

Right now, nearly two-thirds of business and human resources leaders do not consider applicants without bachelor's degrees, even when they meet all other qualifications.[60] Many of these employers see college degrees as signaling soft skills,[61] but, as mentioned above, there is little evidence that these degrees are needed. Recall that some hiring agents look for interns who have done anything besides "sit on their fanny" and then hire them as full-time workers, and that some employers announce that they do not hire based on what students learn in the college classroom. Moreover, it's only recently that a college degree became a requirement for many mid-skilled jobs; for years, people capably completed much of the same work without a degree.[62] Employers in the mid-tier business market could then hire more workers without four-year degrees without sacrificing the quality of their workforce. If they did, they'd resolve two of the luckocracy's disadvantages.[63]

The luckocracy could also be improved by making it more honest. The employers who already advertise pay need to explain whether the posted numbers are based upon a salary or an hourly rate and whether they include projected bonuses. Employers who encourage only some higher-paid workers to post their pay on websites such as Glassdoor need to stop this practice. And employers need to be more honest about job tasks. Right now, the norm is to use job titles that may or may not capture what students will do, post job descriptions that are vague, and sell some positions as more attractive than they are. Instead, employers can be transparent about not knowing what new hires will do by using generalized job titles such as "entry-level financial worker"; using information sessions, career center chats, and interviews to tell students they are uncertain what the work entails; and telling them about the potentially boring roles as well as the interesting ones. These changes would not undermine the luckocracy's equalizing power. Information would still be hidden; employers would just be honest that it is.

Maintaining the Luckocracy

There are several threats to the luckocracy. Advocates will need to guard against them.

The first is simple to say but difficult to enact: advocates of the luckocracy should do what they can to maintain a strong economy. In strong economies, most college graduates are employed.[64] The central inequality then relates to earnings, which the luckocracy helps regulate. But when a recession hits, the central inequality changes and relates to being employed versus unemployed. When the unemployment rate increases, the luckocracy unravels.[65] Class-advantaged job seekers can deploy their larger professional networks to find a job. And while their connections cannot know if that job will be high or low paying for positions like it, they certainly know that having a job pays more than not having one. So to keep the luckocracy, we must keep the labor market strong.

The second threat to the luckocracy is an ironic one: gender equality advocates who see wage transparency as the key to closing the gender pay gap. Different advocates propose different levels of transparency, from posting each company's gender wage gap, to posting all salaries for current employees to see, to exposing all salaries to the public.[66] The first poses no threat to the class-equalizing nature of the luckocracy since employers can post the size of their gender wage gap without revealing salary numbers. Forcing all companies to reveal their wages internally would threaten the luckocracy. In this case, information about which companies pay the most for certain jobs would go to those with the most extensive networks—the class advantaged. Wage information that is publicly available equalizes access to this information but also threatens the luckocracy; once everyone knows which positions pay the most, the class neutrality of the labor market vanishes as the class advantaged use their ties to obtain better-paid positions.

Of course, contrary to equal-pay advocates' claims, these processes would likely work the same way regarding gender. On average, men have more professional contacts than women and would use them to monopolize the highest-paying jobs within a certain kind of work.[67] There's also no guarantee that transparency about wages would produce the public outcry needed to end the gender wage gap—a mechanism some advocates posit.[68] The gender pay gap is calculated by comparing the wages of full-time workers who are men to the wages of full-time workers who are women, not comparing men and women in the same jobs.[69] In fact, most of the gender wage gap stems from men and women doing different jobs and for different lengths of time, the latter due to mothers taking more time off work than fathers and childless men.[70] It seems unlikely that revealing wages will lead the public to pressure employers to close the gender pay gap when "equal pay for equal work" doesn't apply. So, counterintuitively, if we want class origins and gender equality, we need to fight for opacity, not transparency.

The last threat to the luckocracy comes from its own potential advocates. Those who push the luckocracy too far may court blowback that undermines the system. They risk doing so if they do not acknowledge that creating class-origins earnings equality is one value among many, and not always the most important one.

For instance, advocates of the luckocracy should not install it in the low-wage labor market. Establishing a luckocracy there would equalize earnings, just like it does in the mid-tier market. But equalizing the wages of a class-disadvantaged majority and a class-advantaged minority is hardly these workers' most pressing concern. In low-wage labor markets, poverty is common among people who work full-time,[71] schedules are often unpredictable,[72] and work can be dangerous.[73] One way to improve these workers' conditions is to increase transparency in wages, work conditions, and needed skills, thereby allowing workers more information and leverage.[74] These tactics will not promote earnings equality by class origin, but they will help raise the wages and work conditions of low-wage workers from each class origin.

Luckocracy advocates should also not oversell the luckocracy in elite labor markets. These markets are not currently luckocracies. Elite firms more often advertise their pay rather than hide it, letting applicants know that it's high even when not revealing the specific salaries associated with each position.[75] They also set a high bar of employability, one that those with the most resources, the class advantaged, are most likely to meet. But as people in elite positions and at elite firms have great power and influence, those hiring them should look for the best candidates they can find—even at the expense of class-origins earnings equality. After all, we want pharmaceutical companies to hire the scientists most likely to invent lifesaving vaccines and medications, ones that help the advantaged and disadvantaged alike. We want the best surgeons and doctors to treat the poor and the rich, even if they disproportionately come from class-advantaged backgrounds. We want the best journalists to break the most news and do so most accurately, educating people from all classes. We want business leaders who are best at fixing the supply chain, marketing green energy, and financing cybersecurity, tasks that benefit people from across the class spectrum. If luckocracy advocates push too hard for class-origins earnings equality at the top, the pushback they receive may blow over into the places for which its best suited.[76]

And so advocates of the luckocracy should work to preserve it where it best fits: in the mid-tier labor market.[77] The luckocracy's downsides are smallest in this sphere. The luckocracy makes it difficult for workers to maximize their pay, but, unlike in low-wage markets, most workers in this market are paid well already. The luckocracy does not incentivize skill building at work, but workers in these jobs have less responsibility, influence, and power than workers in elite markets. Many mid-tier jobs also do not require high levels of skill, and some barely benefit from excellence over competence. For instance, payroll officers need to administer the payroll correctly and punctually, but beyond meeting these standards, there is no excellent way to do the job. In labor markets for such positions, the luckocracy's downsides are least pressing, allowing for equalizing earnings by class origin at the lowest social cost. Thus, the luckocracy's advocates must do what they can to improve and expand the luckocracy—but only in mid-tier labor markets.

Meritocracy Advocates

Those who value transparency and high skills bars over earnings equality will want to replace the luckocracy with a meritocracy—a weak class-reproduction system built upon high levels of equally available information and class-biased selection processes and criteria. Those who take this stance can draw lessons from the luckocracy to make a better meritocracy.

IMPROVING THE MERITOCRACY

The first way to improve the meritocracy is to recognize that it cannot fulfill its promise of allowing equal opportunities for people from all classes. Its high skills bars will most often be met by those with the most resources. Its transparency allows those with more resources to deploy them to win the most remunerative positions. The meritocracy's advocates should be honest about this. In some labor markets, it is defensible to value transparency and high skills bars over earnings equality. Those who want a meritocracy should advocate for it on these grounds rather than promoting the false narrative that it provides equal opportunities for all.

Those who want meritocracies must also find better ways of measuring merit. When hiring agents evaluate candidates for the same jobs using contradictory standards, it's clear that our current ways of measuring merit are failing. When measures of soft skills are inferred from résumé lines and stories told in interviews, rather than being measured directly, it's again clear that we're not measuring merit well. No measure of soft skills will ever capture merit perfectly or objectively, but there is certainly room to improve.

Those who advocate for meritocracies also need to build them, since they do not currently exist in all mid-tier markets. Meritocracies require that job seekers from all classes have equal access to high levels of information about where and how to get ahead. To do so, employers must be required to post wages in job ads, post hiring criteria in as much detail as they can, and pay the advertised wages for a contractual period.[78] None of this would be easy to accomplish. As mentioned above, much of the luckocracy acts in a self-sustaining manner. Moreover, laws that currently require wage posting allow advertising such large wage ranges that the information can be nearly meaningless; they also include loopholes that let some employers keep wages hidden.[79] To overhaul the system so completely and to compel companies to go against their own interests would require more and stricter laws as well as more enforcement power.[80]

To build a meritocracy in some mid-tier markets, employers would also need to raise their skills bar or start hiring the best of the best. Such a move is in keeping with American values, but it may not be in keeping with the needs of each labor market. Thus, meritocracy advocates need to justify raising the skills bar in mid-tier markets. Would mid-tier jobs change to require the use of more skills? Would promotional opportunities be more transparent and quicker, such that new hires would soon use their greater skills? If current jobs are changed to require more skill, who will do the tasks that do not require high levels of skill?

Those advocating for meritocracies must also limit class biases that are unrelated to a high skills bar. This means following the lead of mid-tier employers who use class-neutral criteria. Specifically, it means ignoring signs of prestige that do not relate to doing the job: disregarding which college students attended, where they interned, how they dress, and what leisure activities they do. It means considering if students learned the same skills from work as internships, and if students really learn more from three internships than two. It means limiting the influence of networks: not favoring applicants who know current employees, not distributing information only to the well connected, and testing applicants' skills in ways that cannot be influenced by their connections. It also means only negotiating with the limited number of students employers cannot afford to lose.

As meritocracies imply that people from all classes have equal opportunities, those who push for them should work toward making this true. They can level the playing field by advocating for redistributive taxes, increasing the earned-income tax credit, expanding the social safety net, improving the work conditions and pay of low-wage parents, and, if the luckocracy does not expand, making college more accessible to the disadvantaged.

Middle-Ground Advocates

There are middle grounds between maintaining a luckocracy and replacing it with a meritocracy. Those who are ambivalent will want to consider these options.

One middle-ground option is to create the weak class-reproduction system mentioned above: to combine low levels of information about where and how to get ahead with a raised skills bar. Advocates of this approach would still need to justify why a higher skills bar is necessary, but they may be able to do so for certain mid-tier jobs. How much inequality this creates depends on how high the skills bar is raised and for how many jobs. It could maintain earnings equality if the changes are slight, but would erase it if the changes are substantial.

Another middle-ground option is to keep all aspects of the luckocracy with one exception: exploding offers. In this scenario, job seekers would be given an extended time period to decide whether or not to accept the offer. During this time frame, they could try to collect additional offers. This allows job seekers a few more chances to get lucky—to receive a high-paying position. It also allows for more negotiation. As class-advantaged students have more experience negotiating with authority figures,[81] this change would likely create class inequality in earnings even as it would give job seekers more leverage.

A final middle-ground option is to force employers to post more about what the job entails, even if they do not post wages. This would allow job seekers more control over their careers while allowing earnings equalization to continue. But implementing it would not be easy. It would require employers to wait to advertise jobs until they know more about what new hires will do, make it nearly impossible for employers to hire large pools of students and later assign them to jobs, and it would limit employers' ability to respond to changing business conditions by reassigning new workers to different tasks. It may also raise students' anxiety; if employers wait to hire until they know what each job entails, fewer students will have jobs lined up before graduation. While this is a middle-ground option, like all other options, it is imperfect too.

Let's Make a Deal

In the game show *Let's Make a Deal*, the host, Wayne Brady, asks contestants like Chona if they want to keep their prize or trade it in for a different, unknown prize—one that could be better or could be worse. You now know the prize we've been given: a luckocracy. It's a system that pulls off a remarkable feat: taking people from different classes—and with unequal connections, money, styles, and strategies—and giving them equal earnings. As if that wasn't enough, it's free and stable, allows workers balance, likely reduces racial and gender inequality, decreases inequality between college- and non-college-educated workers, and, once known, incentivizes advocating for the collective good. It can be expanded to include more people and reformed to be more honest. But despite being the best equalizing system we have, it contains significant downsides as well. It lacks transparency, and without that, students from all classes enter into positions they would not have chosen had they known more. It does not incentivize skill building at work, a downside when one considers investing in work, an upside when considering investing in life outside of work, and perhaps an irrelevancy when considering that many entry-level mid-tier jobs do not require high levels of skill. Other systems exist, ones without these downsides but also without the luckocracy's equalizing power. And so now it's up to all of us to decide which systems we want to maintain or create. If Wayne Brady asked if you want to make a deal, would you trade in the luckocracy for a different prize?[82]

Acknowledgments

This book would not be possible without the participation of Southern State University students and the employers who hire them. I am grateful for their willingness to share their experiences with me.

This book would also not be possible without the Southern State University College of Business staff. I cannot name them here and preserve the participants' confidentiality, but I am indebted to the career center staff and diversity officer who helped me recruit participants and who met with me repeatedly. I also found their commitment to their work inspiring. It is amazing what a small group of people can accomplish.

There is one Southern State University professor who was invaluable in helping me identify employers to interview. Another helped me navigate the IRB process at SSU. I am very grateful for their help.

I am also thankful for the research assistance of several people: Foxx Hart, Michelle Lore, Mari Kate Mycek, Michelle Nguyen, and Elizabeth Vincent. Valerie Duke, Lisa Olds, and Lisa Palmano also provided administrative support.

Several people read entire drafts of the book and provided priceless feedback: Elizabeth Armstrong, Linda George, Anna Holleman, Elizabeth Lee, Nico Restrepo Ochoa, Fabian Pfeffer, and Alford Young Jr. Several other people read parts of the book: Hana Brown, Linda Burton, Michaela DeSoucey, Lisa Keister, Ellen Lamont, Monica Liu, Laura López-Sanders, Anna Manzoni, Abi Ocobock, Jenny Stuber, and Jacklyn Wong. I also thank Ashley Harrell for a useful conversation about the certainty bias—a contribution that is now in chapter 5, and Rob Garlick for many, many conversations about the book. I'm also grateful to Elizabeth Branch Dyson for immediately seeing how such a counterintuitive argument could be true, championing the book, and continually pushing me to improve it. The concluding chapter, especially, is much better due to her advice.

The Spencer Foundation (grant #201500087) funded this project. It would not have been possible without their generous support.

Theoretical Contribution

Beyond demonstrating the existence of a luckocracy and its ability to equalize earnings for college graduates from unequal classes, the main theoretical contribution of this book is to expand Pierre Bourdieu's work. To make the book more readable, I did not use Bourdieu's terms in the main text. Here, I show how we can use his concepts to explain what he rarely mentioned: how people born into different social classes enter the same one.

Bourdieu is perhaps the most famous scholar of class reproduction. In his model, there are fields—areas of social life with particular rules about how to get ahead and particular rewards for doing so.[1] Each field rewards different forms of capital, but most reward the cultural, social, and economic capital that are easiest for the privileged to obtain.[2] Class reproduction occurs as the privileged have the "right" capital to be rewarded in the field, the disadvantaged have the "wrong" capital, and only the privileged know how to use their capital in the "right" way.[3]

There is considerable evidence that Bourdieu's analysis of class reproduction is correct.[4] However, his analysis is also limited: it explains the maintenance of class inequality but not the reduction of it. This book shows we can use Bourdieu's concepts to explain how inequality is reduced as individuals raised in different social classes enter the same one. We can do so by focusing on two aspects of fields: gatekeepers' selection criteria and the information that gatekeepers provide about how to get ahead. In regard to the first, Bourdieu assumed that all fields reward at least one form of capital that the advantaged have more of than the disadvantaged.[5] This, however, is not always true. The mid-tier business employees I talked to did not select applicants on their class-related capitals. To compete in their own fields, they needed people who could do the work, not people who displayed classed signals. They then provided an equal playing field for students with unequal levels of cultural, social, and economic capital.

Second, Bourdieu emphasized that fields vary in the rules of the game and their rewards,[6] but he did not emphasize that fields also vary in the amount of information they provide about their rules and rewards. This was a critical oversight. Capital is only effective if it can be used to gain desired ends. If individuals with high levels of capital do not know how rewards are distributed or where rewards are, they cannot acquire the "right" capital or deploy it to gain the largest rewards.[7]

Of course, not all fields that disperse low but even levels of information about how to get ahead advance equality. For low-information systems to matter, there must be variation in the hidden factors. Without variation in the rewards, individuals' guesses about where to apply would be irrelevant. And without variation in the selection criteria, individuals could quickly figure out what they do not know; if they were offered one job they would know how to receive all others. Variation in selection criteria will do most to level the playing field when it is so extreme that what works in one instance will fail in another, and when opportunity seekers cannot discern each gatekeeper's criteria.

Thus, fields have the power to shape how capital is converted and whether there will be more class inequality or equality. The selection criteria that gatekeepers use shape who will be rewarded, and the information available about rules and rewards shapes whether actors can exchange their capital strategically. When gatekeepers use class-neutral selection criteria and when information on rules and rewards are opaque to opportunity seekers of all classes, previous acquisitions of capital will no longer predict who gets ahead.

There are several implications to recasting Bourdieu's work in this way. First, we need far more emphasis on fields. Fields may have other properties that facilitate the creation of equality. We need to know what they are.

Second, we need to reconsider the role the habitus plays in facilitating class reproduction—that is, we need to reconsider how dispositions internalized by growing up in a particular social class matter for individuals' class trajectories. We tend to ignore that school and college operate differently than the labor market: the former are class-reproducing fields while segments of the latter are luckocracies. This means that as individuals move from college to work, they will enter a new field, one that they were not socialized in, is new to them, and that does not reward the same strategies they used in the past. Given the durability of the habitus, it is likely that even advantaged individuals will not easily adapt to the new system. Instead, they will experience hysteresis—Bourdieu's term for using strategies that were rewarded in fields that actors were once in but that are not rewarded in the fields they enter later.[8] This process should weaken advantaged groups' hold on their class position as they will use strategies that are no longer effective.

Third, we also need to consider what role the habitus plays in internally varied fields. Usually, sociologists portray the habitus as aligned or misaligned with a field. Class-advantaged youths' habitus are usually said to be aligned with fields related to getting ahead and class-disadvantaged youth's habitus are portrayed as misaligned. This combination of alignments and misalignments leads to class reproduction as the advantaged are rewarded for their habitus and the disadvantaged are penalized for theirs. But if ideas of merit vary within a field, then it is possible that no group will have a monopoly on getting ahead. Some people will get ahead when judged by some gatekeepers; those same people will be penalized when judged by others. Class reproduction will not be so smooth.

Fourth, by not taking the field into account, we risk misunderstanding studies of cultural capital. Sociologists often study cultural capital decontextualized from a field.[9] Doing so assumes that we know what counts as capital in each field or that some cultural expressions have a universal exchange rate across fields. This approach leads to measuring individuals' capital and making unfounded assumptions that those with more capital will remain advantaged over those with less capital.[10] Doing so has obvious issues: capital possession is not equal to capital use, exchange rates for capital vary across settings, and fields can block capital's conversion altogether. To understand how individuals born in different classes remain in different classes or enter the same social class, we need to understand capital in the context of a field.[11]

Fifth, sociologists often consider "fit" a code word for discrimination.[12] Fit, in this sense, is used to favor people like oneself—often a person who grew up in the same social class. But as this study has shown, fit can be defined broadly enough to include people from all groups. When defined by broad values such as integrity or broad personality traits such as extroversion and when evaluated superficially, people of all classes may be equally likely to be viewed as good fits.

Sixth, there's a common assumption that individuals' connections can help them get ahead. This assumption is based on other assumptions: that high-status people within a field know how to help and can acquire better outcomes for their connections than actors could have received on their own. It is not clear that these assumptions are correct. Students' connections did not know how to help them, though they spoke as if they did. They also did not know the pay of the positions they helped students obtain or if the pay was higher than the pay the students could have received on their own. Many then offered useless or misleading "help" or funneled students into low-paying positions. By studying fields, we can know if connections are able to be informed enough to provide useful help.

Finally, we need to rethink the role of luck. Social scientists tend to equate luck with a residual—what cannot be explained by measured factors—or as a randomly occurring factor that happens on an individual level.[13] Instead, we need to also view luck as systematically produced. Some fields force luck to matter, allowing for equality across actors with unequal resources.

APPENDIX B

Data and Methods

I began this project intrigued by a puzzle. Studies show that college students from different class backgrounds have different amounts of social capital (connections to people who can help them), cultural capital (knowledge of how to navigate institutions as well as the tastes of the privileged), and economic capital (money).[1] Sociological theories suggest that students who hold unequal amounts of these resources will acquire jobs with unequal earnings.[2] Yet, according to many researchers, students with unequal resources receive jobs with equal earnings.[3] How could it be that students with more social, cultural, and economic capital did not obtain higher-paying positions? How could it be that inequalities in school did not lead to inequalities at work?

I set out to find a college that would allow me to investigate this question by following its students through their job search. I wanted to focus on a university with four criteria: a non-elite university—one that would not usher nearly all students to the top of the labor market; a public university—one meant to symbolize the promise of upward mobility and equalization; a university with some class diversity—not one that touted that 10% percent of its students are the first in their family to attend college when about 60% of American children grow up without a college-educated parent;[4] and a large university—one which had enough students that I could follow many class-disadvantaged and class-advantaged students in the same major.

It was important to me to follow students in one major. While doing so limits the generalizability of the results—as does focusing on one university—I focused on one major because earnings vary considerably by field.[5] Though it would be unlikely given that class-disadvantaged and class-advantaged students are fairly evenly distributed across majors,[6] I did not want to risk comparing class-disadvantaged students in one major and class-advantaged students in another. Business seemed like the best choice because it is the largest major, business students are least likely to go straight to graduate school, and business graduates experience the largest wage variation—allowing class-advantaged students room to use their social and cultural capital to get ahead.[7]

Within business, I also wanted to focus on just one or two specialties. Just as English and business majors systematically earn different amounts, so might marketing and finance specialists. However, focusing in this way proved infeasible. Southern State University had multiple business specialties and had at most seventeen class-disadvantaged seniors in a single specialty per year. There would not be enough students in a single specialty to focus on one. Moreover, the staff at the CoB assured me that students' specialties should not matter. They encouraged all students to think of themselves as business majors who could enter any field, and not as people tied to a business specialty. This turned out not to be the case—students did identify with their specialty and applied to jobs within it. However, earnings variation between specialties turned out to be small and earnings equality by class occurred within most specialties.

With these stipulations in mind, I needed to find a university and students to participate in the study. I first emailed the institutional research manager at one university. I explained what I wanted to do and why I wanted to study students at her university rather than mine. About six weeks later I received a response—you're at Duke, study Duke. I then approached another university using a different tactic. Rather than starting with the institutional research manager—someone I hoped could help me contact a random sample of business students from each social class—I started talking with people who had more contact with students and a larger role in helping them get jobs. I thought these on-the-ground people would be more likely to support the study. At the second university—Southern State University—I spoke first with the business school's diversity officer and then with the career center staff. They agreed to participate and then talked to the dean of the business school on my behalf. With the dean's approval, I then got in touch with the institutional research manager.

I spoke with the institutional research manager because I wanted her help generating a random sample of class-disadvantaged and class-advantaged business majors who were likely to graduate in the coming year. The institutional research manager agreed to help—she would generate this list and send qualifying students an email inviting them to participate in the study. The week before the email was meant to go out, however, the institutional research person I worked with said that her boss would not allow her to send the email. According to her boss, it was a FERPA violation—a violation of students' privacy. I assured the institutional researchers that I would not know anything about the students unless they volunteered to participate in the study and that the IRB had approved my plan, but they still said that they could not go ahead with the emails. I needed a new way to recruit.

After submitting an IRB amendment, I implemented new ways to recruit students for the study. The career center staff and diversity officer emailed all CoB students likely to graduate in the next year who were in two of the three majors at the CoB—business administration and economics, but not accounting, which has a separate labor market. The email told students about the study and asked them to participate. Students who were interested in the study could then review a website I created with information about the study. I also advertised the study with flyers posted in the CoB and made announcements about the study in students' courses and clubs. All recruitment materials said that the study was about how college students found jobs. They did not mention that the study was also about social class.

All students who expressed interest in the study filled out a screening questionnaire. The students answered questions about their parents' or guardians' education and occupation as well as their own major, specialty area, age, nationality, projected graduation date, and plans for attending graduate school. I then contacted all students who were raised in the United States, majored in business or economics, were ages 21–24, and had two or zero parents with at least a bachelor's degree. I focused on students raised in the United States because what counts as useful cultural and social capital varies across place and because international students' job search could be complicated by the need for a visa.[8] I focused on traditional-aged college students because students who graduate at later ages earn less than students who graduate from college shortly after graduating from high school.[9] I included double majors in the sample—of which there were three class-disadvantaged and five class-advantaged students—and included students of all races. When interviewing students, I also asked the same questions again. I dropped all students from the sample who reported that their parents' educations differed from what they said on the eligibility questionnaire or who seemed unsure about their parents' education. I also dropped all students who decided to go to graduate school immediately after college as well as students who did not stay in the study until receiving a job.

I completed several interviews with most respondents. I began interviewing the first group of class-disadvantaged and class-advantaged students in the fall of their senior year. During the first interview, I asked about their university and major choice, career aspirations, work and internship history, how they learned to write cover letters and résumés, who they networked with and how they did so, and their plans for finding a job. I then emailed each student a questionnaire each month—one that asked students to upload the résumés they used to apply to jobs and asked who they talked to about jobs, what they talked about, if they looked for job openings and where, if and what jobs they applied to and how they found out about them, if they attended a job interview, and if they were offered a job. If the student reported interviewing for a position or receiving a job offer, I followed up with a research interview. These in-person or phone interviews asked about how they chose which jobs to apply to, their preparation for interviews as well as what happened in them, the details of their job offers, if and how they negotiated, and how they decided whether or not to take them. In each interview, I probed for how students gathered information, decided what to do, and who they talked to during the process. I sent students monthly questionnaires and repeated the interview process until each student accepted a job offer.

I had three reasons for interviewing the same students multiple times throughout their senior year. First, when I designed the study, I thought that narrow differences in students' job searches might lead to differences in pay. I wanted the play-by-play of their job search to understand these differences, and I worried that students would not remember each part of their job search if I only spoke to them after they were offered a job. Second, I worried that students would be reluctant to tell me about their "failures"—jobs they wanted but did not receive, interviews that did not go well, offers they thought they would get that never came. If I knew where they applied and interviewed before they knew if they received an offer, I could ask about the events that did not go their way. Third, I worried that if I only recruited students after they received jobs, only the most "successful" students would sign up. Thus, I recruited students in the fall. In all, 30 (13 class-disadvantaged and 17 class-advantaged) of the 62 students included in the final sample participated this way.

I wanted to talk to more students, so I also recruited students in the spring. I talked to students who joined the study in the spring about all aspects of their job search. If they had already received a job, I only interviewed them once during their senior year. This interview included the story of how they received their job and the stories of the jobs they applied for but did not receive. If they had not accepted a job offer when I met them in the spring, I sent them the same monthly questionnaire as the fall starters and followed up with a research interview after each of their job interviews or job offers. There were fewer differences between fall and spring starters than I anticipated. Spring starters talked freely of their failures and seemed to remember many of the details of their job searches. I followed this interview process for fall and spring starters in two academic years: 2014–15 and 2015–16.

A year after students graduated from college, I contacted the 62 students who had participated during their senior year. I wanted to know about their work experiences and plans to find new jobs. After trying to

TABLE A1: Respondent Demographics during Their Senior Year

	NUMBER OF RESPONDENTS		AVERAGE EARNINGS ($)	
	Disadvantaged	Advantaged	Disadvantaged	Advantaged
Major/Concentration[a]				
Economics	1	1	30,000	0[b]
Entrepreneurship	0	1	—	72,500
Human Resources	6	3	51,750	48,330
Finance	9	5	44,780	46,200
IT for Business	3	0	57,000	—
Marketing	3	16	56,670	39,390
Operations	6	11	42,000	52,200
Age	22	22		
Gender				
Men	10	18	51,222	46,483
Women	15	19	46,167	42,211
Race				
White	13	35	44,154	43,853
Black	6	1	50,917	38,000
Hispanic	2	0	58,000	—
Asian	3	0	43,000	—
Other	1	1	64,000	60,000
Total/Mean[c]	25	37	47,540	44,289

[a] Some students concentrated in more than one area, so the number of concentrations exceeds the number of students.
[b] This respondent did not hold a job a year after graduating from college.
[c] I reported median salaries in the text: $48,000 for class-disadvantaged students and $45,000 for class-advantaged students.

reach them three times, I convinced 23 of the 37 class-advantaged and 14 of the 25 class-disadvantaged students to participate a final time. I talked to them over the phone or in-person for an hour, asking about their experiences at work and their career plans.

I used the extended case method to design the study and analyzed it accordingly. The extended case method begins with the idea that a theory must be extended to explain an unusual situation.[10] In my case, this was that theories explain how cultural, social, and economic capital create persistent or accumulating inequality, but did not explain the unusual case of how they fail to do so. Thus, when I analyzed the data, I paid particular attention to the capital that students possessed and how they used it. My goal was to build a theory of how the transition from college to work disrupted the transmission of inequality.

I was quickly struck by three findings. The first was that several students told me that they majored in business because they considered it a path to financial stability or riches. Yet when I asked them how they decided where to apply to jobs, they suddenly stopped talking about money. Second, I was struck by class-advantaged students' stories about the mistakes they made. Current theory suggested it was the class-disadvantaged students who should make the most mistakes and the most egregious mistakes. However, class-advantaged students regaled me with the mistakes they made—many of which they admitted were egregious. Third, I was struck by how many of students' outcomes seemed to be accidental—that a student found a high-paying job after trying to take a water bottle or because the company name started with the letter A. I had expected students who received high-paying jobs to tell stories of how they did so intentionally, not how they had lucked into their position.

The combination of these issues prompted me to interrogate the information landscape—why students who said they cared about money did not mention it when talking of their application decisions, why privileged students seemed unable to avoid mistakes, and why advantaged and disadvantaged students alike told so many stories of findings jobs due to chance. Using NVivo, I coded these issues and many more—creating hundreds of codes related to how students gathered information, whom they talked to, what they talked about, and what they said they did to seek a job.

I also spent two years observing events related to the job search process. Southern State University's College of Business operated as a job center—frequently instructing students about how to find jobs and inviting employers to campus to hire them. I observed many of these events. In all, I attended seventeen information sessions and six career fairs—both ones for all business students and for students in particular specialties. I also visited all of the business majors' professionalization clubs, sat in on some courses, and attended networking events. In addition, I observed the information available to students online: I conducted a content analysis of jobs posted on UJobs, looked at how jobs were advertised on company websites, and googled "interview tips for college students" and similar searches to understand what information was available to students online. In most cases, I took notes in real time—sitting in the back of information sessions, standing in the reception area of the career fair, and wandering around the room of networking events. Students were instructed to bring a padfolio—a black padded folder with a notepad—with them to professional events. I fit in by bringing one too and using it to take notes.

I only began interviewing employers after I finished talking to students and analyzing their data. At this point, I had unanswered questions about why some students received jobs that others did not and about why employers gave students so little information. To answer these questions, I recruited employers at career fairs and from LinkedIn groups. I also contacted people who mentioned hiring college students in their LinkedIn profiles and who were in human resources MeetUps and local professional networking groups. During this stage, a Southern State University business professor with relationships with local recruiters introduced me to them and vouched for me and the study. I included all employers who played a role in hiring business students from Southern State University or schools like it. In all, I spoke to thirty-two employers—all of whom I told were participating in a study on how college students find jobs and how employers hire them. Eleven employers were in the technology industry, five in healthcare, five in finance, four in transportation, two in energy, and the rest in an assortment of other industries. The information that the employers whom I formally interviewed provided matched that of the eighty employers whom I talked to briefly at career fairs, after information sessions, and other professionalization events.

Of course, this study does not provide the final word on the earnings equalization process during the transition from college to work. Not all employment sectors hire in the same way and students in other types of universities, majors, and geographic regions may experience different equalization processes. Researchers have much more work ahead of them, especially in finding out where else the role of luck is structurally produced to promote earnings equality among students from unequal origins.

Interview Guides
and Questionnaires

Interview for Fall Starters

Before the Job Search
- Can you tell me the story of how you decided to attend [Southern State University]?
  - › Where else did you apply?
  - › Why did you choose [Southern State University] over your other options?
- Can you tell me the story of how you decided on your major?
- Can you tell me the story of how you decided on your concentration?

Past Job-Related Experiences
- When did you first start thinking about getting a post-college job?
- Can you tell me about what you did since that point, if anything, to prepare for getting a job?
  - › Ask how they thought to do what they did.

Internships
- Have you received any **internships**?
  - › How did you get the position? Can you walk me through every step from how you heard about the position to the point when you received the offer?
    - – How did you find out about the internship/job?
    - – What about the position made you want to apply?
    - – What did you do to apply?
    - – Did you interview?
      - • If so, did you do anything to prepare for the interview? What?

- Did you have any strategies of things you wanted to do in the interview?
- What types of things did the employer ask about? How did you answer?
- What do you think went well in the interview?
- What did you think you could have done better, if anything?

› What types of things did you do in your internship/job? Can you walk me through a typical day?

› What did you learn from your internship/job?

› Were the positions paid or unpaid?

› Did you apply for any internships that you did not receive?
  - How did you find out about these positions?
  - How did you decide which internships to apply for?

› Did you apply for any internships that you thought were scams in any way?

› Did you receive any internship offers that you turned down?
  - What was the position and company?
  - Why did you turn it down?

› Are you interested in continuing to work in a similar type of job after graduation?

› Are you interested in working for the same company after graduation?

Cover Letter and Résumé

- Have you ever written a **résumé**?
  › If yes:
    - When did you first write one?
    - What do you think makes a good résumé? Why?
  › If no:
    - What do you think makes a good résumé? Why?
- Have you ever written a **cover letter** before?
  › If yes:
    - When did you write your first one?
    - What do you think makes a good cover letter? Why?
  › If no:
    - Do you think you will need to write one?
    - What do you think makes a good cover letter?

- If you have written a résumé and cover letter before, did you get any help with them? If so, from whom? What kind of help?

Networking
- Have you done any **networking?**
    › Why/why not?
    › Who do you network with?
    › What do you do when you network? Can you walk me through the last time you did it? What happened?
        – Has it been helpful? How so/why not?
    › Do you use LinkedIn at all?
        – If so, how do you use it?

Career Fair
- Have you ever attended a **career fair?**
    › When did you go to your first one?
    › How many have you been to?
    › How do you decide which employers to talk to there?
    › Can you walk me through what happens when you talk to an employer?
    › Have you ever received an interview from the career fair?
        – For what company and position?

Extracurricular Activities
- Are you involved in any **campus activities** that are related to getting a job?
    › Which ones?
    › How did you decide to join them?
    › How do you see them as helpful for getting a job?
    › Are there other activities you're involved with that are not related to getting a job?
        – If yes, why do you see them as unrelated to getting a job?
    › Have you held any jobs in the past?

Job Expectations
- What kind of job would you like to receive?
    › How did you decide on this type of job?
    › When did you decide to apply for this type of job?

› What is appealing to you about this type of job?
› Who have you talked to, if anyone, to help you decide to apply for this type of job?
  – What did those people say?
› What other types of jobs have you considered?
  – If they don't know, ask about what types of jobs they're considering.
› What do you think it will be like to do this job?
› What do you see as the advantages of this job?
  – Disadvantages?
› For the job you think you are most likely to be in, what do you think the
  – Day-to-day life will be like? Can you walk me through an imagined typical day?
  – Hours?
  – Responsibilities?
  – Salary?
  – Benefits?
› What are your long-term career goals?
  – How does the job you want for next year fit in with your long-term career goals?

Expectations for the Job Search (for a job to work in after graduation)
• How do you think you will find a job?
  › When do you think you will start looking for a job?
  › Where will you find out about job openings?
    – Why these places?
    – (If they say something like "websites" be sure to probe for which ones.)
  › Can you tell me about what you're looking for in a job description?
  › How many jobs do you think you will apply to?
  › What geographical areas will you look for jobs in? Why?
• What do you think an employer wants in an applicant?
  › What kind of skills?
  › What kind of experiences?
  › What kind of character/personality traits?
  › Do you think employers care about your major?
  › Do you think employers care about your GPA?

- › If an employer asked about why they should hire you, what would you say?
- › If in an interview, an employer asked you to name your weaknesses, what answer would you give?
- › If an interviewer asked where you see yourself in five years, what would you say?
- Who have you talked to the most about the process of getting a job in this coming year?
  - › Can you tell me about a conversation you had with that person that was helpful?
- Who do you talk to the next most?
  - › Can you tell me about a conversation you had with that person that was helpful?
- Are there any other people you've talked to that have been helpful?
  - › What have they done or said that has been helpful?
- What is overall the best advice you've received about getting a job?

Next I have questions for you about how your ideas of family relate to your ideas about work.
- Do you have a significant other?
  - › If yes:
    - – Do you talk with him/her about your plans for next year?
    - – Can you tell me about some of the conversations you have?
    - – How do you think s/he will influence your plans?
  - › If no:
    - – Will your job decisions be made at all with the idea of meeting someone in the future? If so, how?
- Do you have children?
  - › If yes:
    - – How will your children influence your ideas about what type of job you look for?
  - › If no:
    - – Do your plans to have or not have kids influence what type of job you want?

Next I have questions for you about the resources you might use as you look for a job.
- Do you have any student debt?
  - › If so, how much?

> ⟩ How much will you need to pay each month after you graduate?
> ⟩ Will debt shape your job decisions?
>> – Why/why not?
- Do you receive financial aid?
  - ⟩ How much?
- Will your parents help you financially if you need it next year?
  - ⟩ Will you support anyone after graduating?
  - ⟩ Are there any other ways that financial resources shape what options you think you have?

Background
- How have you liked college?
- Do you think you will ever go to graduate school?
- Where did you grow up?
- Who did you live with growing up?
- What is each of their highest levels of education?
- What is each of their jobs?
- Approximate income?
- Are your parents married?
- Do you have any older siblings?
  - ⟩ Did they go to college?
  - ⟩ What are their jobs?
- What was the highest level of education and occupation of each of your grandparents?
  - ⟩ Do you talk to your grandparents at all about getting a job?
  - ⟩ Will your grandparents financially support you at all if you need help?

Wrap-Up
- Is there anything about your job search, college experience, or family that we have not covered yet that you think we should know?

Contact Information
We will send you monthly surveys. What is the best email address to send them to?

We may need to occasionally mail payments to you. What address should we use?

Example of Follow-Up Interview

Company 1 Job Interview

- How did the person at [company] who contacted you find out about you?
- What made you interested in the position?
- Did you do anything to prepare for the interview? If so, what?
- Did you have any strategies for this interview?
- What went well?
- What could have gone better?
- Do you remember any specific questions they asked? How did you answer?
- What did you think of the company? The job?
- If you were offered a job, what would factor into your decision about whether or not to take it?

Company 2 Job Interview

- Last time we talked you were going to interview with [company]. How did that go?
- Did you do anything to prepare for the interview? If so, what?
- Did you have any strategies for this interview?
- What happened in the interview?
- What went well?
- What could have gone better?
- Were there any surprises in the interview? If so, what?
- Did you receive an offer?
- Have you had any other interviews in the last few weeks?

Miscellaneous Questions (follow-up questions based on data in monthly surveys)

- Regarding the people you talked to on LinkedIn, how did your contact with them begin?
- How did you decide that the [specific] industry is too hard to get into straight out of college?
- How did you arrange the shadow day at [company]? What did you learn?

Second Example of Follow-Up Interview

Applying

- What do you look for in a job description?
- Did you initially think that [companies you applied to] were different in any ways that were important to you?
- When applying to jobs, can you tell me about jobs like [companies you applied to] that you considered but didn't apply to?

Interviews (repeat for each interview)

- Did you do anything to prepare for the interview? If so, what?
- Did you have any strategies for this interview?
- Do you remember any specific questions they asked? How did you answer?
- Did you have any strategies for this interview?
- What went well?
- What could have gone better?
- Last time you mentioned that you might have an interview with [company]. Did that happen?

Offer

- What will you weigh with whether or not to take it?
- What would you be doing?
- Salary?
- Benefits?
- Hours?
- Location?
- Did you negotiate?
  - › Why?
  - › About what?
  - › Did you get any help preparing to negotiate?
  - › How did it go?
- Did you talk to anyone about whether to accept the position?
  - › Will you wait for other offers to come in?

Reflection

- What do you think was the most important thing you did to get your job offer?
- Is there anything you wish you would have done differently?
- What advice do you have for other students looking for jobs?

Interview for Spring Starters

Before the Job Search

- Can you tell me the story of how you decided to attend [Southern State University]?
  - › Where else did you apply?
  - › Why did you choose [Southern State University] over your other options?
- Can you tell me the story of how you decided on your major?
- Can you tell me the story of how you decided on your concentration?

Past Job-Related Experiences

- When did you first start thinking about getting a post-college job?
- Can you tell me about what you did since that point, up until the start of your senior year, to prepare for getting a job?
  - › For *each* internship or work experience they have, ask:
    - – How did you get the position? Can you walk me through every step from how you heard about the position to the point when you received the offer?
      - • How did you hear about the position?
      - • What made the position seem appealing to you?
      - • What did you do to apply?
      - • Can you tell me about the interview? How did it go? What did you do to prepare, if anything? Did you have any strategies for doing well once in the interview?
      - • Did you talk to anyone about the position or applying for it? If so, who? What did you talk about?
      - • What made you decide to accept the position?
    - – How did the internship go?
      - • What were your responsibilities?
      - • What did you learn through the internship, if anything?
      - • How long was the internship?
    - – Were the positions paid or unpaid?
- Are there any internships or jobs in the past that you were offered but did not take?
  - › How did you hear about the position?
  - › What did you do to apply?
  - › What made the position seem appealing at first?

> Did you talk to anyone about the position or applying for it? If so, what did you talk about?
> What was your reasoning for turning it down?

- Did you apply for any positions that you did not receive? Which ones?
  > What were your reasons for applying for these positions?
  > Did you receive interviews for these positions? If so, how did they go?
  > Why do you think you did not receive these positions?

- Were you involved in any campus activities that were related to getting a job?
  > Which ones?
  > How did you decide to join them?
  > How do you see them as helpful for getting a job?
  > Are there other activities you're involved with that are not related to getting a job?
    – If yes, why do you see them as unrelated to getting a job?
  > Have you held any jobs in the past?

- Did you do any networking?
  > Who do you network with?
  > If you do it, what do you do?
    – Has it been helpful? How so/why not?
  > If you don't do it, what do you imagine it entails?

- Have you ever attended a career fair?
  > When did you go to your first one?
  > How many have you been to?
  > How do you decide which employers to talk to there?
  > Can you walk me through what happens when you talk to an employer?
  > Have you ever received an interview from the career fair?
    – For what company and position?

- Do you use LinkedIn?
  > If so, how?
  > How do you decide who to connect with?
  > Has a recruiter ever contacted you about a job through LinkedIn or UJobs?

- When did you write your first résumé?
  > What do you think makes a good résumé? Why?

- Have you ever written a cover letter before?
  > If yes:
    – When did you write your first one?

  – What do you think makes a good cover letter? Why?
  › If no:
    – What do you think makes a good cover letter?
- If you have written a résumé and cover letter before, did you get any help with them? If so, from whom? What kind of help?
- What is the best advice you've received about how to get a job? From whom?
- The worst? From whom?

Getting a Job for after Graduation: Applying
- How did you decide what type of job to apply for, for your first post-college job?
  › What stood out to you as something you really wanted in a job?
  › Something you didn't want?
  › Did you put any constraints on your job search—that is, did you only apply for positions that met some criteria? What criteria did you use?
- When did you first start applying for jobs that would begin after you graduate?
  › When you started looking for jobs, did you have any companies or types of positions you were particularly interested in? Why these?
  › Any types of jobs that you thought of as backups? Why these?
  › How did you know about these companies?
  › Were there any types of jobs you knew that other people were applying to that you decided not to? If so, what led you not to apply?
- What specific companies and positions did you end up applying for?
  › What stood out about these companies and positions?
- Where did you find out about job openings for these positions?
  › How did you know to look there?
- If you were browsing for job openings, what were you looking for in a job description?
- Did you see any jobs that looked interesting but you decided not to apply for them? If so, what was your reasoning for not applying?
- Did you contact anyone in your network about getting a job? Who? Tell me about how that went.
- Did anyone contact you about a job?
- Did you get any advice about applying?
  › If so, from whom? What kind of advice did that person give? How did you use the advice, if at all?

> Did you get any good advice that you didn't take?
> - What was the advice? Why did you decide not to take it?

Getting a Job for after Graduation: Interviewing

- Of the jobs you applied for or were contacted about, which ones did you interview for?
- Can you walk me through what you did to prepare for the interviews, if anything?
  > Did you talk to anyone who helped you prepare? If so, how did that person help?
- Once you were in the interview, did you have any strategies to help it go well?
- Can you tell me about an interview that went well? What made it go well?
- Can you tell me about an interview that went less well? What do you think happened that made it less good?
- Did anything unexpected happen in the interviews? If so, what? How did you respond?
- What kind of questions did the employers ask? How did you answer?
  > What did you say to questions about your strengths?
  > Weaknesses?
  > Where you want to be in five years?
- What kind of questions did you tend to ask employers, if any?
- What did you wear to interviews?
- Did you have any contact with the employer after the interview? If so, what was said? Who initiated the conversation?

Getting a Job Offer

- Did you receive any job offers? Which ones?
- When did you receive your offer(s)?
- If you had multiple offers, how did you decide which one to accept?
- Did you negotiate at all?
  > If so, what prompted you to negotiate?
  > Can you walk me through what you did to negotiate?
  > Did you end up getting what you wanted?
  > Did you talk with anyone about how to negotiate? What about?
- What were the employers offering in terms of pay? Benefits?
- What will the job you accepted entail in terms of
  > Hours?
  > Responsibilities?

- Do you have any student debt? If so, did that shape what jobs you applied to or what jobs you'd be willing to take?
- If you have not yet received an offer, what will you do next to look for a job?
- What are your long-term career goals? How do you see that as related to the job you recently accepted/job you want out of college?

Family
- Parents
  › What role, if any, did your parents play in your job search?
  › What do they think of your job?
- Significant Other
  › Do you have a significant other?
    - If so, did that person play any role in your job search or decision-making about which jobs to apply for or take?
    - If you do not have a significant other, do ideas of dating shape what types of jobs you applied for or accepted?
- Children
  › Do you have any children?
    - If so, did that shape what types of jobs you applied for or accepted?
    - If not, do your ideas about having or not having kids in the future shape your ideas about what types of jobs to consider?

Finances
- Do you have any student debt?
  › If so, how much?
  › Did having student debt shape any of your decisions? Why/ why not?
- Will your parents pay for anything for you for next year?
  › If so, what?
- Will you need to support anyone next year?
  › If so, did that shape any of your decision-making?

Background and Demographics
- How have you liked college?
- Do you think you will ever go to graduate school?
- Where did you grow up?
- Who did you live with growing up?

- What is each of their highest levels of education?
- What is each of their jobs?
- Approximate income?
- Are your parents married?
- Do you have any older siblings?
  - › Did they go to college?
  - › What are their jobs?
- What was the highest level of education and occupation of each of your grandparents?
  - › Do you talk to your grandparents at all about getting a job?
  - › Will your grandparents financially support you at all if you need help?
- What fraction of your high school class would you guess went to college?
- Do you receive financial aid?
  - › How much?
- What's your GPA?

We will want to contact you again a year after you begin your job to find out about how it's going. What is the best way to get in touch with you?

If we cannot reach you that way, what is an alternative way of getting in touch with you?

If we need to mail you a check, what address should we use?

Monthly Questionnaire

Thank you for participating in this study! We enjoyed talking with you during the interview. We will now begin to send you monthly surveys. You will receive a survey until you receive a job or until a year from now, whichever comes first.

Please note that we are looking for the most accurate information you can provide. We expect that there will be months when you have done nothing in regard to looking for a job. That's fine. Your honest answers are what matter to us, not how much you're doing.

You will receive $5 for every survey you fill out COMPLETELY and $10 for every follow-up interview you complete. We will keep track of how much money you earn and give it to you in lump sums. Please contact us at [email] if you need the money earlier or want to check in about how much you've earned.

First Name:
Last Name:

Did you talk to anyone about jobs in the past month?
   __ Yes
   __ No
If yes: Whom? For everyone you talked to, please list the person's relationship to you, and, if in the workforce, their job title and firm.

Please summarize what each person said and your reaction to it.

Did you <u>look</u> for job openings in the past month?
   __ Yes
   __ No
If yes: Where did you look?

Which places that you looked for jobs seemed like they had the most promising options?

Did you <u>apply</u> for any jobs in the last month?
   __ Yes
   __ No
If yes: About how many jobs did you apply for?

For each job you applied for, please list the job title and firm.

How did you find out about these positions?

Why did you choose to apply for these jobs?

If you used a cover letter to apply to a job in the past month, please upload one of the cover letters you used.

If you used a résumé to apply to a job in the past month, please upload one of the résumés you used.

Did you attend a job interview in the last month?
___ Yes
___ No
If yes: Please list the positions for which you interviewed and the firm.

Did you receive any job offers in the past month?
___ Yes
___ No
If yes: Please list the position and firm from which you received the offer(s).

Did you accept any job offers in the past month?
___ Yes
___ No
If yes: Please list the position and firm from which you received the offer(s).

Did your ideas about what kind of job you want change in the past month?
___ Yes
___ No
If yes: How did your ideas change?

Interview: One Year after Receipt of First Post-College Job

Work Overview

- Tell me about your work experiences over the past year.
  - › Have you stayed in one job? Changed jobs?
  - › What are your responsibilities?
  - › What type of projects have you worked on?
  - › What has gone particularly well?
  - › What has not gone well?
  - › What parts of your job did you feel well prepared for?
  - › What parts of your job did you feel ill prepared for?
  - › What has been the most surprising part of the last year?
- Walk me through what you did yesterday at work.
  - › Was that a typical day? How so?
  - › What did you like about what you did?
  - › What did you not enjoy about what you did?
  - › Tell me about another day that was different.
- Tell me about the last time you did something at work that you found very rewarding.
  - › What percentage of your time at work would you say you're engaged in activities that you find rewarding?
- Tell me about the last time you found something at work to be very frustrating.
  - › Was that experience typical of frustrating experiences?
  - › How often does that happen?
- Are there any new skills you have learned since starting your job?
  - › Are there skills that you learned while in college that you find very useful at work?
  - › Are there skills that you feel like other people who work at your level have that you do not?
  - › Are there skills you feel that you've lost in the last year?
- Is there anything you've learned about office culture? If so, what?
- Is there anything you've learned about how to interact with coworkers, bosses, or clients? If so, what?
- What kind of mistakes have you made in the last year?
- What was the hardest thing to learn or adapt to in your job?

Work—Interaction with Others

- Do you have people at work who are your peers?
  - › Do you talk with them about work-related issues?
    - – If so, what do you talk to them about?
    - – If not, what do you talk with them about?
  - › How often do you talk with them?
- Do you have any mentors?
  - › *If so*, how did you get to know them?
  - › What did you talk about in your last meeting?
  - › What other types of things have you talked about in the past?
  - › What is the best advice you have received?
  - › *If not*, have you tried to build any mentoring relationships? How?
- Tell me about your relationship with your boss.
  - › Tell me about your last interaction with your boss.
    - – Was that typical? How so?
    - – How often does s/he supervise your work?
    - – If you have an idea of something you want to do at work, what would you do?
      - • (Talk to your boss first? Just do it?)
    - – Tell me about a time when your boss asked you to do something differently.
      - • What was it?
      - • How did you react?
- Do you supervise anyone at work?
  - › How many people?
  - › To what extent?
- If you need advice about work, who do you turn to?
  - › What types of things do you ask about?
- Do you talk with people in your industry who are not in your firm?
  - › How do you know them?
  - › What do you talk with them about?
  - › How often do you talk with them?
- Do you talk with anyone about what other industries are like?
  - › Who?
  - › What was your last conversation about?
- Do you talk with your parents about work?
  - › If so, what parts of work do you talk about?
  - › Do they give you advice?

     – If so, what type of advice do they give?
     – What is your reaction to it?

Work—Future
- How has your time at work shaped your ideas of what you want in a job?
- How long do you see yourself staying in this job?
  - › Why?
  - › If you were to stay, what opportunities are there to advance?
    - – Do you see these opportunities as good ones for you?
  - › If you are planning on leaving soon, what are you considering doing next?
    - – How are you planning on doing it?
- How long do you see yourself staying in this industry?
  - › Why?
  - › If you are planning on changing industries, what will you try next?
  - › How are you planning on switching industries?
- Do you want to be promoted?
  - › What is the next position you could have?
  - › How is it different than the one you have now?
  - › Have you been doing anything that would help you be promoted?
  - › What is required to be promoted?
  - › When do you think it is likely you could be promoted?
- If you wanted to change jobs, how would you go about it?

If They Already Changed Jobs
- How did you decide to change jobs?
- How did you decide what the right timing would be to change?
- How did you find out about your new job?
- What was the interview process like?
- How did you decide whether or not to accept the new job?
- Were there any other jobs you were considering?

Work Conditions—Present
- How much are you paid?
  - › Are there sacrifices you have made because of how much you earn?
    - – Which ones?
  - › Do you have any bills you have not been able to pay?

> Do you receive any financial support from your parents?
>> – Do your parents pay any of your bills?
> Do you support anyone else with your pay?
> Do you have student debt?
>> – Are you able to pay it?
>> – Does it shape your decisions about how to advance your career?
- What kind of benefits do you receive?
  > How many sick days do you have each year?
  > How many personal and vacation days do you have each year?
  > Do you have health insurance through your employer?
  > Do you have a retirement account?
  >> – Does your employer contribute?
- What time do you usually begin work? End?
- Overall, how happy are you with your job?
- What do your parents think of your job?
  > Why?

Life Outside of Work
- What is your life like outside of work?
- Who do you live with?
- Do you see your job as allowing you to balance work and life?
  > How so?
  > What are the most important things you do outside of work?
- Are you dating anyone?
  > If yes, how long have you been dating them?
  >> – Are they someone you are serious about?
  >> – What is his/her job?
  >> – Where does s/he live?
  >> – Does your relationship with them have any impact on your work?
  >> – Does your work have any impact on your relationship?
  > If no, do you want to be dating anyone?
  >> – Do your ideas of relationships have any impact on your work?
  >> – Does your work have any impact on your ability or desire to date?

- How often do you see your family of origin?
  - › How do you feel about that?

Reflection
- Is there anything you would have done differently in looking for a job last year?
- Is there anything else we should know about your life in the last year?

Employer Interview

Roles hire for: _____

I want to start out by talking about job ads, especially ones your company uses to recruit recent college graduates. To make it concrete, let's talk about the last job ad you posted in which you were looking to hire recent college graduates and in which business majors were eligible for the job.

- Who [what type of role: marketing, HR, hiring manager, etc.] wrote the ad?
- Do you know how that person decided what to include in the ad?
  - › How did they decide on the job title?
  - › How did they decide on the job description?
- I've also noticed that some job ads include information about pay and others do not. How do you decide whether or not to include earnings information in the ad?
- How did you decide where to post the ad?

I'd like to also ask you about college recruiting.
- How do you decide where to recruit?
- What information do you hope to convey?
- Is there any information you purposefully do not share?

Now I'd like to ask you about your hiring pool.
- How many applications did you receive for the last job you posted that was open to recent college graduates?
  - › How many did you think were qualified?

Now I'd like to ask you about how you select candidates.
- What do you look for when hiring college students?
  - › Can you tell me about a time when the candidate exhibited these traits? When they failed to do so?
  - › What would you say is the most important thing you hire upon?
- When you read a résumé from a college student, what are you looking for?
  - › If they don't bring it up, ask:
    - – Do you care about university attended?
    - – GPA?

- – Internships?
  - Where?
  - How many?
  - – Leadership?
  - – Extracurricular activities?
- How do you decide what to ask in an interview?
  - › What questions do you often ask?
    - – What do you consider a good answer? A bad answer?
  - › Do you and your colleagues ask the same questions, or do each of you ask different ones?
    - – Do you and your colleagues ever disagree about what counts as a good and bad answer? Can you tell me about that?
  - › How do you decide whether to give applicants information about the interview in advance or wait until the interview to ask questions?
- Students tell me there are some questions they are asked often: What do you do when a team member isn't pulling their weight? What setbacks have you faced and how have you overcome them? Tell me about a time when you've shown leadership.
  - › If you've asked questions like this, can you tell me about a student who answered well?
  - › A student who answered poorly?
- I've heard employers say that it's more important how people say things than what they say. Do you agree or disagree? What do you look for in terms of how people talk?
  - › Are there other less tangible things that are important to you when hiring?
- In the interview, what information do you like to tell the candidate about the job?
- Are there questions that you hope a candidate asks you?

Networks
- Do you ever give particular consideration to candidates who others recommended? How does that process work?
  - › Does it matter who recommended them?

Finally, I'd like to ask you about job offers.
- How do you decide what pay to offer candidates?
  - › At what point in the process is this decided?

- Do you allow recent college graduates to negotiate?
  - › What tactics are effective? Ineffective?
  - › What is the most they can get from negotiating?
- How do you decide how long to give students to respond to your offer?
- Once students begin working, what differentiates good hires from bad hires?
- What is the promotional structure like for recent college graduates?
- Would students know how much they could be paid in the future?

Wrap-Up
- What surprised you about hiring when you began doing it?
- What do you wish college students knew about finding a job?

Notes

Chapter One

1. Bourdieu (1980); DiPrete and Eirich (2006).
2. Altintas (2015); Child Trends (2019); Darmon and Drewnowski (2008); Lareau (2011); Phillips (2011).
3. Downey (2020); Lee and Burkam (2002).
4. Cataldi, Bennett, and Chen (2018); Wilbur and Roscigno (2016).
5. Espenshade and Radford (2009); Walpole (2003).
6. Armstrong and Hamilton (2013); Stuber (2011); see findings in chapters 4 and 5.
7. Armstrong and Hamilton (2013); see findings in chapters 4 and 5.
8. Armstrong and Hamilton (2013); Stuber (2011); Terenzini et al. (1996); Walpole (2003); see findings in chapters 4 and 5.
9. Goldrick-Rab (2016); Houle (2014); Schoeni and Ross (2005); Wightman et al. (2013).
10. Bourdieu (1986); DiPrete and Eirich (2006).
11. Chetty et al. (2017; 2020).
12. Chetty et al. (2017; 2020) find an earnings gap when comparing rich and poor former students who attend *any* college—rather than only the same college. However, their sample includes community colleges and focuses on attending rather than graduating from college. Manzoni and Streib (2019) find an approximately $4,000 class wage gap for women and a $7,000 wage gap for men ten years after graduating. However, most of these gaps relate to where first-generation and continuing-generation graduates live, suggesting the gaps may disappear when controlling for cost of living. Witteveen and Attewell (2017) find an earnings gap by class origin, but their study is restricted to students whose parents funded their college education. The remaining 40% of the college-going population is not in their sample. Hurst (2019) observes an earnings gap one year after graduation for students of liberal arts colleges. However, her response rate is 25%, and she does not use techniques to account for missing data. Other studies that identify class wage gaps do so in regard to other countries (Friedman and Laurison 2019) or measure earnings gaps during recessions (Giani 2016). The exception is Witteveen and Attewell (2020), who argue that there is a small wage gap between students from different class backgrounds—one that other studies miss due to their sample size. Still, many studies using a variety of data sources have found that earnings equalization occurs for all students with undergraduate

degrees, including Bloome, Dyer, and Zhou (2018); Cataldi, Bennett, and Chen (2018); Choy (2001); Ford (2019); Hout (1988); Ishida, Muller, and Ridge (1995); Pascarella et al. (2004); Pfeffer and Hertel (2015); Thomas (2000); Torche (2011).

13. Attewell et al. (2007); Bloome, Dyer, and Zhou (2018); Cataldi, Bennett, and Chen (2018); Choy (2001); Ford (2019); Hout (1988); Ishida, Muller, and Ridge (1995); Pascarella et al. (2004); Pfeffer and Hertel (2015); Radford and Cataldi (unpublished manuscript); Thomas (2000); Thompson (2019, for some colleges only); Torche (2011).

14. Hout (1988, 1358).

15. Torche (2011, 764).

16. Breen and Jonsson (2007); Hout (1988); Ishida, Muller, and Ridge (1995); Tomaszewski et al. (2018); Torche (2011).

17. Cataldi, Bennett, and Chen (2018); Chetty et al. (2017); Choy (2001); Pascarella et al. (2004); Pfeffer and Hertel (2015); Thomas (2000); Torche (2011).

18. Attewell et al. (2007); Bloome, Dyer, and Zhou (2018); Cataldi, Bennett, and Chen (2018); Ford (2019); Hout (1988); Ishida, Muller, and Ridge (1995); Pascarella et al. (2004); Pfeffer and Hertel (2015); Thomas (2000); Thompson (2019, for some colleges only); Torche (2011).

19. Chetty et al. (2017).

20. Some studies suggest that earnings equalization occurs due to the selection of students into college. They argue that since it is easier for the class advantaged to graduate from college than the class disadvantaged, both excellent and mediocre class-advantaged students graduate while only excellent class-disadvantaged students graduate (Mare 1981). One study finds partial support for this idea, showing that earnings equalization is due to selection among students who attend lower-tier universities but not mid- and upper-tier universities (Zhou 2019). Other studies find no support for the selection argument. One finds that selection cannot explain occupational equalization by class origin (Karlson 2019), while another finds that students from different classes do not differentially select into college based on their non-cognitive skills (Smith, Grodsky, and Warren 2019). To the best of my knowledge, no study finds that college selects class-disadvantaged and class-advantaged students with equal cultural and social capital or that it equalizes these resources while students are in college. Therefore, we still need to explain how cultural and social capital differences do not lead to earnings differences as students transition from college to work.

21. Manzoni and Streib (2019).

22. Bowen, Kurzweil, and Tobin (2005); Pascarella et al. (2004); Terenzini et al. (1996); Walpole (2003). But see Manzoni and Streib (2019) for evidence that college GPA may not always differ by class background.

23. Students at elite universities are more likely to enter elite labor markets, ones that do not operate as luckocracies.

24. Carnevale, Cheah, and Hanson (2015).

25. See the episode on February 15, 2019.

26. Barth et al. (2016); Song et al. (2015); Xie, Killewald, and Near (2016).

27. When comparing students with the same credentials, work histories, jobs, and employment locations and (not included above) when one worked for a start-up and another at an established firm, this difference rose to $58,000 a year.

28. There is no objectively "right" set of experiences, skills, and styles. Employers define each according to their perceived needs. Experiences might include internships, work experience, course work, course projects, or participation in leadership roles or extracurricular

activities. Skills are the abilities and traits that employers believe are needed to conduct job tasks. They include "soft" skills such as communication, teamwork, and perseverance as well as "hard" skills such as the ability to create macros in Excel or knowledge of the project management life cycle. Styles are ways of speaking, dressing, and interacting. What counts as a desirable style varies widely. As an anthropologist put it, "The qualities that make you seem like a great team member in one company culture can make you seem like an asshole in another company culture" (Gershon 2017, 170).

29. Erickson (1996) also finds that mid-tier business employers do not care about the status of employees' leisure activities.

30. Calarco (2018); Streib (2011).

31. Of course, this assumes that the skills rewarded in the market are equally available to individuals of all classes. This may be true in some markets and untrue in others.

32. For example, lotteries and seniority systems are class neutral but not merit based.

33. See, for example, Castilla (2008, 1484), who writes: "Meritocracy is thus one possible way of assigning rewards. . . . Seen through this lens, the question at issue in the article is whether the process is consistent and, therefore, whether employees get the same reward for the same level of merit regardless of their gender, race, or nationality."

34. Altenhofen, Berends, and White (2016); Diamond and Gomez (2004); Lareau and Goyette (2014); Walters (2018).

35. Kalmijn (1991; 1998).

36. Streib (2015).

37. Fernández and Rogerson (2001).

38. Lareau (2011); Radford (2013).

39. Buchmann, Condron, and Roscigno (2010); Karabel (2005); Stevens (2009).

40. Dearden et al. (2017); Golden (2007); Kahlenberg (2010); Karen (1990); Lieber (2019).

41. Hoxby and Avery (2012); Lareau (2011); Persell and Cookson (1985); Radford (2013).

42. Bailey and Dynarski (2011), refers to the 1979–82 birth cohorts.

43. Fry (2021).

44. Chetty et al. (2017; 2020).

45. Each of these remain unequal after class-advantaged and class-disadvantaged students graduate from college (Charles, Hurst, and Killewald 2013; Fry 2021; Gugushvili et al. 2021; Mullen, Goyette, and Soares 2003; Musick, Brand, and Davis 2012; Pfeffer and Killewald 2018; Schoeni and Ross 2005).

46. Bailey and Dynarski (2011).

47. I use "wages" and "earnings" interchangeably.

48. Armstrong and Hamilton (2013); Beasley (2012); Bowen, Kurzweil, and Tobin (2005); Kim and Sax (2009); Pascarella et al. (2004); Pike and Kuh (2005); Stuber (2009); Terenzini et al. (1996); Walpole (2003); Wilbur and Roscigno (2016).

49. Scholars who consider luck as more than a residual often consider it as an individual-level factor: some individuals just happen to get luckier than others (Frank 2016; Pluchino, Biondo, and Rapisarda 2018).

50. Sauder (2020, 198) argues that sociologists prefer to explain away luck or treat it as an "explanatory junk drawer" as doing otherwise threatens sociologists' focus on social structure and rationality. But luck can also be produced by structure, as the idea of the luckocracy shows. Jencks et al. (1979) also saw luck as structurally produced. They note that firms pay different wages for similar workers who do similar work, and that luck is responsible for

whether one worker is paid more than another with similar skills, tastes, and personal characteristics.

51. Koppman (2016); Friedman and Laurison (2019); Rivera (2015); Rivera and Tilcsik (2018). Torche (2011; 2018) also found that people with graduate degrees—with the exception of PhDs—do not experience earnings equalization. These workers may be more likely to enter elite labor markets, where class-biased selection criteria is more common.
52. Bourdieu (1984); Koppman (2016).
53. Giani (2016) examined whether earnings equalization happens among recent college graduates who enter the labor market during a recession. He found that earnings equalization does not hold.
54. First-generation college graduates who major in healthcare fields have about the same average salaries as continuing-generation graduates (Gesing, Pant, and Burbage 2022).
55. The College of Business, or CoB, is also a pseudonym.
56. Carnevale, Cheah, and Hanson (2015).
57. Manzoni and Streib (2019).
58. Manzoni and Streib (2019) show that there is no statistically significant difference in the earnings that class-advantaged and class-disadvantaged male business majors receive ten years after graduating. Class-advantaged women who major in business earn about $4,000 more than class-disadvantaged women in the same major. However, this gap disappears when comparing class-advantaged and class-disadvantaged women who are similar in terms of race and motherhood status, among other factors.
59. Carnevale, Cheah, and Hanson (2015). I exclude accounting majors as many move straight into master's degree programs.
60. I also included one "chief people officer." None of the people I interviewed were contractors; all were full-time employees. Upon occasion, students were also interviewed by CEOs; I did not conduct interviews with CEOs.
61. Davis and Binder (2019) and Rivera (2015) also find that elite employers do not recruit college students at public universities.
62. Abramson (2015); Chetty et al. (2017); DiPrete and Eirich (2006).
63. Lareau and Conley (2008).
64. Pfeffer and Hertel (2015); Torche (2011); see Jacob and Klein (2019) for evidence of equal occupational prestige by class background among British college graduates.
65. Mastekaasa and Birkelund (2022).
66. Weininger, Lareau, and Conley (2015).
67. Lareau and Conley (2008).
68. See Chetty et al. (2017) for earnings equalization among students who attend the same college. For studies about all four-year college graduates—not just those attending the same college—see Bloome, Dyer, and Zhou (2018); Hout (1988); Ishida, Muller, and Ridge (1995); Pascarella et al. (2004); Thomas (2000); Torche (2011).
69. When possible, I checked respondents' self-reported earnings against posted earnings. In each case that I could check, respondents' self-reports aligned with the posted wages.
70. Means among sampled students are barely different: $47,540 for class-disadvantaged students and $44,289 for class-advantaged students. Each is somewhat higher than the starting salaries among business majors nationally (Carnevale, Cheah, and Hanson 2015). The salary numbers I use do not include bonuses since students did not know in advance if they

would receive a bonus or how much it would be. Salary is self-reported. Studies suggest that most subjects tell the truth (Abeler, Nosenzo, and Raymond 2019).

71. The student with zero earnings tried to find a professional job. She did find several but was usually fired or quit within a week. She did not always receive a paycheck for the time she worked, sometimes because she was working on commission and other times because she did not pick it up.

72. Backhaus (2004); Feldman and Klaas (2002); Young and Foot (2006).

73. WorkSpan Daily (2018).

74. Selingo (2016).

75. Cappelli (2015).

76. Finlay and Coverdill (2002).

77. Nowicki and Rosse (2002).

78. Judge, Higgins, and Cable (2000); Selingo (2016).

79. Finlay and Coverdill (2002); Gershon (2017).

80. Of course, the idea that job seekers have little information is at odds with some economists' assumptions that they have full information (Mortensen 2010; Löfgren, Persson, and Weibull 2002). However, other economists have challenged this view (Belot, Kircher, and Muller 2018; Carranza et al. 2022; Conlon et al. 2018), as have a variety of other researchers (Backhaus 2004; Cappelli 2015; Finlay and Coverdill 2002; Feldman and Klaas 2002; Gershon 2017; Young and Foot 2006).

81. Koppman (2016); Rivera (2015).

82. Erickson (1996, 248).

83. DiMaggio (1987); Lizardo (2006).

84. Cohen, March, and Olsen (1972).

85. Graeber (2019) writes that many professional employees do little work; Moss-Pech (unpublished manuscript) finds that entry-level business and engineering workers mostly do clerical work; Rivera (2015) finds hiring agents at elite businesses also see jobs for new college graduates as needing little skill.

86. Calarco (2018); Diamond and Lewis (2015).

87. Duffy, Binder, and Skrentny (2010); Lareau, Evans, and Yee (2016). It may also be difficult to believe that a luckocracy equalizes earnings because this requires thinking that a structure is more important for individuals' outcomes than their resources and strategies. Stratification research tends to focus on these resources and strategies (Blau and Duncan 1967; Bourdieu 1986; Lareau 2011).

88. Davis and Binder (2019); Rivera (2015).

89. Pedulla (2020).

90. I don't mean to imply that selection plays no role in earnings equality, only that selection alone cannot account for it.

91. Armstrong and Hamilton (2013); Mullen (2011); Stuber (2011).

92. Karlson (2019); Torche (2011); Zhou (2019). Note that Zhou finds that selection does not explain earnings equalization at selective universities, only at unselective universities.

93. It's also important to note that Rivera's (2015) findings do not contradict the idea of earnings equalization. Disadvantaged students who did not apply to or who were denied jobs at the firms she studied could find high-paying jobs at other firms and in other sectors, thereby earning the same average pay as advantaged students.

94. They attribute the class inequalities they observe to students entering different majors, among other factors. But it is unlikely that major plays a large role in producing earnings inequality. Studies using nationally representative data show that students from each class origin are fairly evenly distributed across majors (Manzoni and Streib 2019). It is also worth noting the differences between their sample and my own. Many of the disadvantaged women in Armstrong and Hamilton's (2013) study came from and returned to rural areas—places with few jobs—while the advantaged women in their study came from and returned to large and expensive cities. In my sample, the geographic differences by class were not as wide. Most students of each class background grew up in state and a larger portion of class-disadvantaged students moved out of state after graduating. Few students from either class moved to the United States' most expensive cities. In addition, many of Armstrong and Hamilton's class-disadvantaged respondents transferred universities—not graduating from the same university as the class-advantaged students. The students I followed all graduated from the same university.

Chapter Two

1. This information came from my observations at Southern State University and from what employers told me. Davis and Binder (2016) also note that employers form relationships with colleges in order to hire students.
2. Gershon (2017) makes the same point.
3. Rossetti and Dooley (2010) discovered that even supply chain professors cannot identify which job titles are associated with supply chain jobs.
4. Several hiring agents told me that they wished they didn't need to hire so early, referring both to hiring sophomores as interns who may later become full-time workers and to hiring full-time workers in the fall of students' senior years. They hired early because they believed other employers were doing so, and they wanted to compete for the same students.
5. The quotes come from field notes that I wrote while watching the videos at the information session. I quoted as accurately as I could, but I cannot guarantee that I captured each word correctly.
6. Maurer, Howe, and Lee (1992) also observe that information sessions for engineering students provide little information about salaries, benefits, and opportunities for promotions, raises, and bonuses. Breaugh and Billings (1988) similarly find that information sessions provide job seekers with little specific information and little information that they did not already know.
7. Cable et al. (2000) find little correlation between companies' culture and what they advertise it to be.
8. Davis and Binder (2019); Rivera (2015).
9. Backhaus (2004); Brenčič (2012).
10. Marinescu and Wolthoff (2016). Job ads for college-educated workers are less likely to include earnings information than job ads for workers without four-year degrees (Hall and Krueger 2008). Thus, among job ads that participants viewed, these numbers likely overestimate the percentage of jobs that included earnings information. Indeed, in a sample of job ads collected by Burning Glass Technologies, Deming and Kahn (2017) found that 87% of jobs for college graduates did not include information on wages.
11. UJobs is a pseudonym.

12. It is not new that employers post little information about wages for entry-level jobs. Rynes and Boudreau found the same in a 1986 study.

13. Data is from my analysis of all UJobs ads posted between August 1, 2015, and May 1, 2016, and listed under filters related to business, economics, and each business specialization.

14. Young and Foot (2006) find that Fortune 500 companies do not provide pay information on their corporate websites either.

15. One recruiter told students what they would be paid for a summer internship. However, to win students' trust, he told them that the salary was half its real amount. As Employer 2 (technology, sales) said: "A lot of times I'll have to tell them they're going to make $10,000, so then later, I tell them, 'It's actually 20.' Because sometimes they just don't believe me." In general, however, pay information for internships was hidden too, with only about a quarter of business internships on UJobs listing an hourly pay rate. Moreover, even if internship pay rates were listed, students would not know how much the entry-level job would pay if their internship led to one.

16. A few hiring agents I spoke to said they used Glassdoor when they searched for a job as a college student and were dismayed to find out that the pay they were offered was much lower than the site led them to believe.

17. Winkler and Fuller (2019).

18. I am referring to the fact that pay information is not typically publicly available to employees in a firm. However, in some firms, employers prohibit or discourage employees from discussing it, despite that it is illegal to do so (Rosenfeld 2017).

19. Researchers have noted that undergraduates at other business schools also tend to have a few days to two weeks to decide whether to accept a job offer (Cortés et al. 2020).

20. Xie, Killewald, and Near (2016).

21. Avent-Holt and Tomaskovic-Devey (2014); Barth et al. (2016); Song et al. (2015).

22. Rosenfeld (2021) also observes that individuals' earnings are partly due to luck. However, he does not connect this argument to how college graduates from unequal classes receive equal pay.

Chapter Three

1. Other studies have found that employers who focus on how to get hired are rated as more intimidating by students than employers who focus on the company (Turban and Dougherty 1992). The hiring agents I spoke to did not raise this reason for giving little information about the hiring process, but it is possible it weighed on their minds.

2. Indeed, Feldman and Klaas (2002) find that many companies do not give out employees' contact information. When trying to identify hiring agents to interview, I also found it difficult to figure out who to speak to at a company. While some recruiters were easily identifiable on LinkedIn, many recruiters and hiring managers were not marked on company websites or LinkedIn.

3. Nationally, continuing-generation students are more likely to complete internships than first-generation college students, but the difference is not large (Shandra 2022).

4. One study finds that, nationally, students who complete internships have a 2.2 percentage point higher likelihood of being invited to an interview (Nunley et al. 2016). While this number may be an underestimate since the study looks at people who applied to jobs four years after graduating from college, it does suggest that the returns to internships are lower

than is often thought. It is also consistent with my findings that not all employers care about whether college students complete internships.

5. National Association of Colleges and Employers (2018).

6. I focus on how employers evaluate students' skills in interviews. However, different teams also used different techniques to evaluate the same skills. For instance, teams varied on how they evaluated students' communication skills. Some employers put students in front of their CEO to test whether they could speak clearly under pressure. Others had students give an impromptu presentation to the hiring team. Some asked students to write an email or an essay to test their written communication abilities. Others asked students how they handled specific communication issues. Employer 17 (transportation, management), for example, asked job candidates: "Tell me about a time that you had to work in a group and you had a breakdown in communication that affected you. From that, how did you fix the breakdown in communication and what was the end result?"

7. Taylor and Sniezek (1984) also find that interviewers rarely agree on what questions to ask job candidates. Interviewers' differences related to their own ideas of how to interview rather than the type of job for which they hired.

8. Other studies have found that employers' interview processes and evaluation procedures vary within firms, too. Judge, Higgins, and Cable (2000, 384–85) write: "There is low reliability among interviewers regarding what questions should be asked of applicants and how applicants are evaluated," and "interviewers base their decisions on different factors, have different hiring standards, and differ in the degree to which their actual selection criteria match their intended criteria." Others find that managers admit not knowing what questions to ask, do little to prepare for interviews, and ask what amounts to a random set of questions (Nowicki and Rosse 2002; Selingo 2016). Moreover, such agreements appear not to be new. In 1984, Taylor and Sniezek found that interviewers disagreed about what topics to cover and did not consistently cover the topics they thought were important.

9. Wilbur and Roscigno (2016).

10. Stuber (2009).

11. Breen and Jonsson (2007) assume that more highly educated individuals are hired on meritocratic grounds. My findings support their assumption that employers use class-neutral criteria while not supporting the idea that the post-college labor market is meritocratic.

12. Most of the Southern State University students I followed did not receive internships that led into jobs. It's also important to note a downside to internships created for students by their parents' and parents' friends: these internships were never designed to lead into jobs. Indeed, no student I followed who had an internship created just for them was later offered a job in the same company.

13. These employers' low bars are consistent with research showing that IQ is unrelated to occupational status and income among college graduates (McGue et al. 2022).

14. Radford and Cataldi (unpublished manuscript) studied the college and career paths of high school valedictorians. They found that college students' leadership activities and work experiences do not relate to their post-graduate earnings.

15. Class-disadvantaged students tend to be less comfortable holding a conversation with employers than class-advantaged students. However, class-disadvantaged students can still hold these conversations, despite feeling less comfortable.

16. This is different than how elite employers define fit (Koppman 2016; Rivera 2015).

17. I did not ask employers how they considered racial or gender diversity. The hiring agents

who brought it up almost always did so in the context of recruiting a diverse pool. They mentioned purposefully recruiting at historically black colleges, women's colleges, and colleges that they considered racially diverse. They also mentioned recruiting at clubs that were diverse and using job ads with words that would draw people from a variety of backgrounds. No one brought up affirmative action.

18. Employers that considered university rank tended to recruit computer science or engineering majors as well as business majors.

19. Some employers also told me that they stayed away from the highest-ranked universities. They needed to generate a return on their investment—they needed to find as many hires as they could from the universities they visited. Their company was less likely to stand out at highly ranked universities, so they believed recruiting there did not make financial sense.

20. Deming et al. (2016) conducted an audit study that reinforces this point. Fictional résumés from low- and high-status public universities received the same callback rates. Mihut (2021) also conducted an audit study and found that employers call back more applicants with high skills who attend unranked universities than low-skilled applicants from highly ranked universities.

21. Chetty et al. (2017).

22. Hiring agents held different opinions about whether to screen applicants by the university they attended. The majority told me the university did not matter. Employer 26 (technology, many business roles) claimed: "We will hire any student from any university." Employer 29 (healthcare, supply chain) said: "We're open as long as it's a school that's accredited." Employer 20 (energy, hourly trader) agreed: "It really doesn't make much of a difference to the hiring managers where the degree comes from. It's more just showing that the student does have the degree." Employer 32 (transportation, management) agreed and explained why: "The school that they attended doesn't really carry a whole lot of weight. We want to make sure they meet those basic qualifications and then we want to interview them and make sure they meet our competencies. . . . A lot of times the school doesn't necessarily dictate those competencies." However, some employers did screen applicants by the university they attended. Employer 24 (technology, many business roles), like other employers, favored students from the universities where they recruited: "We really focus on our schools because we made a big investment to participate in the school. Many people wanna work for [company]. If they didn't go to our school [where we recruit], they would apply to a repository online. But we only went to the repository if we were desperate, and we were never desperate." Only a few employers focused on university rank and defined it as the higher the better. These employers hired engineers and computer scientists along with business majors, and thought technical abilities were correlated with university rank.

23. Stuber (2009).

24. Armstrong and Hamilton (2013); Goldrick-Rab (2016).

25. Remember that hiring agents believed the jobs they were recruiting for were so easy that most college graduates could do them or so specific that they couldn't expect any applicants to already have the right training. In this context, it makes sense that they view having three internships as no better than having one. Students with one internship would still be able to do most jobs and, for very specific jobs, students with three internships would still need to be trained.

26. Armstrong and Hamilton (2013); Pascarella et al. (2004); Terenzini et al. (1996); Yee (2016).

27. Bowen, Kurzweil, and Tobin (2005); Terenzini et al. (1996); but see Manzoni and Streib (2019) for evidence of similar GPAs by class origin.
28. Most employers reimburse interns for their moving and housing expenses (National Association of Colleges and Employers 2019).
29. Stuber (2009).
30. Masters (1989); Stephens-Davidowitz (2018); Stevens (2009).
31. Astin and Oseguera (2004); Semuels (2017); Stevens (2009).
32. Armstrong and Hamilton (2013); Kim and Sax (2009).
33. Based on my review of respondents' résumés.
34. Interestingly, the internships that students' parents and parents' friends created for them tended to provide students with less fodder for stories about skill use. For example, Kathy's (class advantaged) father created an internship for her in which she moved boxes, Logan's (class advantaged) neighbor designed an internship for him in which he entered data, Levi (class advantaged) did busy work for his mother's company, and Jim (class advantaged) said that the internship he received from a family friend "wasn't really that beneficial." Students could try to recast these experiences as showing evidence of skills but tended to draw upon other experiences instead.
35. In my sample, class-disadvantaged students more often found internships through applying on UJobs, while class-advantaged students more often used their connections.
36. Weiss and Roksa (2016); Wilbur and Roscigno (2016). In my study, class-disadvantaged students reported telling interviewers more about their working-class jobs than did class-advantaged students.
37. Armstrong and Hamilton (2013); Stuber (2009).
38. Class-disadvantaged students are more likely to pay for college themselves (Goldrick-Rab 2016; McCabe and Jackson 2016).
39. Khan (2010); Rivera (2015).
40. Lareau (2011).
41. Entitlement could also prevent students from converting internships into jobs. Employer 19 (technology, many business roles) explained that interns who did not receive offers acted like "'I'm hot shit. I got this job offer from [company 19].' And they come in acting like they know it all."
42. Aries and Seider (2007).

Chapter Four

1. For example, Chetty et al. (2017); Torche (2011).
2. Armstrong and Hamilton (2013); Beasley (2012); Goldrick-Rab (2016); Houle (2014); Kim and Sax (2009); Pascarella et al. (2004); Pike and Kuh (2005); Stuber (2009); Walpole (2003); Wilbur and Roscigno (2016).
3. The game selects applicants on showing up, wearing a homemade or rented costume, and appearing well on camera (https://on-camera-audiences.com/shows/Lets_Make_a_Deal; https://www.liveabout.com/contestant-on-lets-make-a-deal-1396398).
4. Disadvantaged and advantaged students do not have the same chances of entering graduate school (Mullen, Goyette, and Soares 2003), implying that college itself doesn't equalize. The systems that come after it are more relevant to equalization. Some are luckocracies and others are strong or weak class-reproduction systems.

5. This is a fake title.
6. Colbeck, Campbell, and Bjorklund (2000); Glenn (2011); Moshiri and Cardon (2014).
7. Pascarella et al. (2004); Soria, Hussein, and Vue (2014); Wilbur and Roscigno (2016).
8. Armstrong and Hamilton (2013); Rivera (2015); Stuber (2009).
9. Yee (2016).
10. Calarco (2018); Kusserow (2004).
11. Bauer-Wolf (2018).

Chapter Five

1. Refers to jobs posted between August 1, 2015, and May 1, 2016.
2. Marinescu and Wolthoff (2016).
3. Several students accidentally applied for jobs they later considered scams. These included pyramid schemes; door-to-door sales jobs in which employees had to buy the product and lose money on items they did not sell; and jobs that did not have a website, a physical address, or in which "interviewers" spoke in thick accents and refused to answer questions about the job. Career center staff told me that they believed the latter were scams to obtain students' social security numbers.
4. Students' skepticism about the value of Glassdoor reviews is for good reason. Some companies ask recently promoted employees to post a review while not asking employees who are less likely to post positively. The same person can also post multiple reviews and managers can promote the company with their own reviews. See Widdicombe (2018) for more on this topic.
5. I focus on the job search in this chapter, but the process is similar for students who search for internships that turn into jobs.
6. Of course, some class-disadvantaged students did know some professionals, including those with whom the university put them in touch. However, class-disadvantaged students, unlike class-advantaged students, tended to wait for professionals to approach them rather than approaching them themselves.
7. Class-disadvantaged participants tended to think that their parents could not help them. Ben (class disadvantaged) said of his parents: "I talk to them but not about job stuff. So my mom graduated high school but nothing beyond that. She works a retail job, not professional. Dad dropped out in eighth or ninth grade.... So for obvious reasons I don't consult them for work advice." Avery (class disadvantaged) did not turn to her parents for career advice either: "Neither of them had gone to college and neither of them work in a business setting. My mom is a hairstylist and my dad paints houses and drives for Greyhound, so they just have different environments. And so I just want to do it on my own." Asked if she talked to her father much, Rebecca (class disadvantaged) said: "Not about jobs." Asked if she received career advice from her parents, Anna (class disadvantaged) said: "Nothing is super memorable."

    As they prepared to leave college, class-disadvantaged students also tended to say that they knew few professionals. Avery (class disadvantaged) explained her situation: "I think it's only my aunt I know that has gone to college, and she's a teacher." Peter (class disadvantaged) mentioned that his only relevant network ties were to his instructors. Eli (class disadvantaged) said he did not know three professionals he could list as references.

    In college, they reached out to few professionals as well. They often reported feeling

221

intimidated by them and then avoiding networking opportunities. For instance, Karen (class disadvantaged) met a professional she thought could help her but did not activate the tie: "I was like, 'Okay, he's this big businessman, and I don't even know what I want to do yet, so what am I supposed to talk to him about?' So it was just intimidating." She decided to wait and see if he emailed her rather than emailing him first. Amy (class disadvantaged) said she was hesitant to build a network of professionals: "When we see people in the professional field, we're so afraid to talk to them. I'll see the opportunity, but then I don't go talk to them." Eli (class disadvantaged) didn't feel at home at the networking events—places designed to help students meet those who can help them: "It's really not my setting." Connor (class disadvantaged) said: "Other than career fairs and information sessions, I haven't gone to any networking events." Shawna (class disadvantaged) summed up: "Honestly, I hate networking."

8. This is an example Andrea (class disadvantaged) used.

9. Kusserow (2004); Streib (2015).

10. In Hurst's (2019, 174) review of studies on student debt, she writes of the same phenomena: "Students express a surprising lack of concern and knowledge of the full contours of their indebtedness while in college."

11. Tversky and Kahneman (1986).

12. Class-advantaged respondents were more likely than class-disadvantaged respondents to say they knew many professionals. For example, Cody (class advantaged) said he could speak to "my dad's friends, my girlfriend's dad's friends, people who are established in the industry and have a good reputation." Levi (class advantaged), like other class-advantaged students, had his parents' contacts to turn to for help: "My dad was in corporate for thirty-plus years, my mom is a real estate agent, so they come across a lot of people in multiple industries doing real estate. So I can utilize their contacts." Tyler (class advantaged), like other class-advantaged students, had his friends' parents to turn to: "I went to a private school, so a lot of people who run the companies around here, they have kids in the school, so we all know each other."

13. Class-advantaged respondents, more often than class-disadvantaged respondents, considered their parents to have useful advice. For instance, Chloe (class advantaged) said: "My mom, she has to interview and fire a lot of people so she is obviously a great resource." Carter (class advantaged) said of the role his father played in his career preparation: "He's very influential on me." Ethan (class advantaged) mentioned: "My uncle and my dad have been in finance and accounting for their entire lives, so I talk to them a lot about career opportunities." Brooke (class advantaged) added: "My dad is my biggest professional mentor." Caroline (class advantaged) said: "I did go to [my parents] for advice a lot." Katelyn (class advantaged) said of her father: "He is vice president of his company. He was an engineer but he has his master's in business, so he's basically played a part in every role in every area of business in his company. He knows about recruiting, he knows about financing, he knows about all those things. I can learn a lot from him." Kathy (class advantaged) agreed: "My dad has been my biggest network."

14. There's another reason why class-advantaged students may not have benefited from their parents' help as much as is commonly assumed. Given the differences in their parents' work histories, class-advantaged students tended to see their fathers as better positioned to help them than their mothers. However, they said that for most of their lives, their mothers provided them with more advice than their fathers. While some class-advantaged students

reported that their fathers provided detailed and ongoing career advice, others said that their fathers' advice was vague, not actionable, or given in a manner that made it difficult to accept. That fathers tended to have less practice giving their children advice may have made the advice they did give less effective.

15. This raises the question of why class-advantaged students did not receive more interviews despite sending out more résumés. Part of the reason is likely that they sent more résumés to elite firms and to firms that recruit from other schools, sending them to places where they were unlikely to be interviewed.

16. Within each class, men were more likely than women to reach out to people they did not know, approach employers, use their parents' networks, and feel comfortable at the career fair. Women were more likely than men to wait for others to come to them, to turn down their network's offers to help, and to find the career fair intimidating. Women's greater reluctance to use their networks to find a job may relate to their worries about and experiences with harassment. A handful of women who were contacted by men on LinkedIn believed that the men were interested in romantic or sexual relationships rather than work. For example, I had the following conversation with Jill (class advantaged):

JESSI: Who else has contacted you on LinkedIn?

JILL: Sometimes random professionals will just message you and say, "Oh, your profile picture looks great. It looks like you have a lot of experience." And you're like, "I don't know you."

JESSI: They comment on your picture?

JILL: Yeah. It's kind of strange. It's older middle-aged men, and so then you just delete them, but that's happened to me and my friends who are women as well, so that's kind of sketchy. You don't want strangers messaging you on LinkedIn of all places, because Facebook is one thing, it's creepy, but LinkedIn you're like, "I don't know you." But that's only happened once or twice. I just ignore that, but yeah, mainly recruiter-type people are the ones with actual information.

JESSI: Yeah. How do you figure out who is creepy and who is not?

JILL: Creepy is obviously my definition of creepy, because I'm a twenty-year-old girl, so it's creepy old men and things like that, but usually I would look at their profile. Like the lady who emailed me who was a generalist, I looked at her profile, it was like generalist at [company] and she had all her other things. I was like, 'Okay, well, this lady, she's real,' and you can tell. The man who messaged me, we had a few connections in common, and he had a real job and everything, but I don't feel comfortable about you reaching out to me because you're not in HR and there's no reason that you'd be seeking an employee.

Despite Jill's opinion that it was obvious who was creepy and who was not, not all women felt that way. Avery (class disadvantaged) dismissed a recruiter on LinkedIn who she thought was creepy: "I already had somebody message me and they didn't really have business motives. I mean, it's guys on there—it's hit-or-miss with those. So I just didn't say anything." A friend who had met the same recruiter later told Avery that he did have business motives. She later responded to him, worked for him, and did not find him to be a creepy boss. Another respondent did not think that a situation would be problematic but found that it was. Alice (class advantaged) attended a job interview. The male interviewer decided it would occur over dinner at a hotel restaurant. Alice reported that the interviewer wanted to take her upstairs to his hotel room. By the end of the evening, she was not even sure if the job posting was real. Alice declined his advances but was shaken by the experience.

17. Two class-advantaged students learned from their connections to students at nearby elite universities that companies advertised "better" jobs there. They tried applying to these jobs but were not hired.

18. To class-advantaged students, large companies were high status because if they told someone they worked there, they wouldn't ask what the company does. Binder (2014) also observes that college students equate status with working for a company that others know.

19. Kusserow (2004); Streib (2015).

20. It's possible that Claire was also thrown off by the interviewer's framing of the company. By the time Claire interviewed, the company was nationally known.

21. Ryan could have received a larger paycheck working in sales positions at other firms. Employer 2 and Employer 23 told me that their door-to-door sales interns made an average of $20,000 in a summer—an average they said included the employees who quit. Employer 23, who broke the rookie sales record for his door-to-door sales job, said he earned $117,000 in a summer—over twice as much in one summer than Ryan would make in a year. His assertion seemed likely to be true; he posted it on his LinkedIn account, one that his employer could see. He also told me that he brought his paystubs to campus recruitment events to show skeptical students.

22. Other research finds that students who apply to jobs via referrals are paid less than those who apply through formal means (Greenberg and Fernandez 2016).

23. Within each class, men more often said they were not allowed to negotiate, while women more often said that they did not negotiate because they were grateful for the offer.

24. Kahn (2010); Manzoni, Härkönen, and Mayer (2014).

25. Bui (2016).

26. Kroeger, Cooke, and Gould (2016).

27. The term "satisfice" comes from March and Simon (1958).

28. Pedulla (2020) finds that hiring agents want to know applicants' reasons for having nonstandard work histories. They evaluate these stories closely.

29. Wanberg, Ali, and Csillag (2020).

30. Faberman et al. (2022).

Chapter Six

1. Other studies have found mixed results about if mentorship varies by new hires' race and gender (Blake-Beard, Murrell, and Thomas 2006; Murrell and James 2002). Most of the students I talked to had positive mentorship relationships when they were assigned a mentor, regardless of their race or gender.

Chapter Seven

1. Other studies have also found that few companies tell employees how a new job, promotion, or raise will increase their pay (Day 2012; Mulvey et al. 2002; Shields et al. 2009).

2. Backhaus (2004, 131).

3. Backhaus (2004).
4. Young and Foot (2006, 52).
5. Cappelli (1999; 2012).
6. One study finds that managers and workers describe their employees' work so differently than the employees that many are describing fundamentally different jobs (Mathiowetz 1992). If this holds true, it's no wonder why job titles are misleading and job descriptions are unclear.
7. Punctuality can be classed, as low-income people have less access to reliable transportation. But college graduates were paid enough to avoid transportation issues.
8. When referring to inappropriate attire, employers mentioned extreme cases—cases that were unlikely to be classed. They talked of swear words on shirts, clothes with many holes, or shirts that showed women's stomachs. After years in a business school, students of all class backgrounds knew that these clothes were considered unprofessional.
9. Researchers have found that professional parents train their children to become professionals by teaching them to be assertive and autonomous (Kohn 1977). However, this training may not be helpful in the early stages of their careers. Before becoming managers, they are usually workers—people who need to fit into a hierarchy.
10. There is a long line of research showing class-disadvantaged students exhibit deference from a young age (Calarco 2018; Kohn 1977; Kusserow 2004; Streib 2011).
11. Some may wonder how long the luckocracy will last given that more experienced workers have more opportunities to negotiate, and workers from class-advantaged backgrounds are more likely to be taught to negotiate by their parents (Lareau 2011). Research finds that earnings equalization among college graduates from different class backgrounds lasts through midlife (Chetty et al. 2017; Torche 2011). It is likely that any class-origin difference in workers' propensity to negotiate or skill at negotiating is small compared to the large difference in salaries offered for similar work at different firms. It is also likely to be offset by the combination of other factors that influence pay: whether workers decide to leave the workforce to take care of children or parents; fall ill unexpectedly; switch fields; decide to scale back or increase their hours; experience layoffs; work under bosses who believe pay is a main motivator; work at organizations with few or many promotional opportunities; as well as the timing of their job searches in relationship to the economy and whether they join industries that later benefit from market forces, government regulations or subsidies, or random shocks.

Chapter Eight

1. Altintas (2015); Lareau (2011); Phillips (2011).
2. Lareau (2011); Snellman et al. (2015); Weininger, Lareau, and Conley (2015).
3. Darmon and Drewnowski (2008).
4. Child Trends (2019).
5. García and Weiss (2017); Lee and Burkam (2002).
6. Downey (2020).
7. Fry (2021).
8. Armstrong and Hamilton (2013); Beasley (2012); Bowen, Kurzweil, and Tobin (2005); Kim and Sax (2009); Pascarella et al. (2004); Pike and Kuh (2005); Stuber (2009); Terenzini et al. (1996); Walpole (2003); Wilbur and Roscigno (2016).

9. Dynarski (2017); Russakoff (2015).
10. Lee and Burkam (2002).
11. García and Weiss (2017).
12. Dynarski and Wiederspan (2012); Perna and Leigh (2018); Tough (2019).
13. Cataldi, Bennett, and Chen (2018); Wilbur and Roscigno (2016).
14. Wilbur and Roscigno (2016).
15. Kim (2015); Rege and Solli (2014).
16. Some cities and states have mandated wage posting, but allow such wide wage ranges as to be almost meaningless. They also include loopholes that allow some companies to get around posting wages (Cutter 2022).
17. Cohen, March, and Olsen (1972).
18. Cohen, March, and Olsen (1972); Sauder, Chun, and Espeland (2021); Zahariadis (1994).
19. Lazear, Shaw, and Stanton (2018).
20. Frank (2016) offers an example of this process: Bryan Cranston's career took off because a better-known actor first turned down the lead part in the television hit *Breaking Bad*.
21. Weinstein (2022).
22. Some students also have the luck of inheriting genes that relate to good health, physical attractiveness, deferred gratification, and grit—genes associated with obtaining high levels of educational attainment and high earnings (Harden 2021).
23. Rivera (2015).
24. Wildhagen (2015).
25. Haskins (2013); Murray (2013).
26. Lubrano (2004); Streib (2015).
27. Murray (2013).
28. Streib (2017).
29. Beasley (2012); Charles and Bradley (2009).
30. Beasley (2012); Cornwell and Cornwell (2008).
31. Campbell (1988); McDonald, Lin, and Ao (2009).
32. The idea here is based upon Rawls's (1971) veil of ignorance. He suggests that if individuals could be denied information about their personal circumstances and identities, they would design more fair and egalitarian systems.
33. Sandel (2020) argues that a major problem with so-called meritocracies is that they create "winners" who have too much hubris and "losers" who feel too much shame. They also do not incentivize the winners to help the losers. Instead, the winners believe the losers could match winners if they worked harder.
34. These conjectures are hypotheses that deserve further study. For more on market failures, including ones caused by one party's limited information, see Salanié (2000); Cowen and Crampton (2004).
35. Kenny (2012); Shrider et al. (2021).
36. Autor (2014).
37. Alesina and Perotti (1993).
38. Fry (2021).
39. Snellman et al. (2015).
40. Stevens (2009).
41. Arum and Roksa (2010).

42. Of course, several steps could be taken to make college less expensive. But it would still be expensive in terms of the time it takes to earn a degree and its opportunity costs.

43. See Moss and Tilly (2003) regarding employers' process of hiring low-wage workers.

44. Armstrong and Hamilton (2013); Rivera (2015).

45. This is true among the students I followed. Others have found the same (Khan 2010; Rivera 2015).

46. Mijs (2016) also writes about the unfulfillable promise of meritocracy.

47. Sandel (2020).

48. Even more than that, we can't tell if someone has merit without understanding their environment. Some interns receive more opportunities to generate results than others. Students' GPAs reflect not only their effort and skills but also which classes they take, how easy or hard their professors grade, how well their professors teach the material, if they are assigned group projects with stellar or free-riding peers, and what obligations they have outside of school. The ability for a student to lead is influenced by the desire of others to follow, the successes and failures of prior leaders, and potentially the budget that others award them. In one environment, we might think one set of students is meritorious—however we define that. In another environment, we'd pick a different set of students. See Rosenfeld (2021) for a similar critique of meritocracy.

49. Quillian, Lee, and Oliver (2020).

50. Klein (2019); Markovits (2019).

51. Many of these arguments come from Markovits (2019).

52. This is common for overqualified workers (Erdogan et al. 2011).

53. See Rivera (2015) for elite employers' argument for why they should hire people who share their cultural tastes.

54. Indeed, couples who grow up in different classes find ways to connect with each other (Streib 2015), suggesting that workers from different classes can too.

55. Jaffrelot (2006).

56. Friedersdorf (2020); Kramer (2019).

57. See Jaffrelot (2006) for a review of the issues that India's quota system has raised and Vaid (2014) for a review of the quota system's limited ability to equalize economic outcomes in India.

58. Hansen and Quintero (2017).

59. Hansen and Quintero (2017).

60. Fuller and Raman (2017).

61. Fuller and Raman (2017).

62. Fuller and Raman (2017).

63. Arum and Roksa (2010) show that many students learn little in college, especially business majors.

64. US Census Bureau (2019).

65. Indeed, during the Great Recession, college graduates from advantaged backgrounds out-earned college graduates from disadvantaged backgrounds (Giani 2016).

66. Tomaskovic-Devey (2022).

67. It is also possible that men's greater ties to workers may be offset by other factors that wage transparency brings, such as women knowing which jobs pay women less than men (Bennedsen et al. 2019).

68. There is some evidence that posting wages lowers the gender wage gap. However, these studies have primarily focused on academia or more liberal countries, places where there is more pressure to be gender equal (Baker et al. 2019; Bennedsen et al. 2019; Obloj and Zenger 2022).
69. *The Economist* (2017).
70. England (2005; 2010).
71. Brady, Baker, and Finnigan (2013).
72. Schneider and Harknett (2021).
73. Baron et al. (2014).
74. See the Shift Project's efforts at making wages transparent for low-wage work: https://shift.hks.harvard.edu/the-company-wage-tracker.
75. Rivera (2015).
76. Luckocracies also do not operate in labor markets in which applicants are chosen based upon their tastes, such as markets for museum curators, publishers, film directors, advertisers, and graphic designers. Though not always recognized as such, "good taste" often means the taste of the advantaged groups, and so these industries tend to use class-biased hiring criteria (Bourdieu 1984; Koppman 2016; Thomas 2018). Changing these systems to luckocracies would be beneficial but difficult.
77. Some may wonder if it is possible to have different opportunity structures in different labor markets. I would argue that we already do.
78. Employers would be better able to provide transparency if they hire soon before the new employee starts working. Several of the employers I talked to would welcome this change. They bemoan that other firms begin hiring early in the fall and choose interns earlier and earlier in their college career. They match other firms' timelines to compete with them, though they would prefer to hire later.
79. Cutter (2022).
80. There is precedent for such an approach. New York City, California, and Colorado mandate that wage ranges be posted for every job (New York City Commission on Human Rights 2022; Valdez 2022). But, as mentioned, these laws contain substantial loopholes.
81. Calarco (2018); Lareau (2011); Streib (2011).
82. Of course, this is not exactly how *Let's Make a Deal* works. The game does not reveal any information about what contestants receive if they trade in their prize.

Appendix A

1. Bourdieu and Wacquant (1992).
2. Bourdieu and Wacquant (1992).
3. Bourdieu (1980; 1984).
4. Armstrong and Hamilton (2013); Calarco (2018); Lareau (2011); Rivera (2015); Streib (2011).
5. Bourdieu and Wacquant (1992).
6. Bourdieu and Wacquant (1992).
7. This point is also made by Lareau, Evans, and Yee (2016).
8. Bourdieu (1988).
9. Survey research often measures tastes decontextualized from fields.
10. For example, see Bathmaker et al. (2016) and Burke (2016).
11. Of course, this was Bourdieu's point as well (Bourdieu and Wacquant 1992).

12. Rivera (2012).
13. As Sauder (2020, 198) puts it, "The default approach to luck, then, is to treat it as something that should be explained away rather than studied." Likewise, Denrell, Fang, and Liu (2015, 923) write that management scholars dismiss luck for the same reason: "Management scholars often consider chance and randomness as a nuisance to be eliminated." These authors argue against what they see as the dominant approach; they believe we should not dismiss luck as an unexplained residual. Of course, other scholars see luck as a chance encounter that happens to individuals and that meaningfully relates to their outcomes (Frank 2016; Pluchino, Biondo, and Rapisarda 2018; Sauder 2020).

Appendix B

1. Armstrong and Hamilton (2013); Hamilton (2016); Pascarella et al. (2004); Rivera (2015); Stuber (2011).
2. Bourdieu (1984).
3. Chetty et al. (2017); Torche (2011).
4. National Center for Education Statistics (2019), refers to co-residential parents only.
5. Carnevale, Cheah, and Hanson (2015).
6. Manzoni and Streib (2019).
7. Carnevale, Cheah, and Hanson (2015).
8. Lee and Kao (2009).
9. Elman and O'Rand (2004).
10. Burawoy (1998).

References

Abeler, Johannes, Daniele Nosenzo, and Collin Raymond. 2019. "Preferences for Truth-Telling." *Econometrica* 87 (4): 1115–53.

Abramson, Corey. 2015. *The End Game: How Inequality Shapes Our Final Years*. Cambridge, MA: Harvard University Press.

Alesina, Alberto, and Roberto Perotti. 1993. "Income Distribution, Political Instability, and Investment." NBER Working Paper 4486.

Altenhofen, Shannon, Mark Berends, and Thomas G. White. 2016. "School Choice Decision Making among Suburban, High-Income Parents." *AERA Open* 2 (1): 1–14.

Altintas, Evrim. 2015. "The Widening Education Gap in Developmental Child Care Activities in the United States, 1965–2013." *Journal of Marriage and Family* 78 (1): 26–42.

Aries, Elizabeth, and Maynard Seider. 2007. "The Role of Social Class in the Formation of Identity: A Study of Public and Elite Private College Students." *Journal of Social Psychology* 147 (2): 137–58.

Armstrong, Elizabeth, and Laura Hamilton. 2013. *Paying for the Party: How College Maintains Inequality*. Cambridge, MA: Harvard University Press.

Arum, Richard, and Josipa Roksa. 2010. *Academically Adrift: Limited Learning on College Campuses*. Chicago: University of Chicago Press.

Astin, Alexander, and Leticia Oseguera. 2004. "The Declining 'Equity' of American Higher Education." *Review of Higher Education* 27 (3): 321–41.

Attewell, Paul, David Lavin, Thurston Domina, and Tania Levey. 2007. *Passing the Torch: Does Higher Education for the Disadvantaged Pay Off across the Generations?* New York: Russell Sage Foundation.

Autor, David. 2014. "Skills, Education, and the Rise of Earnings Inequality among the 'Other 99 Percent.'" *Science* 344 (6186): 843–51.

Avent-Holt, Dustin, and Donald Tomaskovic-Devey. 2014. "A Relational Theory of Earnings Inequality." *American Behavioral Scientist* 58 (3): 379–99.

Backhaus, Kristin. 2004. "An Exploration of Corporate Recruitment Descriptions on Monster .com." *Journal of Business Communication* 41 (2): 115–36.

Bailey, Martha, and Susan Dynarski. 2011. "Educational Expectations and Attainment." In *Whither Opportunity? Rising Inequality, Schools, and Children's Life Chances*, ed. Greg Duncan and Richard Murnane, 117–32. New York: Russell Sage Foundation.

Baker, Michael, Yosh Halberstam, Kory Kroft, Alexandre Mas, and Derek Messacar. 2019. "Pay Transparency and the Gender Gap." NBER Working Paper 25834.

Baron, Sherry, Sharon Beard, Letitia K. Davis, Linda Delp, Linda Forst, Andrea Kidd-Taylor, Amy K. Liebman, Laura Linnan, Laura Punnett, and Laura S. Welch. 2014. "Promoting Integrated Approaches to Reducing Health Inequities among Low-Income Workers: Applying a Social Ecological Framework." *American Journal of Industrial Medicine* 57:539–56.

Barth, Erling, Alex Bryson, James Davis, and Richard Freeman. 2016. "It's Where You Work: Increases in Earnings Dispersion across Establishments and Individuals in the U.S." *Journal of Labor Economics* 34 (2): S67–S97.

Bathmaker, Ann-Marie, Nicola Ingram, Jessie Abrahams, Anthony Hoare, Richard Waller, and Harriet Bradley. 2016. *Higher Education, Social Class, and Social Mobility: The Degree Generation*. London: Palgrave Macmillan.

Bauer-Wolf, Jeremy. 2018. "More Growth for Handshake." *Insider Higher Ed*, April 30.

Beasley, Maya. 2012. *Opting Out: Losing the Potential of America's Young Black Elite*. Chicago: University of Chicago Press.

Belot, Michèle, Philipp Kircher, and Paul Muller. 2018. "Providing Advice to Jobseekers at Low Cost: An Experimental Study on Online Advice." *Review of Economic Studies* 86:1411–47.

Bennedsen, Morten, Elena Simintzi, Margarita Tsoutsoura, and Daniel Wolfenzon. 2019. "Do Firms Respond to Gender Pay Gap Transparency?" NBER Working Paper 25435.

Binder, Amy. 2014. "Why Are Harvard Grads Still Flocking to Wall Street?" *Washington Monthly*, August 21.

Blake-Beard, Stacy, Audrey Murrell, and David Thomas. 2006. "Unfinished Business: The Impact on Understanding Mentoring Relationships." Harvard Business School, Working Paper No. 06-060.

Blau, Peter, and Otis Dudley Duncan. 1967. *The American Opportunity Structure*. New York: John Wiley & Sons.

Bloome, Deirdre, Shauna Dyer, and Xiang Zhou. 2018. "Educational Inequality, Educational Expansion, and Intergenerational Income Persistence in the United States." *American Sociological Review* 83 (6): 1215–53.

Bourdieu, Pierre. 1980. *The Logic of Practice*. Palo Alto, CA: Stanford University Press.

Bourdieu, Pierre. 1984. *Distinction: A Social Critique of the Judgement of Taste*. Cambridge, MA: Harvard University Press.

Bourdieu, Pierre. 1986. "The Forms of Capital." In *Handbook of Theory and Research for the Sociology of Education*, ed. John G. Richardson, 241–58. Westport, CT: Greenwood.

Bourdieu, Pierre. 1988. *Homo Academicus*. Cambridge: Polity Press.

Bourdieu, Pierre, and Jean-Claude Passeron. 1977. *Reproduction in Education, Society and Culture*. New York: Sage.

Bourdieu, Pierre, and Loïc Wacquant. 1992. *An Invitation to Reflexive Sociology*. Chicago: Chicago University Press.

Bowen, William, Martin Kurzweil, and Eugene Tobin. 2005. *Equity and Excellence in American Higher Education*. Charlottesville: University of Virginia Press.

Brady, David, Regina Baker, and Ryan Finnigan. 2013. "When Unionization Disappears: State-Level Unionization and Working Poverty in the United States." *American Sociological Review* 78 (5): 872–96.

Breaugh, James, and Robert Billings. 1988. "The Realistic Job Preview: Five Key Elements and

Their Importance for Research and Practice." *Journal of Business and Psychology* 2 (4): 291–305.

Breen, Richard, and Jan Jonsson. 2007. "Explaining Change in Social Fluidity: Educational Equalization and Educational Expansion in Twentieth-Century Sweden." *American Journal of Sociology* 112 (6): 1775–810.

Brenčič, Vera. 2012. "Wage Posting: Evidence from Job Ads." *Canadian Journal of Economics* 45 (4): 1529–59.

Buchmann, Claudia, Dennis Condron, and Vincent Roscigno. 2010. "Shadow Education, American Style: Test Preparation, the SAT and College Enrollment." *Sociology of Education* 89 (2): 435–61.

Bui, Quoctrung. 2016. "The One Question Most Americans Get Wrong about College Graduates." *New York Times*, June 5.

Burawoy, Michael. 1998. "The Extended Case Method." *Sociological Theory* 16 (1): 1–33.

Burke, Ciaran. 2016. *Culture, Capitals, and Graduate Futures: Degrees of Class*. New York: Taylor & Francis.

Cable, Daniel, Lynda Aiman-Smith, Paul Mulvey, and Jeffrey Edwards. 2000. "The Sources and Accuracy of Job Applicants' Beliefs about Organizational Culture." *Academy of Management Journal* 43 (6): 1076–85.

Calarco, Jessica McCrory. 2018. *Negotiating Opportunities: Social Class and Children's Help-Seeking in Elementary School*. New York: Oxford University Press.

Calarco, Jessica McCrory. 2020. "Avoiding Us versus Them: How Schools' Dependence on Privileged 'Helicopter' Parents Influences Enforcement of Rules." *American Sociological Review* 85 (2): 223–46.

Campbell, Karen. 1988. "Gender Differences in Job-Related Networks." *Work and Occupations* 15 (2): 179–200.

Cappelli, Peter. 1999. *The New Deal at Work: Managing the Market-Driven Workforce*. Cambridge, MA: Harvard University Press.

Cappelli, Peter. 2012. *Why Good People Can't Get Jobs: The Skills Gap and What Companies Can Do about It*. Philadelphia: Wharton Digital Press.

Cappelli, Peter. 2015. *Will College Pay Off? A Guide to the Most Important Financial Decision You'll Ever Make*. New York: Public Affairs.

Carnevale, Anthony, Ban Cheah, and Andrew Hanson. 2015. "The Economic Value of College Majors." Georgetown University Center on Education and the Workforce. https://cew .georgetown.edu/cew-reports/valueofcollegemajors/.

Carranza, Eliana, Robert Garlick, Kate Orkin, and Neil Rankin. 2022. "Job Search and Hiring with Limited Information about Workseekers' Skills." *American Economic Review* 112 (11): 3547–83.

Castilla, Emilio. 2008. "Gender, Race, and Meritocracy in Organizational Careers." *American Journal of Sociology* 113 (6): 1479–526.

Cataldi, Emily, Christopher Bennett, and Xianglei Chen. 2018. "First-Generation Students: College Access, Persistence, and Postbachelor's Outcomes." Washington, DC: US Department of Education.

Centers for Disease Control and Prevention. 2021. "Childhood Lead Poisoning Prevention: Populations at Higher Risk." October 29. https://www.cdc.gov/nceh/lead/prevention/ populations.htm.

Charles, Kerwin Kofi, Erik Hurst, and Alexandra Killewald. 2013. "Marital Sorting and Parental Wealth." *Demography* 50 (1): 51–70.

Charles, Maria, and Karen Bradley. 2009. "Indulging Our Gendered Selves? Sex Segregation by Field of Study in 44 Countries." *American Journal of Sociology* 114 (4): 924–76.

Chetty, Raj, John Friedman, Emmanuel Saez, Nicholas Turner, and Danny Yagan. 2017. "Mobility Report Cards: The Role of Colleges in Intergenerational Mobility." *Equality of Opportunity Project*, http://www.equality-of-opportunity.org/papers/coll_mrc_paper.pdf.

Chetty, Raj, John Friedman, Emmanuel Saez, Nicholas Turner, and Danny Yagan. 2020. "Income Segregation and Intergenerational Mobility across Colleges in the United States." *Quarterly Journal of Economics* 135 (3): 1567–633.

Chetty, Raj, and Nathaniel Hendren. 2018. "The Impacts of Neighborhoods on Intergenerational Mobility I: Childhood Exposure Effects." *Quarterly Journal of Economics* 133 (3): 1107–62.

Child Trends. 2019. *Adverse Experiences.* https://www.childtrends.org/?indicators=adverse-experiences.

Choy, Susan. 2001. "Students Whose Parents Did Not Go to College: Postsecondary Access, Persistence, and Attainment." *Condition of Education 2001.* Washington, DC: National Center for Education Statistics.

Cohen, Michael, James March, and Johan Olsen. 1972. "A Garbage Can Model of Organizational Choice." *Administrative Science Quarterly* 17 (1): 1–25.

Colbeck, Carol, Susan Campbell, and Stefani Bjorklund. 2000. "Grouping in the Dark." *Journal of Higher Education* 71 (1): 60–83.

Conlon, John, Laura Pilossoph, Matthew Wiswall, and Basit Zafar. 2018. "Labor Market Search with Imperfect Information and Learning." NBER Working Paper 24988.

Cornwell, Erin, and Benjamin Cornwell. 2008. "Access to Expertise as a Form of Social Capital: An Examination of Race- and Class-Based Disparities in Network Ties to Experts." *Sociological Perspectives* 51 (4): 853–76.

Cortés, Patricia, Jessica Pan, Laura Pilossoph, and Basit Zafar. 2020. "Gender Differences in Job Search and the Earnings Gap: Evidence from Business Majors." NBER Conference Paper. https://conference.nber.org/conf_papers/f141273.pdf.

Cowen, Tyler, and Eric Crampton. 2004. *Market Failure or Success: The New Debate.* Cheltenham, UK: Edward Elgar.

Cutter, Chip. 2022. "JPMorgan, Macy's and Other Companies Reveal What They Pay Workers as Deadline Looms." *Wall Street Journal,* October 30.

Darmon, Nicole, and Adam Drewnowski. 2008. "Does Social Class Predict Diet Quality?" *American Journal of Clinical Nutrition* 87:1107–17.

Davis, Daniel, and Amy Binder. 2016. "Selling Students: The Rise of Corporate Partnership Programs in University Career Centers." *Research in the Sociology of Organizations,* ed. Elizabeth Popp Berman and Catherine Paradeise, 46:395–422.

Davis, Daniel, and Amy Binder. 2019. "Industry, Firm, Job Title: The Layered Nature of Early-Career Advantage for Graduates of Elite Private Universities." *Socius* 5:1–23.

Day, Nancy. 2012. "Pay Equity as a Mediator of the Relationships among Attitudes and Communication about Pay Level Determination and Pay Secrecy." *Journal of Leadership & Organizational Studies* 19 (4): 462–76.

Dearden, James, Suhui Li, Chad Meyerhoefer, and Muzhe Yang. 2017. "Demonstrated Interest: Signaling Behavior in College Admissions." *Contemporary Economic Policy* 35 (4): 630–57.

Deming, David, and Lisa Kahn. 2017. "Skill Requirements across Firms and Labor Markets: Evidence from Job Postings for Professionals." NBER Working Paper 23328.

Deming, David, Noam Yuchtman, Amira Abulafi, Claudia Goldin, and Lawrence Katz. 2016. "The Value of Postsecondary Credentials in the Labor Market: An Experimental Study." *American Economic Review* 106 (3): 778–806.

Denrell, Jerker, Christina Fang, and Chengwei Liu. 2015. "Chance Explanations in the Management Sciences." *Organization Science* 26 (3): 923–40.

Dey, Farouk, and Christine Cruzvergara. 2014. "Evolution of Career Services in Higher Education." *New Directions for Student Services* 148:5–18.

Diamond, John, and Kimberly Gomez. 2004. "African American Parents' Educational Orientations: The Importance of Social Class and Parents' Perceptions of Schools." *Education and Urban Society* 36 (4): 383–427.

Diamond, John, and Amanda Lewis. 2015. *Despite the Best Intentions: How Racial Inequality Thrives in Good Schools.* New York: Oxford University Press.

DiMaggio, Paul. 1987. "Classification in Art." *American Sociological Review* 52 (4): 440–55.

DiPrete, Thomas, and Gregory Eirich. 2006. "Cumulative Advantage as a Mechanism for Inequality: A Review of Theoretical and Empirical Developments." *Annual Review of Sociology* 32:271–97.

Downey, Douglas. 2020. *How Schools Really Matter: Why Our Assumption about Schools and Inequality Is Mostly Wrong.* Chicago: Chicago University Press.

Duffy, Meghan, Amy Binder, and John Skrentny. 2010. "Elite Status and Social Change: Using Field Analysis to Explain Policy Formation and Implementation." *Social Problems* 57 (1): 49–73.

Dynarski, Mark. 2017. "It's Not Nothing: The Role of Money in Improving Education." *Brookings Institute*, March 2. https://www.brookings.edu/research/its-not-nothing-the-role-of-money-in-improving-education/.

Dynarski, Susan, and Mark Wiederspan. 2012. "Student Aid Simplification: Looking Back and Looking Ahead." NBER Working Paper 17834.

The Economist. 2017. "Men, Women, and Work: The Gender Pay Gap." October 7.

Elman, Cheryl, and Angela O'Rand. 2004. "The Race Is to the Swift: Socioeconomic Origins, Adult Education and Mid-Life Economic Attainment." *American Journal of Sociology* 110 (1): 123–60.

England, Paula. 2005. "Gender Inequality in Labor Markets: The Role of Motherhood and Segregation." *Social Politics: International Studies in Gender, State and Society* 12 (2): 264–88.

England, Paula. 2010. "The Gender Revolution: Uneven and Stalled." *Gender & Society* 24 (2): 149–66.

Erdogan, Berrin, Tayla N. Bauer, José María Peiró, and Donald Truxillo. 2011. "Overqualified Employees: Making the Best of a Potentially Bad Situation for Individuals and Organizations." *Industrial and Organizational Psychology* 4: 215–32.

Erickson, Bonnie. 1996. "Culture, Class, and Connections." *American Journal of Sociology* 102 (1): 217–51.

Espenshade, Thomas, and Alexandria Walton Radford. 2009. *No Longer Separate, Not Yet Equal: Race and Class in Elite College Admission and Campus Life.* Princeton, NJ: Princeton University Press.

Faberman, Jason, Andreas I. Mueller, Ayşegül Şahin, and Giorgio Topa. 2022. "Job Search Behavior among the Employed and Non-Employed." *Econometrica* 90 (4): 1743–79.

Feldman, Daniel, and Brian Klaas. 2002. "Internet Job Hunting: A Field Study of Applicant Experiences with Online Recruiting." *Human Resource Management* 41 (2): 175–92.

Fernández, Raquel, and Richard Rogerson. 2001. "Sorting and Long-Run Inequality." *Quarterly Journal of Economics* 116 (4): 1305–41.

Finlay, William, and James Coverdill. 2002. *Headhunters: Matchmakers in the Labor Market*. Ithaca, NY: Cornell University Press.

Ford, Karly. 2019. "Persisting Gaps: Labor Market Outcomes and Numeracy Skill Levels of First-Generation and Multi-Generation College Graduates in the United States." *Research in Social Stratification and Mobility* 56: 21–27.

Frank, Robert. 2016. *Success and Luck: Good Fortune and the Myth of Meritocracy*. Princeton, NJ: Princeton University Press.

Friedersdorf, Connor. 2020. "Why California Rejected Racial Preferences, Again." *The Atlantic*, November 10.

Friedman, Sam, and Daniel Laurison. 2019. *The Class Ceiling: Why It Pays to Be Privileged*. Chicago: Policy Press.

Fry, Richard. 2021. "First-Generation College Graduates Lag Behind Their Peers on Key Economic Outcomes." Pew Research Center, May 18. https://www.pewresearch.org/social -trends/2021/05/18/first-generation-college-graduates-lag-behind-their-peers-on-key -economic-outcomes/.

Fuller, Joseph, Christina Langer, Julia Nitshke, Layla O'Kane, Matt Sigelman, and Bledi Taska. 2022. "The Emerging Degree Reset." The Burning Glass Institute. https://www.hbs.edu/ managing-the-future-of-work/Documents/research/emerging_degree_reset_020922.pdf.

Fuller, Joseph, and Manjari Raman. 2017. *Dismissed by Degrees*. Accenture, Grads of Life, Harvard Business School. https://gradsoflife.org/wp-content/uploads/2020/07/Dismissed-by -Degrees-10.26.17-1.pdf.

García, Emma, and Elaine Weiss. 2017. "Education Inequalities at the School Starting Gate: Gaps, Trends, and Strategies to Address Them." Economic Policy Institute, September 27. https://www.epi.org/publication/education-inequalities-at-the-school-starting-gate/.

Gershon, Ilana. 2017. *Down and Out in the New Economy: How People Find (or Don't Find) Work Today*. Chicago: University of Chicago Press.

Gesing, Peggy, Mohan Pant, and Amanda Burbage. 2022. "Health Occupations Salary Outcomes: Intersections of Student Race, Gender, and First-Generation Status." *Advances in Health Sciences Education*.

Giani, Matt. 2016. "Are All Colleges Equally Equalizing? How Institutional Selectivity Impacts Socioeconomic Disparities in Graduates' Labor Outcomes." *Review of Higher Education* 39 (3): 431–61.

Glenn, David. 2011. "The Default Major: Skating through B-School." *New York Times*, April 14.

Golden, Daniel. 2007. *The Price of Admission: How America's Ruling Class Buys Its Way into Elite Colleges—and Who Gets Left Outside the Gates*. New York: Random House.

Goldrick-Rab, Sara. 2016. *Paying the Price: College Costs, Financial Aid, and the Betrayal of the American Dream*. Chicago: University of Chicago.

Graeber, David. 2019. *Bullshit Jobs: A Theory*. New York: Simon & Schuster.

Greenberg, Jason, and Roberto Fernandez. 2016. "The Strength of Weak Ties in MBA Job Search: A Within-Person Test." *Sociological Science* 3:296–316.

Gugushvili, Alexi, Grzegorz Bulczak, Olga Zelinska, and Jonathan Koltai. 2021. "Socioeconomic

Position, Social Mobility, and Health Selection Effects on Allostatic Load in the United States." *PLoS ONE* 16 (8): e0254414.

Hall, Robert, and Alan Krueger. 2008. "Wage Formation between Newly Hired Workers and Employers: Survey Evidence." NBER Working Paper 14329.

Hall, Robert, and Alan Krueger. 2010. "Evidence on the Determinants of the Choice between Wage Posting and Wage Bargaining." NBER Working Paper 16033.

Hamilton, Laura. 2016. *Parenting to a Degree: How Family Matters for College Women's Success.* Chicago: University of Chicago Press.

Hansen, Michael, and Diana Quintero. 2017. "Scrutinizing Equal Pay for Equal Work among Teachers." Brookings, September 7. https://www.brookings.edu/research/scrutinizing-equal -pay-for-equal-work-among-teachers/.

Harden, Kathryn Paige. 2021. *The Genetic Lottery: Why DNA Matters for Social Equality.* Princeton, NJ: Princeton University Press.

Haskins, Ron. 2013. "Three Simple Rules Poor Teens Should Follow to Join the Middle Class." Brookings, March 13. https://www.brookings.edu/opinions/three-simple-rules-poor-teens -should-follow-to-join-the-middle-class/.

Houle, Jason. 2014. "Disparities in Debt: Parents' Socioeconomic Status and Young Adult Student Loan Debt." *Sociology of Education* 87 (1): 53–69.

Hout, Michael. 1988. "More Universalism, Less Structural Mobility: The American Occupational Structure in the 1980s." *American Journal of Sociology* 93 (6): 1358–400.

Hoxby, Caroline, and Christopher Avery. 2012. "The Missing 'One-Offs': The Hidden Supply of High-Achieving, Low Income Students." NBER Working Paper 18586.

Hurst, Allison. 2019. *Amplified Advantage: Going to a "Good" College in an Era of Inequality.* New York: Lexington Books.

Ishida, Hiroshi, Walter Muller, and John M. Ridge. 1995. "Class Origin, Class Destination, and Education: A Cross-National Study of Ten Industrial Nations." *American Journal of Sociology* 101 (1): 145–93.

Jacob, Marita, and Markus Klein. 2019. "Social Origin, Field of Study, and Graduates' Career Progression: Does Social Inequality Vary across Different Fields?" *British Journal of Sociology* 70 (5): 1850–73.

Jaffrelot, Christophe. 2006. "The Impact of Affirmative Action in India: More Political than Socioeconomic." *India Review* 5 (2): 173–89.

Jencks, Christopher, et al. 1979. *Who Gets Ahead?: The Determinants of Economic Success in America.* New York: Basic Books.

Judge, Timothy, Chad Higgins, and Daniel Cable. 2000. "The Employment Interview: A Review of Recent and Recommendations for Future Research." *Human Resource Management Review* 10 (4): 383–406.

Kahlenberg, Richard. 2010. *Affirmative Action for the Rich: Legacy Preferences in College Admissions.* New York: Century Foundation.

Kahn, Lisa. 2010. "The Long-Term Labor Market Consequences of Graduating from College in a Bad Economy." *Labour Economics* 17 (2): 303–16.

Kalmijn, Matthijs. 1991. "Intermarriage and Homogamy: Causes, Patterns, Trends." *Annual Review of Sociology* 24 (1): 395–421.

Kalmijn, Matthijs. 1998. "Status Homogamy in the United States." *American Journal of Sociology* 97 (2): 496–523.

Karabel, Jerome. 2005. *The Chosen: The Hidden History of Admission and Exclusion at Harvard, Yale, and Princeton.* New York: Houghton Mifflin Harcourt.

Karen, David. 1990. "Toward a Political-Organizational Model of Gatekeeping: The Case of Elite Colleges." *Sociology of Education* 63 (4): 227–40.

Karlson, Kristian Bernt. 2019. "College as Equalizer? Testing the Selectivity Hypothesis." *Social Science Research* 80:216–29.

Kearney, Melissa S., Benjamin H. Harris, Elisa Jácome, and Lucie Parker. 2014. "Ten Economic Facts about Crime and Incarceration in the United States." Brookings. https://www .brookings.edu/wp-content/uploads/2016/06/v8_thp_10crimefacts.pdf.

Kenny, Charles. 2012. "We're All the 1 Percent." *Foreign Policy*, February 27.

Khan, Shamus. 2010. *Privilege: The Making of an Adolescent Elite at St. Paul's School.* Princeton, NJ: Princeton University Press.

Kim, Marlene. 2015. "Pay Secrecy and the Gender Wage Gap in the United States." *Industrial Relations* 54 (4): 648–67.

Kim, Young, and Linda Sax. 2009. "Student-Faculty Interaction in Research Universities: Differences by Student Gender, Race, Social Class, and First-Generation Status." *Research in Higher Education* 50 (5): 437–59.

King, Michael. 2021. "College as a Great Equalizer? Marriage and Assortative Mating among First- and Continuing-Generation College Students." *Demography* 58 (6): 2265–89.

Klein, Ezra. 2019. "Work as Identity, Burnout as Lifestyle." *Vox Conversations* (podcast), April 22.

Khurana, Rakesh. 2010. *From Higher Aims to Hired Hands: The Social Transformation of American Business Schools and the Unfulfilled Promise of Management as a Profession.* Princeton, NJ: Princeton University Press.

Kohn, Melvin. 1977. *Class and Conformity: A Study in Values.* Chicago: University of Chicago Press.

Koppman, Sharon. 2016. "Different Like Me: Why Cultural Omnivores Get Creative Jobs." *Administrative Science Quarterly* 61 (2): 291–331.

Kramer, Margaret. 2019. "A Timeline of Key Supreme Court Cases on Affirmative Action." *New York Times*, March 30.

Kroeger, Teresa, Tanyell Cooke, and Elise Gould. 2016. "The Class of 2016: The Labor Market Is Still Far from Ideal for Young Graduates." Economic Policy Institute, April 21. https://www .epi.org/publication/class-of-2016/.

Kusserow, Adrie. 2004. *American Individualisms: Child Rearing and Social Class in Three Neighborhoods.* New York: Palgrave Macmillan.

Lareau, Annette. 2011. *Unequal Childhoods: Class, Race, and Family Life.* 2nd ed. Berkeley: University of California Press.

Lareau, Annette, and Jessica McCrory Calarco. 2012. "Class, Cultural Capital, and Institutions: The Case of Families and Schools." In *Facing Social Class: Social Psychology of Social Class*, ed. Susan Fiske and Hazel Markus, 61–86. New York: Russell Sage.

Lareau, Annette, and Dalton Conley. 2008. *Social Class: How Does It Work?* New York: Russell Sage.

Lareau, Annette, Shani Adia Evans, and April Yee. 2016. "The Rules of the Game and the Uncertain Transmission of Advantage: Middle-Class Parents' Search for an Urban Kindergarten." *Sociology of Education* 89 (4): 279–99.

Lareau, Annette, and Kimberly Goyette, eds. 2014. *Choosing Homes, Choosing Schools.* New York: Russell Sage Foundation.

Lazear, Edward P., Kathryn L. Shaw, and Christopher T. Stanton. 2018. "Who Gets Hired? The Importance of Competition among Applicants." *Journal of Labor Economics* 36 (S1): S133–S181.

Lee, Elizabeth, and Grace Kao. 2009. "Less Bang for the Buck? Immigration and Cultural Capital Effects on Kindergarten Academic Outcomes." *Poetics* 37 (3): 201–26.

Lee, Valerie, and David Burkam. 2002. *Inequality at the Starting Gate: Social Background Differences in Achievement as Children Begin School.* Washington, DC: Economic Policy Institute.

Lieber, Ron. 2019. "Another Admissions Advantage for the Affluent: Just Pay Full Price." *New York Times*, March 15.

Lizardo, Omar. 2006. "How Cultural Tastes Shape Personal Networks." *American Sociological Review* 71:778–807.

Löfgren, Karl-Gustaf, Torsten Persson, and Jörgen W. Weibull. 2002. "Markets with Asymmetric Information: The Contributions of George Akerlof, Michael Spence and Joseph Stiglitz." *Scandinavian Journal of Economics* 104 (2): 195–211.

Lubrano, Alfred. 2004. *Limbo: Blue-Collar Roots, White-Collar Dreams.* Hoboken, NJ: Wiley.

Manzoni, Anna, Juho Härkönen, and Karl Ulrich Mayer. 2014. "Moving On? A Growth-Curve Analysis of Occupational Attainment and Career Progression Patterns in West Germany." *Social Forces* 92 (4): 1285–312.

Manzoni, Anna, and Jessi Streib. 2019. "The Equalizing Power of a College Degree for First-Generation College Students: Disparities across Institutions, Majors, and Achievement Levels." *Research in Higher Education* 60 (5): 577–605.

March, James, and Herbert Simon. 1958. *Organizations.* New York: John Wiley & Sons, Inc.

Mare, Robert. 1981. "Change and Stability in Educational Stratification." *American Sociological Review* 46 (1): 72–87.

Marinescu, Ioana, and Ronald Wolthoff. 2016. "Opening the Black Box of the Matching Function: The Power of Words." NBER Working Paper 22508.

Markovits, Daniel. 2019. *The Meritocracy Trap: How America's Foundational Myth Feeds Inequality, Dismantles the Middle Class, and Devours the Elite.* New York: Penguin.

Mastekaasa, Arne, and Gunn E. Birkelund. 2022. "The Intergenerational Transmission of Social Advantage and Disadvantage: Comprehensive Evidence on the Association of Parents' and Children's Educational Attainments, Class, Earnings, and Status." *European Societies.*

Masters, Brooke. 1989. "Minority Recruitment Vexes Scouts." *Washington Post*, August 13.

Mathiowetz, Nancy. 1992. "Errors in Reports of Occupation." *Public Opinion Quarterly* 56 (3): 352–55.

Maurer, Steven, Vince Howe, and Thomas Lee. 1992. "Organizational Recruiting as Marketing Management: An Interdisciplinary Study of Engineering Graduates." *Personnel Psychology* 45 (4): 807–33.

McCabe, Janice, and Brandon Jackson. 2016. "Pathways to Financing College: Race and Class in Students' Narratives of Paying for School." *Social Currents* 3 (4): 367–85.

McDonald, Steve, Nan Lin, and Dan Ao. 2009. "Networks of Opportunity: Gender, Race, and Job Leads." *Social Problems* 56 (3): 385–402.

McGue, Matt, Elise L. Anderson, Emily Willoughby, Alexandros Giannelis, William G. Iacono, and James J. Lee. 2022. "Not by G Alone: The Benefits of a College Education among Individuals with Low Levels of General Cognitive Ability." *Intelligence* 92:101642.

Mihut, Georgiana. 2021. "Does University Prestige Lead to Discrimination in the Labor Market?

Evidence from a Labor Market Field Experiment in Three Countries." *Studies in Higher Education* 47 (6): 1227–42.

Mijs, Jonathan. 2016. "The Unfulfillable Promise of Meritocracy: Three Lessons and Their Implications for Justice in Education." *Social Justice Research* 29:14–26.

Mortensen, Dale. 2010. "The Nobel Prize Banquet Speech." https://www.nobelprize.org/prizes/economic-sciences/2010/mortensen/biographical/.

Moshiri, Farrokh, and Peter Cardon. 2014. "The State of Business Communication Classes: A National Survey." *Business and Professional Communication Quarterly* 77 (3): 312–29.

Moss, Philip, and Chris Tilly. 2003. *Stories Employers Tell: Race, Skill, and Hiring in America.* New York: Russell Sage.

Moss-Pech, Corey. Unpublished manuscript. "How College Students Find Jobs."

Muhit, Georgiana. 2021. "Does University Prestige Lead to Discrimination in the Labor Market? Evidence from a Labor Market Field Experiment in Three Countries." *Studies in Higher Education* 47 (6): 1227–42.

Mullen, Ann. 2011. *Degrees of Inequality: Culture, Class, and Gender in American Higher Education.* Baltimore: John Hopkins University Press.

Mullen, Ann, Kimberly Goyette, and Joseph Soares. 2003. "Who Goes to Graduate School? Social and Academic Correlates of Educational Continuation after College." *Sociology of Education* 76 (2): 143–69.

Mulvey, Paul, Peter LeBlanc, Robert Heneman, and Michael McInerney. 2002. "Study Finds That Knowledge of Pay Process Can Beat Out Amount of Pay in Employee Retention, Organizational Effectiveness." *Journal of Organizational Excellence* 21 (4): 29–42.

Murray, Charles. 2013. *Coming Apart: The State of White America, 1960–2010.* New York: Crown Forum.

Murrell, Audrey, and Erika Hayes James. 2002. "Gender and Diversity in Organizations: Past, Present, and Future Directions." *Sex Roles* 45 (5–6): 243–57.

Musick, Kelly, Jennie Brand, and Dwight Davis. 2012. "Variation in the Relationship between Education and Marriage: Marriage Market Mismatch?" *Journal of Marriage and Family* 74 (1): 53–69.

National Association of Colleges and Employers. 2018. "Employers Want to See These Attributes on Students' Resumes." December 12. https://www.naceweb.org/talent-acquisition/candidate-selection/employers-want-to-see-these-attributes-on-students-resumes/.

National Association of Colleges and Employers. 2019. "2019 Internship & Co-op Survey Report." Bethlehem, PA.

National Center for Education Statistics. 2019. "The Conditions of Education." https://nces.ed.gov/programs/coe/indicator_cce.asp.

New York City Commission on Human Rights. 2022. "Salary Transparency in Job Advertisements." https://www1.nyc.gov/assets/cchr/downloads/pdf/publications/Salary-Transparency-Factsheet.pdf.

Nowicki, Margaret, and Joseph Rosse. 2002. "Managers' Views of How to Hire: Building Bridges between Science and Practice." *Journal of Business and Psychology* 17 (2): 157–70.

Nunley, John, Adam Pugh, Nicholas Romero, and R. Alan Seals Jr. 2016. "College Major, Internship Experience, and Employment Opportunities: Estimates from a Résumé Audit." *Labour Economics* 38:37–46.

Obloj, Tomasz, and Todd Zenger. 2022. "The Influence of Pay Transparency on (Gender) Inequity, Inequality and the Performance Basis of Pay." *Nature Human Behavior.*

Owens, Ann. 2018. "Income Segregation between School Districts and Inequality in Students' Achievement." *Sociology of Education* 91 (1): 1–27.

Pascarella, Ernest, Christopher Pierson, Gregory Wolniak, and Peter Terenzini. 2004. "First-Generation College Students: Additional Evidence on College Experiences and Outcomes." *Journal of Higher Education* 75 (3): 249–84.

Pedulla, David. 2020. *Making the Cut: Hiring Decisions, Bias, and the Consequences of Nonstandard, Mismatched, and Precarious Employment*. Princeton, NJ: Princeton University Press.

Perna, Laura, and Elaine Leigh. 2018. "Understanding the Promise: A Typology of State and Local College Promise Programs." *Educational Researcher* 47 (3): 155–80.

Persell, Caroline, and Peter Cookson. 1985. "Chartering and Bartering: Elite Education and Social Reproduction." *Social Problems* 33 (2): 114–29.

Pfeffer, Fabian, and Florian Hertel. 2015. "How Has Education Shaped Social Mobility Trends in the United States?" *Social Forces* 94 (1): 143–80.

Pfeffer, Fabian, and Alexandra Killewald. 2018. "Generations of Advantage: Multigenerational Correlations in Family Wealth." *Social Forces* 96 (4): 1411–42.

Phillips, Meredith. 2011. "Parenting, Time Use, and Disparities in Academic Outcomes." In *Whither Opportunity: Rising Inequality, Schools, and Children's Life Chances*, ed. Greg Duncan and Richard Murnane, 207–28. New York: Russell Sage.

Pike, Gary, and Gregory Kuh. 2005. "First- and Second-Generation College Students: A Comparison of Their Engagement and Intellectual Development." *Journal of Higher Education* 76 (3): 276–300.

Pluchino, Alessandro, Alessio Biondo, and Andrea Rapisarda. 2018. "Talent versus Luck: The Role of Randomness in Success and Failure." *Advances in Complex Systems* 21 (3–4).

Quillian, Lincoln, John Lee, and Mariana Oliver. 2020. "Evidence from Field Experiments in Hiring Shows Substantial Additional Racial Discrimination after the Callback." *Social Forces* 99 (2): 732–59.

Radford, Alexandria. 2013. *Top Student, Top School?: How Social Class Shapes Where Valedictorians Go to College*. Chicago: University of Chicago Press.

Radford, Alexandria, and Emily Cataldi. Unpublished manuscript. "Top Student, Top Career? How Undergraduate Alma Mater Shapes Valedictorians' Lives."

Rawls, John. 1971. *A Theory of Justice*. Cambridge, MA: Harvard University Press.

Rege, Mari, and Ingeborg Foldøy Solli. 2014. "Lagging Behind the Joneses: The Impact of Relative Earnings on Job Separation." Working Paper.

Ridgeway, Cecilia. 2011. *Framed by Gender: How Gender Inequality Persists in the Modern World*. New York: Oxford.

Rivera, Lauren. 2012. "Hiring as Cultural Matching: The Case of Elite Professional Service Firms." *American Sociological Review* 77 (6): 999–1022.

Rivera, Lauren. 2015. *Pedigree: How Elite Students Get Elite Jobs*. Princeton, NJ: Princeton University Press.

Rivera, Lauren, and András Tilcsik. 2018. "Class Advantage, Commitment Penalty: The Gendered Effect of Social Class Signals in an Elite Labor Market." *American Sociological Review* 81 (6): 1097–131.

Roksa, Josipa, Eric Grodsky, Richard Arum, and Adam Gamoran. 2007. "Changes in Higher Education and Social Stratification in the United States." In *Stratification in Higher Education: A Comparative Study*, ed. Yossi Shavit, Richard Arum, and Adam Gamoran, 165–91. Stanford, CA: Stanford University Press.

Rosenfeld, Jake. 2017. "Don't Ask or Tell: Pay Secrecy in U.S. Workplaces." *Social Science Research* 65:1–16.

Rosenfeld, Jake. 2021. *You're Paid What You're Worth and Other Myths of the Modern Economy.* Cambridge, MA: Harvard University Press.

Rossetti, Christian, and Kevin Dooley. 2010. "Job Types in the Supply Chain Management Profession." *Journal of Supply Chain Management* 46 (3): 40–56.

Russakoff, Dale. 2015. *The Prize: Who's in Charge of America's Schools?* New York: Houghton Mifflin Harcourt.

Rynes, Sara, and John Boudreau. 1986. "College Recruiting in Large Organizations: Practice, Evaluation, and Research Implications." *Personnel Psychology* 39 (4): 729–57.

Salanié, Bernard. 2000. *Microeconomics of Market Failures.* Cambridge, MA: MIT Press.

Sandel, Michael J. 2020. *The Tyranny of Merit: Can We Find the Common Good?* New York: Picador.

Sauder, Michael. 2020. "A Sociology of Luck." *Sociological Theory* 38 (3): 193–216.

Sauder, Michael, Hyunsik Chun, and Wendy Espeland. 2021. "The Garbage Can Model and Organizational Metrics." *Research in the Sociology of Organizations* (Worlds of Rankings) 74:175–97.

Schneider, Daniel, and Kristen Harknett. 2021. "Hard Times: Routine Schedule Unpredictability and Material Hardship among Service Sector Workers." *Social Forces* 99 (4): 1682–709.

Schoeni, Robert, and Karen Ross. 2005. "Material Assistance Received from Families during the Transition to Adulthood." In *On the Frontier of Adulthood: Theory, Research, and Public Policy,* ed. Richard Settersten Jr., Frank Furstenberg Jr., and Ruben Rumbaut, 396–416. Chicago: University of Chicago Press.

Selingo, Jeffrey. 2016. *There Is Life after College: What Parents and Students Should Know about Navigating School to Prepare for the Jobs of Tomorrow.* New York: HarperCollins.

Semuels, Alana. 2017. "Poor Girls Are Leaving Their Brothers Behind." *The Atlantic,* November 27.

Shandra, Carrie. 2022. "Internship Participation in the United States by Student and School Characteristics, 1994 to 2017." *Socius* 8.

Shields, John, Dow Scott, Richard Sperling, and Thomas Higgins. 2009. "Rewards Communication in Australia and the United States: A Survey of Policies and Programs." *Compensation & Benefits Review* 41 (6): 14–26.

Shrider, Emily, Melissa Kollar, Frances Chen, and Jessica Semega. 2021. "Income and Poverty in the United States: 2020." *United States Census Bureau,* Report Number P60-273.

Smith, Christian Michael, Eric Grodsky, and John Robert Warren. 2019. "Late-Stage Educational Inequality: Can Selection on Noncognitive Skills Explain Waning Social Background Effects?" *Research in Social Stratification and Mobility* 63:100424.

Snellman, Kaisa, Jennifer Silva, Carl Frederick, and Robert Putnam. 2015. "The Engagement Gap: Social Mobility and Extracurricular Participation among American Youth." *Annals of the American Academy of Political and Social Science* 657 (1): 194–207.

Song, Jae, David Price, Fatih Guvenen, Nicholas Bloom, and Till von Wachter. 2015. "Firming Up Inequality." NBER Working Paper 21199.

Soria, Krista, Deeqa Hussein, and Carolyn Vue. 2014. "Leadership for Whom? Socioeconomic Factors Predicting Undergraduate Students' Positional Leadership Participation." *Journal of Leadership Education* 13 (1): 14–30.

Stephens-Davidowitz, Seth. 2018. *Everybody Lies: Big Data, New Data, and What the Internet Can Tell Us about Who We Really Are.* New York: Dey Street Books.

Stevens, Mitchell. 2009. *Creating a Class: College Admissions and the Education of Elites*. Cambridge, MA: Harvard University Press.

Streib, Jessi. 2011. "Class Reproduction by Four Year Olds." *Qualitative Sociology* 34 (2): 337–52.

Streib, Jessi. 2015. *The Power of the Past: Understanding Cross-Class Marriages*. New York: Oxford University Press.

Streib, Jessi. 2017. "The Unbalanced Theoretical Toolkit: Problems and Partial Solutions to Studying Culture and Reproduction but Not Culture and Mobility." *American Journal of Cultural Sociology* 5 (1–2): 127–53.

Stuber, Jenny. 2009. "Class, Culture, and Participation in the Collegiate Extra-Curriculum." *Sociological Forum* 24 (4): 877–900.

Stuber, Jenny. 2011. *Inside the College Gates: How Class and Culture Matter in American Higher Education*. New York: Lexington Books.

Taylor, Susan, and Janet Sniezek. 1984. "The College Recruitment Interview: Topical Content and Applicant Reactions." *Journal of Occupational Psychology* 57 (1): 57–168.

Terenzini, Patrick, Leonard Springer, Patricia Yaeger, Ernest Pascarella, and Amaury Nora. 1996. "First-Generation College Students: Characteristics, Experiences, and Cognitive Development." *Research in Higher Education* 37 (1): 1–22.

Thomas, Kyla. 2018. "The Labor Market Value of Taste: An Experimental Study of Class Bias in U.S. Employment." *Sociological Science* 5:562–95.

Thomas, Scott. 2000. "Deferred Costs and Economic Returns to College Major, Quality, and Performance." *Research in Higher Education* 41 (3): 281–313.

Thompson, Jason. 2019. "Mobility in the Middle: Bachelor's Degree Selectivity and the Intergenerational Association in Status in the United States." *Research in Social Stratification and Mobility* 60:16–28.

Tomaskovic-Devey, Donald. 2022. "Pay Transparency Can Close the Gender Gap—If Done Correctly." The Hill, March 10. https://thehill.com/opinion/civil-rights/597539-pay-transparency-can-close-the-gender-gap-if-done-correctly/.

Tomaszewski, Wojtek, Francisco Perales, Ning Xiang, and Matthias Kubler. 2018. "Beyond Graduation: Socio-Economic Background and Post University Outcomes of Australian Graduates." Life Course Centre Working Paper Series No. 2018-22.

Torche, Florencia. 2011. "Is a College Degree Still the Great Equalizer? Intergenerational Mobility across Levels of Schooling in the US." *American Journal of Sociology* 117 (3): 763–807.

Torche, Florencia. 2018. "Intergenerational Mobility at the Top of the Educational Distribution." *Sociology of Education* 91 (4): 266–89.

Tough, Paul. 2019. *The Years That Matter Most: How College Makes or Breaks Us*. New York: Houghton Mifflin Harcourt.

Turban, Daniel, and Thomas Dougherty. 1992. "Influences of Campus Recruitment on Applicant Attraction to Firms." *Academy of Management* 35 (4): 739–65.

Tversky, Amos, and Daniel Kahneman. 1986. "Rational Choice and the Framing of Decisions." *Journal of Business* 59 (4.2): S251–S278.

US Census Bureau. 2019. "44.6 Percent of High School Dropouts and 72.3 Percent of College Graduates Employed in August 2019." September 11. https://www.bls.gov/opub/ted/2019/44-6-percent-of-high-school-dropouts-and-72-3-percent-of-college-graduates-employed-in-august-2019.htm.

Vaid, Divya. 2014. "Caste in Contemporary India: Flexibility and Persistence." *Annual Review of Sociology* 40:391–410.

Valdez, Jonah. 2022. "New California Law Will Require Job Postings to Include Salary Ranges." *Los Angeles Times*, September 29.

Walpole, Mary. 2003. "Socioeconomic Status and College: How SES Affects College Experiences and Outcomes." *Review of Higher Education* 27 (1): 45–73.

Walters, Christopher. 2018. "The Demand for Effective Charter Schools." *Journal of Political Economy* 126 (6): 2179–223.

Wanberg, Connie, Abdifatah A. Ali, and Borbala Csillag. 2020. "Job Seeking: The Process and Experience of Looking for a Job." *Annual Review of Organizational Psychology and Organizational Behavior* 7:315–37.

Weininger, Elliot, Annette Lareau, and Dalton Conley. 2015. "What Money Doesn't Buy: Class Resources and Children's Participation in Organized Extracurricular Activities." *Social Forces* 94 (2): 479–503.

Weinstein, Russell. 2022. "Firm Decisions and Variation across Universities in Access to High-Wage Jobs: Evidence from Employer Recruiting." *Journal of Labor Economics* 40 (1).

Weiss, Felix, and Josipa Roksa. 2016. "New Dimensions of Educational Inequality: Changing Patterns of Combining College and Work in the U.S. Over Time." *Research in Social Stratification and Mobility* 44:44–53.

Widdicombe, Lizzie. 2018. "Improving Workplace Culture, One Review at a Time." *New Yorker*, January 15.

Wightman, Patrick, Megan Patrick, Robert Schoeni, and John Schulenberg. 2013. "Historical Trends in Parental Financial Support of Young Adults." Population Studies Center, Report 13-801. https://www.psc.isr.umich.edu/pubs/pdf/rr13-801.pdf.

Wilbur, Tabitha, and Vincent Roscigno. 2016. "First-Generation Disadvantage and College Enrollment/Completion." *Socius* 2.

Wildhagen, Tina. 2015. "'Not Your Typical Student': The Social Construction of the 'First-Generation' College Student." *Qualitative Sociology* 38:285–303.

Winkler, Rolfe, and Andrea Fuller. 2019. "How Companies Secretly Boost Their Glassdoor Ratings." *Wall Street Journal*, January 22.

Witteveen, Dirk, and Paul Attewell. 2017. "Family Background and Earnings Inequality among College Graduates." *Social Forces* 95 (4): 1539–76.

Witteveen, Dirk, and Paul Attewell. 2020. "Reconsidering a 'Meritocratic Power of a College Degree.'" *Research in Social Stratification and Mobility* 66:100479.

WorkSpan Daily. 2018. "Lack of Pay Transparency Tops Applicants' List of Frustrations." World at Work, September 25. https://www.worldatwork.org/workspan/articles/lack-of-pay-transparency-tops-applicants-list-of-frustrations.

Xie, Yu, Alexandra Killewald, and Christopher Near. 2016. "Between- and Within-Occupation Inequality: The Case of High-Status Professions." *Annals of the American Academy of Political and Social Science* 663 (1): 53–79.

Yee, April. 2016. "The Unwritten Rules of Engagement: Social Class Differences in Undergraduates' Academic Strategies." *Journal of Higher Education* 87 (6): 831–58.

Young, Jun, and Kristen Foot. 2006. "Corporate E-Cruiting: The Construction of Work in Fortune 500 Recruiting Web Sites." *Journal of Computer-Mediated Communication* 11 (1): 44–71.

Zahariadis, Nikolaos. 1994. "Garbage Cans and the Hiring Process." *PS, Political Science* 27 (1): 98–101.

Zhou, Xiang. 2019. "Equalization or Selection? Reassessing the 'Meritocratic Power' of a College Degree in Intergenerational Income Mobility." *American Sociological Review* 84 (3): 459–85

Index